To dearest Dick
a very happy Christmas
1974

Lots of love from

Septimus

& Nicky

Paradise of Exiles

Paradise of Exiles

TUSCANY AND THE BRITISH

Olive Hamilton

ANDRE DEUTSCH

First published 1974 by
André Deutsch Limited
105 Great Russell Street London WC1

Printed in Great Britain by
T & A Constable Ltd Edinburgh

ISBN 0 233 96531 9

To Denis

Acknowledgments

THE ILLUSTRATIONS

Thanks are due to the National Portrait Gallery for kind permission to reproduce
    the portrait of Smollett by an unknown Italian artist
    the portrait of Mary Wollstonecraft Shelley by R. Rothwell
    the portraits of Elizabeth Barrett Browning and of Robert Browning by Gordigiani
    the portrait of Walter Savage Landor by R. Faulkner
    the portrait of Frances Trollope by A. Hervieu
    the portrait of D. H. Lawrence by J. Juta

to the Radio Times Hulton Picture Library for
    the portrait of Byron by Count d'Orsay
    the portrait of Teresa Guiccioli by Count d'Orsay
    the portrait of Alice Keppel by Ellis Roberts

to the Mary Evans Picture Library for
    the drawing of Ouida

to Edizione Alinari for
    the photographs of Palazzo Lanfranchi (photo. Buonarroti), Villa Farinola, Villa Fabbricotti, Villa Palmieri, and the Castle at Montegufoni

to the Mills College Library for
    the painting of the Brownings' sala in Casa Guidi by George Mignaty

To Laurence Pollinger Ltd, the Estate of the late Mrs Frieda Lawrence and William Heinemann Ltd, for permission to reprint extracts from the works of D. H. Lawrence and Frieda Lawrence.

ACKNOWLEDGMENTS

To Maddison: the University of Wisconsin Press; © 1959 by the Regents of the University of Wisconsin; for permission to quote from Edward Nehls, ed. *D. H. Lawrence: a Composite Biography*, vol. III.

To Barrie and Jenkins Ltd for permission to reproduce from *The Autobiography of Leigh Hunt*, ed. J. E. Morpurgo (Cresset Press, 1949).

To John Murray, 'sole legal representative of the late Lord Byron deceased', for permission to quote from Lord Byron's letters; from *The Last Attachment* by Iris Origo; and from *Castle in Italy* by Lina Waterfield.

To Dr Michael E. Mallett for permission to use the text and adapt a map from *The Florentine Galleys in the Fifteenth Century* published by the Clarendon Press, Oxford.

To David Higham Associates for permission to use extracts from various books by Sir Osbert Sitwell, published by Macmillan.

To Mrs Laura Huxley and Chatto and Windus for permission to quote from *Letters of Aldous Huxley*.

To Carola Oman and Hodder and Stoughton Ltd for permission to quote from *Nelson*.

To the Longman Group Ltd for permission to quote from *The Golden Ring* by Giuliana Artom Treves, translated by Sylvia Sprigge.

To Methuen and Co Ltd for permission to quote from *More Memoirs of an Aesthete* by Harold Acton.

To the gracious permission of Her Majesty the Queen to republish extracts from *The Letters of Queen Victoria*, Third Series, vol. I, ed. G. E. Buckle, published by John Murray.

To the Gabinetta Fotografica degli Uffizi, Florence, for permission to reproduce the photograph of the Grinling Gibbons wood carving now in the Bargello Collection, from the catalogue of the Exhibition of 1972, *Firenze Restaura*.

To Mr Henry Moore for permission to print extracts from a letter.

I am also deeply grateful to many friends whose names do not appear in the text. First to Mr Leonard Russell who read the manuscript and gave unlimited help and advice; to Professor Andrea Tacchi of Florence for his spontaneous assistance in helping to find the houses of the Anglo-Florentines; to Mrs John Primavesi and Mrs Trevor Fenwick for accompanying me; and to Signora Giuliana Artom Treves, Dr Hannah Keil of Florence, Mrs Inge Feltrinelli, Dr and Mrs G. Fischer, Contessa Muzi Falconi, Mr Herbert Handt, Conte G. Tadini, Mr Ian Greenlees, and Architetto and Signora Donatella Papi. Finally I must express my gratitude to Mr Matthews and the staff of the London Library for unfailing assistance, and to Miss Diana Athill of André Deutsch Ltd for her enthusiasm.

Contents

Introduction   *page* 13

I How It All Began   17

II Sir John Hawkwood and the Mercenaries   26

III Antonio Bonvisi: Robert Dudley   33

IV In Search of Smollett at Livorno   49

V The Grand Tour and the Shelley Circle   62

VI Byron and his Friends   83

VII Walter Savage Landor   98

VIII Ouida   120

IX The Brownings   137

X The Trollopes   144

XI Queen Victoria   150

XII D. H. Lawrence   157

XIII The Sitwells   175

XIV Henry Moore   182

XV The Floods of 1966   190

    Maps and Town Plans   194

    A List of Books   202

    Index   213

List of Illustrations

Sir John Hawkwood	*facing page*	32
Sir Robert Dudley		33
I Rinieri, Dudley's country house		33
Carving by Grinling Gibbons		48
Tobias Smollett		49
Percy Bysshe Shelley		64
Mary Wollstonecraft Shelley		64
Pallazzo Lanfranchi		65
Byron		80
Teresa Guiccioli		80
Walter Savage Landor		81
Villa Gherardescha		96
Villino Trollope		96
Frances Trollope		97
Thomas Adolphus and Anthony Trollope		97
Elizabeth Barrett Browning		112
Robert Browning		112
The Brownings' salon in the Casa Guido		113
Ouida		128
Villa Farinola, Scandicci		129
Ouida's tomb		129
Memorial to Florence Nightingale		144
Queen Victoria's continental travelling coach		145
Lawrence and Frieda in Italy		160
Villa Mirenda		161
The Lawrences' house at Lerici		161
Alice Keppel		176
Montegufoni		177

Henry Moore   177

LIST OF MAPS AND TOWN PLANS

The routes of the Florentine galleys   194
Tuscany today   195
Florence (centre)   196
The Florentine countryside   197
Pisa   198
Livorno   199
Bagni di Lucca   200
Bay of La Spezia   201

Introduction

WE have a little house in Tuscany. It is our retreat from the modern world and our place of physical and spiritual rejuvenation.

We knew and loved parts of Greece, Turkey, the Middle East, North Africa, Spain and Sicily, and had a deep attachment to France begun when post-war family holidays were enchanting escapes from the austerity of life in England, but there was never any real question as to which country we would choose. We knew in our hearts that it would be Italy, and only had to decide on the region.

We loved Venice, but found the climate enervating in summer; the South, but found it too harsh. Rome was where we had spent a long-delayed honeymoon immediately after the war, and it has never lost its magic for us; but because we must continue to live in London for the greater part of the year, we didn't want our retreat in Europe to be in another great city. So Tuscany it had to be.

It is green, like our native land, but its warm sunshine is reliable; both mountains and sea are close; it is easily accessible by air. But even more important than these practical advantages, is the endless historic and artistic interest it provides, its unequalled concentration of painting, sculpture and architecture.

We started with no word of Italian, but sensed a warmth in the people which made us eager to express ourselves in their language. We also sensed that they have retained a certain quality and flavour in their life which we, in our welfare state, have somehow lost or failed to achieve, and this transmitted to us a feeling of peace and harmony. On each of our Italian holidays we had experienced this inward joy and contentment, and the first time we motored up 'our valley' I had an inexplicable feeling of coming home.

13

Our footsteps were led there by Henry Moore, who like innumerable sculptors before him was using the marble quarries of Carrara and the workshops and foundries of Pietrasanta. He too had succumbed to the gentle beauty of this part of Tuscany—the hills clothed with olives and chestnut forests, the sea and the mountains. He too was fascinated by the character of the Tuscans, with their craftsmanship and sense of beauty, their individual kindness, their pride, stubborness, wilfulness, intelligence and suspicion, unchanged since the time of Dante. And they have a deep sense of history. It does not surprise a Tuscan, for example, that the chemist in our small town has written a two-volume work on the region from early Etruscan times.

The grace of the women is particularly impressive, and I never tire of watching them carry water on their heads up the steep hill from the simple but pleasing washing cisterns—in spite of deploring the bureaucratic inadequacy which fails to supply piped water to the mountain villages although there is plenty in the small town below us and the mountain streams never seem to run dry. (It is an article of faith in many Tuscan villages that the *aquedotto* will be finished next year. . . .)

The Tuscans we met when we were preparing our house were certainly proud, intelligent and stubborn—but so graceful in defeat when a point has been proved. Equally certainly, their craftsmanship was unimpaired. Things done in our absence in England were accomplished with exquisite taste, such as the terrace of old bricks with depressed Roman arches which links the old house and the addition to it into an impeccable unity. It made us conscious that our English forebears were almost barbarians at a time when the ancestors of these people, the Etruscans, had evolved a great civilisation. The *muratore* who was responsible for the terrace loved to point out the eleven ancient churches visible on a clear day from our house, and local pride in our village's beautiful church is strong. They claim that the apse is ninth century, the font is an early Roman marble sarcophagus, and the triptych is by Battista da Pisa, 1443.

Our provincial capital is the ancient walled city of Lucca, which fortunately is not on the mass tourist route and is almost unchanged externally since the Middle Ages. We can reach it quickly on the *autostrada*, but prefer to drive there (on the slightest pretext) by the old road through the hills. It was a remark made by a distinguished classical historian who has made his home there which first suggested to me the theme of this book. When I asked him why he liked living in Tuscany, he answered 'Because they like the English'; and the links between Great Britain and Tuscany have become increasingly evident with every visit. When, during the war, the penalty for sheltering British soldiers and airmen from the Germans was death, a great many Tuscans risked it without hesitation.

On the short flight between London and Pisa (there is a daily flight all summer and a twice-weekly service in winter) I began thinking back to the hazardous journeys of the past, taking weeks or even months, on foot or on horseback, in wagon or coach. For hundreds of years clerics, merchants, soldiers, bankers, scholars and tourists braved this journey. The only alternative was the galleys which started a twice-monthly run in the fifteenth century, carrying wool and other cargo to Pisa from Southampton or London, and returning with the finished cloth. The sea journey took about twenty-one days each way and was no less hazardous than the land journey, owing to storms, pirates and the lack of precise navigational instruments.

I wanted to find out how this traffic between the two countries began and continued. What sort of people established the friendship between the Tuscans and the English which has persisted through all the turbulence of history? The more I learnt about the men and women from England who had walked the streets of the ancient towns of Tuscany, the more these towns came alive for me. It was astonishing how much there was to explore; how many of our countrymen had made their homes here, some to escape persecution of one sort or another, some to do their finest work. Without any particular plan I found myself following an historical-literary trail—a pilgrimage, if you like— to places associated with them, the houses in which they lived, and sometimes to their graves.

I began, naturally, with the more famous. I saw the statue of Shelley in the square at Viareggio, not far from where his body was burned on the beach; I remembered the romantic elopement of Robert Browning and Elizabeth Barrett and the new life and health she found in Tuscany; I read much on the era of the Grand Tour, of which Florence was the highlight, and by which young Englishmen of means and fashion completed their education. And these, I knew, were mere beginnings. . . .

So it was that during winter weekends in England I began to haunt the second-hand bookshops in pursuit of books on Tuscany. Many of them were written at the turn of the century, and even if they happened to be verbose and undistinguished, were still fascinating in their leisurely descriptions of people, customs, history and the countryside. The more I learnt, the more there was to learn.

Many English still choose to make a home in Tuscany. These pages set out the discoveries and reflections of two such new settlers in the hope that they will interest readers who share their love of the place, and will provide enjoyment and guidance for others as yet unlearned in the lore of this great region. It is by no means a complete account of the English in Tuscany—if it were that, it would be a very much longer book—and I don't doubt that I have omitted characters and incidents whose absence will be deplored. I can claim only to have chosen those who most interested me, in the hope of being able to share the great pleasure I discovered in my quest.

O. H.

CHAPTER 1

How It All Began

EVER since the establishment of the Papacy and the Church there were comings and goings of ecclesiastics between the republics which made up Tuscany, and Britain; but it was with the development of trade and finance that the long historic process of building up mutual understanding really began, developing after the passage of centuries into English support for the fight for Italian freedom—the *Risorgimento*.

In Tuscany, up to the twelfth century, the old system of dependence on agriculture, which entailed barter without the necessity for money, slowly but surely gave way to commerce and industry so that the towns again became the centre of life as they had been in antiquity. The old Roman towns (and Lucca dates even earlier, from Etruscan times) were repopulated as the merchant class established itself; yet, despite the fact that the merchant was a free man with legal status, the feeling that it was degrading to live by commercial transactions died hard, and the travelling merchant undoubtedly felt a sense of social inferiority. The landed classes, however, soon adapted to these changing conditions and became rich not only by trading but also by becoming moneylenders. Dante, a son of Florence, deplored their thrusting greed in his *Paradiso*.

The wars of Edward I of England, and the extravagance of his Court in Aquitaine, forced him to borrow from the merchant families of Lucca and then of Florence. These Italian merchants were the most useful of Edward's advisers, naturally enough when one remembers that they were in the vanguard of a great commercial revolution and at the centre of an intricately woven system of Papal finance and world trade, based on cities whose methods of trade and culture were a hundred years in advance of those in Britain.

English and Scottish wools were imported into Flanders even

earlier than the Norman Conquest, and were purchased by the Tuscan merchants through middlemen. English wool was unrivalled in the thirteenth century for strength and quality, and as time went by the Italians came to purchase it direct from England, having carried spices of the East and the luxury manufactured articles of their own cities to the great fairs of the Low Countries and Champagne. The lay brothers of Cistercian monasteries were the greatest wool producers. Because the Pope's collectors of his tax, the 'Papal tenth', came regularly to the monasteries, the wool trade and Papal finances were soon intermingled, and Tuscan merchants became familiar figures, and the monopolists of the wool trade. Until the opening up of the sea route for trade from Pisa and Livorno to Flanders and England in the fifteenth century nearly all the wool was sent overland.

In February 1303, an important charter was issued at Windsor by Edward I to all foreign merchants who traded in England. This was the *Carta Mercatoria*, confirming their rights and privileges in return for additional dues at half the present customs on wool, wool-fells and leather. There were also dues on wine, cloth and wax, and an *ad valorem* duty of threepence in the pound sterling on all other exports. By the charter the foreign merchants were placed under the King's special care and protection.

Some of the foreign bankers in England were able to live like great landowners. One of these, Amerigo Frescobaldi, was described by Edward I as his 'yeoman'. By 1308 he was Warden of the English Exchange as English Constable of Bordeaux, and he became a Lincolnshire landholder.

They had to be careful not to offend the English, however, One of the Frescobaldi wrote in a sonnet of advice:

> *Wear no bright colours, be humble;*
> *Appear stupid but be subtle in act.*
> *Spend freely and do not show yourself mean;*
> *Pay as you go and collect your debts courteously pleading your need.*
> *Do not be too inquisitive, busy as good occasion offers,*
> *But have no dealings with the men of the court.*
> *Be obedient to the powerful,*
> *Keep on good terms with your fellow-countrymen,*
> *And bolt your doors early.*

18

The firms of the Bardi and Peruzzi of Florence took the place of the Frescobaldi in the finances of the English government, but their spectacular bankruptcy in 1345, owing to the King's inability to pay his debts, shook the business world in Florence to its depths. The Black Death, which followed a few years later, in 1349, took its terrible toll of the population, and for a time trade with England languished.

In Tuscany, meanwhile, there was progress. Lucca was one of the first Italian towns in which silk was manufactured; there is some evidence that there was a silk factory there in AD 846, but it is usually supposed that the craft was not introduced to Italy from the East before 1148.

In return for wool, Lucca and Florence sent to England magnificent cloths of gold and silver, a more delicate silk, finely spun, known as *sandali*, and a thin gauze striped with gold, called *pleasaunce*; as well as the finest goldsmith's work, the tradition for which remains to this day. For the Church came ecclesiastical vestments; for the scholar bales of parchment and reams of writing paper.

By the end of the thirteenth century there had been a change in commercial methods: the travelling Italian merchant was superseded by the Italian board of directors, as we should call it, who remained in their settled centres of business in Italy and from there directed their international business interests, with offices in important towns like London, much as merchant banking is carried on today with headquarters in the respective capital cities.

The privileges granted to the Italians in London began, not unnaturally, to alarm the workers there, and demonstrations caused the Italian merchants to move for a time to certain ports, of which Southampton was the chief. By 1251, according to Matthew Paris, they had bought expensive houses and possessions there. Some of them brought their wives to England, others married Englishwomen. A few even brought their slaves, acquired from the Orient or from Africa. Their place of worship was St John's Church in French Street, Southampton, to which some of them bequeathed legacies. This church was demolished in the nineteenth century and incorporated in the Norman church of St Michael. Southampton was unique in granting the privilege of burgess status to a relatively large number of Italians; the foreigners could be more easily assimilated there than in London, where jealousy of their skills forced them to seek protection in segregated areas.[1]

To the Tuscan merchants the towns of England, with their muddy and insanitary unpaved streets, their strange half-timbered houses and thatched roofs, and their cold damp climate, must have seemed uninviting. Their own towns had been paved as early as the thirteenth century. All Tuscan cities were surrounded by walls, and as the population expanded these were rebuilt. Pisa had completed her new walls by 1158, Piacenza earlier than this and Florence by 1174. Last of all was Lucca, by 1260. The walls were maintained and defended by the people: their safety depended on them. At regular intervals round the walls were gateways at which all goods entering the city were taxed, whether produce from the local peasants or imports from distant lands. Outside the walls stood inns for travellers arriving late, after the gates were closed at sunset. Five hundred years later Smollett and his delicate wife, returning to Florence late at night, endured a four-mile walk around the walls before they found a gate which could admit them. In the fourteenth century Florence probably had a population of 100,000 (as compared with 40,000 in London), but three-fifths of this number were carried off by the Plague in 1349. In all probability, however, the population of Florence had increased almost to its former total within a generation. Rents were high as trade developed, and every bit of land on narrow streets was occupied by the houses and the palaces of the rich. The most successful and influential Tuscans, however, often built villas with gardens in an outer circle, such as the Villa Guinigi in Lucca, now a museum.

The places where people gathered and from which the streets radiated were squares descended from the Roman forum (such as the Piazza San Michele in Lucca), with a neighbouring centre of government and court of justice. There would also be another important piazza, that of the Cathedral. In Tuscany the piazza can be quite small, or of architectural grandeur like the splendid

---

[1] The timber-framed wool house on the quay at Southampton where the 'pokes' of wool were stored ready for loading on to the galleys has been superbly adapted as a maritime museum.

Piazza of Siena. Jealousies and feuds between rich families sometimes resulted in their building high towers on their houses to overlook their rivals (San Gimignano is the most striking example), but they do not seem to have had the idea of building upwards in the modern apartment-block manner because land was expensive.

The new Tuscan men of merchant wealth became the burghers, gradually assuming the executive power, headed by a *podesta* often from another State and appointed for a limited time.

In the middle of the twelfth century the municipal bodies founded schools for the children of the burghers, the first lay schools since classical times. The ability to read and write had become the exclusive preserve of the clergy, who still retained a monopoly of higher education, but it was now essential that the layman should have a rudimentary education for the conduct of business. The 'lay clerks' who benefited from this took over the city accounts, communications, and the many details of commerce. At first Latin was the language used, but by the beginning of the thirteenth century the speech of the people came into use; and it was Dante's language, the Tuscan tongue, which came to be regarded as the purest Italian. Despite this Italy's most glorious poet was exiled for life from his native Florence in one of the civil wars and bloody inter-family struggles which constantly bedevilled the city states of Tuscany.

The people of Lucca, the Lucchesi, were the first Tuscans to be involved in trade with England on a large scale. They were always an industrious people, and in addition to their superb olive oil and their wine, they specialised in the art of silk weaving, which was governed by strict laws. As a result of participation in the Crusades, they learned the art of weaving damask from Damascus—and from Spain, China, India, Asia Minor and Georgia, too, according to Marco Polo. Any weaver guilty of inferior work would be fined and declared a forger, and his silk burned in the public square, the Piazza San Michele. Florence, meanwhile, developed the making and finishing of woollen cloth into a speciality, learning the art of silk weaving later from Lucchese settlers. Her hills, like those of England, were suitable for sheep, and the villages and monasteries around Florence were used for sheep-rearing.

Florence used the religious Houses of the Humiliati Order particularly, and set up a training school for wool workers, leading all Europe in carding, combing, trimming, and especially in dyeing, for which plants and minerals were brought in from all over the world. To this day, in my opinion, her materials for the fashion trade are still pre-eminent in their beauty of colour and taste in blending it. The Florentine historian Villani says that in 1308 there were 30,000 people in the industry and two hundred shops turning out annually 80,000 bolts of cloth. But until 1406 Florence lacked that most essential prerequisite of export-import business—a port. In that year she gained an outlet for her trade by subduing Pisa and making it her port.

Industry from the middle of the twelfth century was in the hands of the guilds, or *Arti*, who controlled capital and directed labour, production and distribution, prices and wages. To start with the craft guilds were democratic, and members of each guild lived in the same part of the town. But their oligarchic power grew and finally all independent labour was eliminated and no one could remain outside the guilds; in their power to judge and fine members the guilds had powers not unlike those of our trade unions in Britain.

After their capture of Pisa in 1406 the Florentines seem to have relied on foreign or hired shipping. In the fifteenth century it took the galleys two or three days to reach the sea, yet throughout that century the ship-building yards remained in the old citadel of Pisa. The communal galleys were kept on the Arno 'between the bridges', the bridge at the western end being raised to allow vessels to pass down river. The stretch of river between this bridge, the Ponte a Mare, and the next, the Ponte Nuovo, ran beside the commercial heart of the city, the Piazza S. Niccola, where the galleys were moored.

Porto Pisano was the outlet to the sea, but as it became silted up attention was focussed on Livorno. Despite money spent on both Porto Pisano and Livorno, first by Pisans then by Florentines, and despite tax concessions, neither of them grew in size until the end of the fifteenth century. The merchants were not drawn to settle in the ports, mainly because of the unhealthy air of the marshes behind them, and the warehouse and customs facilities were limited. In 1421 the population of Livorno was estimated at between six hundred and eight hundred, and it had not increased by the end of the century: the people who lived there were workers, fishermen and a few reluctant Florentine officials. The *febbra livornina*, as the fever was called, struck down no fewer than eight Florentine Captains of Livorno at their post, and six of them died. Under Florence, Pisa continued to be the administrative centre of the area and the residence of the Sea Consuls who controlled the trade.

All merchandise exported from Florence passed through Pisa, and by the fifteenth century the incoming cargoes had to be unloaded into flat-bottomed boats, which could only go as far as Signa; for the last ten miles the cargoes were transferred to mules or carts. The Florentine galleys left Pisa not more than half full, chiefly with luxury wool and silk cloths, and then travelled round the western Mediterranean picking up cargoes of madder, almonds, dates, raisins, rice, wax, silk, cochineal and saffron.

Owing to the dangers of sea piracy the Florentines could never afford to send more than three galleys in a fleet; single galleys and often pairs were sometimes held up for months, or even cancelled, if pirates were reported to be active.

From the diary of a Captain of the galleys, one Luca di Maso degli Albizzi, for 1429-30, we learn something of the life of a son of a leading Florentine politician. He was born in 1382 and carefully educated, and at the age of twenty-one he accompanied his father on an embassy to Rome. The following year he fought in a campaign against Pisa. In 1410 he had his first experience of the sea on a pilgrimage to the Holy Land which took two years. In 1423 and the following year he went to sea as commander of one of the new communal wool galleys in her trials off Provence, and he then became a special ambassador to the King of Aragon (ambassadors in those days were still appointed temporarily to negotiate some particular business, and Luca appears to have done this well). In 1425 he held the post of Captain of Livorno. Two years later he became a prior and was sent to Hungary as envoy to the Emperor Sigismondo. He was one of the judges in the great tournament held in the Florentine Piazza Santa Croce in April 1429. At the age of forty-seven, in the same year, he was considered an ideal choice for Captain of the Galleys, and on his first voyage to England and the west 'he took a supply of clothing and armour and eight cross-bows, bedding, his pennant and flag, his copy of the Epistles of St Paul, and a pair of slippers' says Michael E. Mallett in his book *The Florentine Galleys in the Fifteenth Century* (1967). 'On the voyage he bought: in Majorca six small baskets, in Cadiz silk handkerchiefs, in Bruges and Southampton a considerable quantity of cloth of all kinds, candlesticks, brass bowls and jugs and birettas for ecclesiastical friends. In Spain some hair-nets for his wife.' He kept the most detailed and precise accounts for Florence, apparently formed friendships at Southampton with his English confrères, and made the observations of a trained diplomat wherever he travelled.

His diary throws much light on the Florentine galleys. The normal complement was 210: 160 oarsmen and 50 others. His suite was laid down in regulations: a chaplain, a barber-surgeon, two trumpeters, two servants and four squires, young men of good family. It was general practice in Italy then to divide the day into twenty-four hours, starting at sunset. There were three watches for the day and three for the night and whenever rowing was required it was done by some fifty of the oarsmen at a time. The maximum time allowed in any port on the route, except for Sluys and Southampton, was three days.

It is interesting that the pilots of these galleys often misjudged the distance they had travelled across the Bay of Biscay, continuing to sail northwards long after they should have turned north-east into the Channel, to find themselves in Mousehole Bay in the south-west.

It was obligatory for the captains and patrons of the galleys to be accommodated in the houses of the leading citizens of Southampton, who were to some extent responsible for them. Luca's diary tells us that after a night or two at the inn, during which time he was probably supervising the unloading of the cargo, he moved into the home of William Soper, a wealthy merchant and shipowner and one of the most influential figures in the town. Soper had been mayor of Southampton twice and was Member of Parliament many times between 1413 and 1449. He was also chief Customs Officer for many years.[1] On the

[1] 'Alien Hosting in Southampton in the Fifteenth Century', *Economic History Review xvi*, 1946. A. A. Ruddock.

first day of loading alone 290 'pokes of wool' were weighed. After the loading the captain rode to London carrying amongst other things finely wrought Milanese armour for Humphrey, Duke of Gloucester, who acted as Regent for his young nephew, Henry. Great honours seem to have been showered on Luca by the Florentine community in London.

There is insufficient information in his diary to distinguish between the sailing and rowing time of the galleys, but they were very rarely rowed for long periods. From these details one can form an impression of the fortitude necessary to accomplish one of these journeys from Pisa to Southampton and back:

Navigation time	776½ hours
Provisioning & stop	470
Bad weather delays	750
	————
	1,997 hours

outward Pisa 14 Sept.
                    83 days 5 hours
arrive Sloys 6 Dec.

Navigation time	532½ hours
Provisioning & trade	74
Bad weather	772½

return Southampton
                    23 Feb.
arrive Porto
Pisano   27 Mar.
    32 days 4½ hours

On his return Luca visited the church of Santa Maria in Livorno *in pleno gratiae*, so fulfilling the first of a number of vows he had made before the voyage. Finally, the consuls audited the accounts of the voyage and heard any complaints against the conduct of the expedition by Luca and the patrons. Thus were the early links established between Tuscany and England, by primitive and courageous sea-faring.

CHAPTER II

Sir John Hawkwood and the Mercenaries

WE have met an outstanding Tuscan; now we find an Englishman who carries the story forward. Although trained fighting men have accepted jobs as 'mercenaries' in many wars (the 1939-45 war was no exception), it is doubtful whether any of them achieved the riches, glory and glamour of Sir John Hawkwood, who even earned that most rare of gifts, gratitude.

Born in Essex, he fought in Edward III's campaigns in France, and he was knighted on the field by the King. After the Peace of Brétigny in 1360 he collected a company described by the Italian historian Villani as

> lusty young men, most of them brought up in the long wars between France and England; warm, eager and practised in rapine and slaughter . . . with very little care for their personal safety but in matters of discipline very obedient to their commanders. In their camps and cantonments, however, they lay scattered about with so little caution that a bold resolute body of men might give them a shameful defeat in that state.

It was amazing to Villani that they could continue fighting in the closed winter season, 'a thing unusual even among the Romans', and he could only find Hannibal to compare with them. The White Company, as it was called, of which Hawkwood eventually took command, had both cavalry and infantry, but in battle the horses were usually left out of sight in the charge of the pages, while the soldiers formed a tight circle, lightly accoutred by comparison with men of arms of other nationalities: a cuirass instead of a breastplate, sleeves of mail and a gorget (a piece of armour for the throat). Each lance was held by two people, the knight and his squire, and the formation advanced slowly with terrifying shouts. Although not a romantic means of achieving victory, it was practical, because if the attack did not succeed they were still a close disciplined force ready for defence. Apparently the White Company was noted for its appearance, the squires taking great pride in the polishing of their arms. There is in Froissart a recipe of the year 1402 to prevent rust: 'Cut off the legs of a goat from the knee downward; let them stay in the smoke for a day, then keep them 15 to 25 days. When you require them break the legs and take out the marrow from the bones and grease the arms with it and they will always keep bright even when wet.' They provisioned by means of plunder and menaces, thus extorting large sums of money from the cities.

Froissart says in his 'Chronicles': 'At this time there was in Tuscany a right valiant English knight, called Sir John Hawkwood who had there performed many most gallant deeds of arms. . . . This Sir John Hawkwood was a knight much inured to war which he had long followed, and had gained great renown in Italy from his gallantry.' And the irrefutable evidence that Froissart was not exaggerating has remained in the Duomo of Florence for five hundred years: an enormous fresco, the work of one of her greatest artists, Paolo Uccello, showing a bronze equestrian statue of Sir John Hawkwood above a marble tomb, which it had been the intention of the Commune to erect to his memory. Undoubtedly they would have carried this out but for the wish he expressed in old age, not long before his death, to be allowed to return to his native land. When death overtook him it was at the express desire of his King—Richard II—that his body was returned to England.

The Italians, then as now, had difficulty with English names, especially with H and W. In one inscription Hawkwood became Aguto or Acuto, his Christian name being translated into Italian —Giovanni. In another, the simple Latin inscription on the tomb in the fresco, it reads:

JOANNES ACUTUS EQUES BRITANNICUS DUX AETATIS SUAE CAUTISSIMUS ET REI MILITARIS PERITISSIMU HABITUS EST.

Below on an elegant base: 'PAULO UCCELLO OPUS'.

From this fresco, in which he wears a short doublet over his armour and carries in his right hand the baton of command, one can see that he was a strong, rather thick-set man, clean-shaven, and that his hair was cut short below the ear. From floor level it is impossible to examine the features properly, but from a photograph in the Berenson Library I was struck by the resemblance of his sharp features to those of that great soldier of our own day, Field-Marshal Montgomery of Alamein.

Hawkwood assisted the Pisans against Florence in 1364 and the Visconti of Milan against Pisa, Florence and other enemies. In 1368 he was in Milan for the marriage of Lionel, Duke of Clarence, son of Edward III of England, to Violante, daughter of Galeazzo Visconti. In all their contracts the English mercenaries stipulated that fighting against the King of England was excluded.

Later, resenting the interference of a council of war, Hawkwood fought for the Papacy against the Visconti from 1373 to 1375. It was at this time that, according to the archives of the State of Lucca, on October 18, 1375, '*Il Commune di Lucca concede la cittadinanza onoraria a Giovanni Hawkwood e delibera pagamenti a suo favore*'. These payments to great Condottieri for protecting States were quite usual, of course, but Lucca's grant of honorary citizenship seems an unusual favour. Six years later '*Il Commune di Lucca concede un'annua provvigione e una casa in citta a Giovanni Hawkwood*': again the payment, this time an annual one, but greater than that a house in the city, when the mercenaries were usually kept strictly outside the walls, even though the commanders might sleep within.

It seems that in this same year of 1381 the Florentines agreed to pay Hawkwood and his companion 130,000 gold florins within three months on condition that he did not fight against them; and the governing body of the republic—the Signoria, composed of representatives of the Trade Guilds—awarded him a pension of 12,000 florins a year. Hawkwood and his mercenaries had become a nuisance, but since inter-city rivalries and suspicions did not allow the Florentines to organise an alliance to get rid of him, he was obviously regarded as an increasingly expensive necessity. An attempt was made to persuade him to lead his band on a Crusade, but this failed; even Saint Catherine of Siena tried personally to influence Sir John: 'There I pray you sweetly, that you who so delight in wars should no longer war against

28

Christians... but go and oppose the Turks for it is a great cruelty that we who are Christians should persecute each other'. Hawkwood replied courteously that he would indeed concur with her suggestion when Pope Gregory could arrange it. But as the Pope was far too committed in Italy to spare time for Palestine, the suggestion came to nothing.

It is not known when Hawkwood was born but he must have been about forty years old when he entered Italy. In 1376, while in the service of the Church, he made war on Bologna. The English were encamped at Medicina, and for three days Hawkwood led 400 lancers, sacking, burning and taking 400 peasants prisoner on the way to Ponte Maggiore. The Bolognese replied by imprisoning all the English in the city, including the two little sons of the English captain. Paternal affection accomplished what no amount of money or persuasion could achieve: a truce of sixteen months was arranged while the prisoners were released. During this time Sir John seems to have consolidated his territorial acquisitions and arranged his private affairs. He took up residence at Bagnacavallo, a well-fortified town in the Romagna where Byron's little daughter was to die five hundred years later. He also enlarged his possession of Cotignola, near by. It was a ruined fortress which he surrounded with new walls, a deep moat and defences. Besides several small forts he erected 'a large royal palace with dungeons like a great stronghold'. Only a tower remains.

The Florentines were very anxious to woo Hawkwood away from the service of the Church and their opportunity came after the 'massacre of Caesena'. Hawkwood found himself involved in this massacre while under the orders of Roberto, Count of Geneva, a legate of the legitimate Gregory XI, commissioned to restore the temporal power of the Pope. Roberto was ugly and deformed in body and in character, and he insisted on such excesses in the helpless town of Caesena that even Hawkwood was disgusted and afterwards joined the anti-Papal League.

In 1377 he married the illegitimate daughter of the favourite mistress of Bernabo Visconti of Milan (this was probably Hawkwood's second wife), the beautiful Donnina. Bernabo probably thought to tie down the services of the great English captain, who must have been well into his fifties at the time of this marriage. One assumes his bride was a young girl. For the next two years he was constantly in the field of battle, but he quarrelled with Bernabo, left Milan and entered the service of Florence, and later made his home at San Donato in Polveroso, close to the city.

The Florentine war cabinet, in employing mercenaries, stipulated that the entire company pass, fully equipped, in parade before the Commissioners of the State, who rejected all equipment, men and horses which failed to come up to the required standard. Horses were examined and branded to prevent any future substitution of inferior animals. When Florence was a republic the custom was to have a grand parade at which the Captain-General received his baton of command with great ceremony and rode out of the city at the head of the army. This was doubly necessary: to show the citizens their protectors and to demonstrate how the money had been used. In order to defeat dishonest usurers who stripped them of money, arms and horses when they went off the rails, the republic formed a bank and placed 15,000 florins at its disposal to begin operations. Since the mercenaries were not citizens, punishment for crimes had to be adapted to their circumstances, and a fine—which did not prevent the loss of service—was imposed for crimes sometimes even including murder.

In 1388 Hawkwood made an unsuccessful attack against Gian Galeazzo Visconti of Milan, who had murdered Bernabo. The Florentines took up the war against Galeazzo and appointed Hawkwood commander-in-chief. Though he was nearly eighty, his campaign against the Milanese army was a triumph of generalship, and he was hailed by his contemporaries as equal to the Roman generals.

Despite the enormous sums he and his companions had already been paid, the Florentines were generous to him in his old age: 'That Hawkwood together with his wife and family shall be received as a perpetual friend of the Commune, and deputed its captain of war; that besides the pensions of 1200 gold florins conceded since 1375 he shall, during his life, receive a new annual pension of 2000 gold florins without any deduction, and the first year of this annuity shall begin with May 1st 1392'. Donnina was not overlooked:

Moreover after the death of the said Sir John, which God grant may be a peaceful and happy one after a long life, and meanwhile may he give him good fortune and direct his steps happily,—that the noble Lady Donnina, wife of Sir John, as long as she is a widow, and remains in the city, country or district of Florence, shall have every year of her widowhood the pension and gift of 1000 gold florins in honour of the memory of that noble and brave man her husband.

Whenever, however, she lives away from her son or daughters, or out of the city and country, the pension shall be deducted pro rata of the time.

And that the said Sir John and his sons and descendants in the male line born, or yet to be born, shall enjoy the privilege of Florentine citizenship and shall only be excluded from the power and ability of holding office in the commune or city.

Marriage portions of 2000 florins were voted to each of his three daughters, and as soon as the war ended on March 14, 1392, this was ratified in a public deed.

On August 22, 1393, a year before Hawkwood died, there was an almost unanimous vote in the Council of the Podesta and Commune, in favour of constructing, as soon as possible, 'in a conspicuous place, high and honourable as shall appear best to them, a worthy and handsome tomb for the ashes of the great and brave knight Sir John Hawkwood, English captain-general. . . .'

The following year, 1394, it seems that the old general had a longing for his native land, and a '*provvisione*' was approved by the Council: 'Considering that Hawkwood, weary by reason of his great age and as he asserts, weighed down by his infirmities, wishes to return to his old country and to dispose of his pension as well as the under-mentioned among others of his possessions . . .'. Five days later he died of a stroke. A commission of citizens was elected 'to order and provide splendid obsequies, without regard to expense'. The Signoria provided handsome black dresses for his wife and family and all the household. The coffin was covered with rich drapery of crimson velvet and gold and was first placed in the Piazza della Signoria, where the funeral procession formed. It included soldiers of Hawkwood's lances with fourteen caparisoned horses carrying flags and pennants embroidered with his arms, his helmet with its crest, and his sword and shield. The coffin was raised by the cavaliers of Florence, and was carried to fetch the body, which was laid on the open bier, robed in cloth of gold. Then the cavaliers carried it to San Giovanni (the Baptistery) and placed it on the baptismal font covered with cloth of gold. The body was then carried into the Duomo and placed under the catafalque. All the shops of Florence were closed. The ashes, as has been said, were returned to England at the order of King Richard II, and the tomb envisioned on the fresco was never erected.

IOANNES·ACVTVS·EQVES·BRITANNICVS·DVX·AETATIS·S
VAE·CAVTISSIMVS·ET·REI·MILITARIS·PERITISSIMVS·HABITVS·EST

·PAVLI·VCCELLI·OPVS·

Sir John Hawkwood: the Florentines intended this statue to stand above his tomb, but he wished to be buried in England so there was no tomb. Fortunately Paolo Uccello's painting of how it would be is still in the Duomo at Florence.

Sir Robert Dudley: an engraving
after the miniature by Nicholas
Hilliard.

I Rinieri, the country house where for many years Dudley found 'delicious repose'

CHAPTER III

Antonio Bonvisi: Robert Dudley

A VISIT we paid to Lucca on a New Year's Day provided the opportunity to find out about the family of Antonio Bonvisi, whose friendship for Sir Thomas More was one of the most touching in the history of Anglo-Tuscany. I knew that Bonvisi was a merchant banker from a cultured family of Lucca; and that he had settled in London buying Crosby Hall[1] from More in 1513. When Sir Thomas, Henry VIII's Chancellor, was imprisoned in the Tower by the King, Antonio kept him supplied with meat and wine, and at the end sent him 'a warm camelot gown', soft and silky for his skin, to wear for the execution. Apparently More would have worn it but for the dissuasion of the Lieutenant of the Tower.

Just before his trial he sat down to write to Antonio in Latin, and his words are so vivid and human that they sound across the centuries:

> Sith my mind doth give that I shall not have long liberty to write unto you by this little epistle of mine how much I am comforted with the sweetness of your friendship . . . when I consider in my mind that I have been almost this forty years not a guest, but a continual nursling in Master Bonvisi's house . . . now I comfort myself with this, that I never had occasion to do you pleasure. For such was always your great wealth that there was nothing left in which I might be unto you beneficial.
>
> . . . I therefore my dear friend of all mortal men dearest do . . . earnestly . . . pray that for his mercy sake he will bring us from this wretched and stormy world into his rest, where shall need no letters, where no wall shall dissever us, where no porter shall keep

---

[1] Built about 1460 of stone, it was taken down and recreated in 1908 in Chelsea, where it can be seen today.

us from talking together . . . and as I was wont to call you the apple of mine eye, right heartily fare ye well. And Jesus Christ keep safe and sound and in good health all your family which be of like affection toward me as their master is.[1]

A visit to the State Archives of Lucca revealed that Antonio, born in 1484, was the eldest of four brothers, and that he did not marry but left his estate to a nephew, according to a copy of his will which had been sent from Louvain, where he died in 1559. He was driven out of England in 1544 in a period of Catholic persecution, and Crosby Hall was seized.

I had only to mention my interest in the Bonvisi family to Professor Gino Arrighi, who though he taught mathematics in Lucca was immersed in the history of his native city, and we were off through the narrow streets to the romanesque basilica of San Frediano, which houses the Bonvisi family chapel. In the darkening winter afternoon the professor brought to life the inhabitants of the old medieval city, pointing out details like the tiny circular nursery windows of a beautiful palace, placed at a lower level than the ordinary windows.

The Bonvisi chapel is the one nearest to the entrance on the north side, and in contrast to the purity of the architecture of the church, built in 1150, it is in a more renaissance style, made of warm-toned marbles. It was built by Benedetto, father of Antonio, in 1511. As I entered I looked up at the three high arches to find suspended in each a cardinal's hat: this, then, was not only a rich but an illustrious family. A baroque memorial on the east wall is that of the first of the Bonvisi cardinals, born in Lucca in 1561. Two marble busts commemorate the others, who were also appointed bishops of Lucca: Girolamo, born at Lucca in 1607 and his nephew, Francesco, nineteen years later. The family crest or *stemma* is incised in low relief in the marble floor of the chapel— a star with long radiating points of which the lower centre is the longest—and this I was to find on many of the most beautiful villas around Lucca, as well as on the Palazzo Bonvisi at Bagni di Lucca. (Here the 'Old Pretender' to the throne of England, James Edward Stuart, stayed with his wife and large retinue in 1722 and much to the annoyance of the English government

---

[1] *Sir Thomas More, Letters*, edited by R. W. Chambers.

held the ceremony—the young Samuel Johnson knew all about the rite—of 'touching for the king's evil', said to cure the disease of scrofula. Here, too, a century later, came Lord Byron: he has the distinction of a plaque to his memory on the façade.)

Professor Arrighi pointed out further memorials which had associations with England. First, the Roman sarcophagus in which lay the bones of a Saxon King Richard of the ninth century which had been removed from the earlier church beneath San Frediano; an exquisite stone altar of five niches surmounted it, carved by the great sculptor Jacopo della Quercia. On from this altar to the chapel of Santa Zita we hurried, the professor talking in rapid Italian about Santa Zita, the saint of the servant girls beloved of the Lucchese, whose 'incorruptible body' lay beneath glass. He pointed to a missing little toe and laughed at the generosity of his forebears who could only spare this small relic to send to Eagle, a hamlet chapel in Lincolnshire, in honour of the Saint.

Sir Thomas More was one of the early classical scholars of the English Renaissance, and whilst England continued to receive Tuscan scholars, as well as artists and teachers of fencing, dancing and music, throughout the reigns of Henry VIII and his children, it was not until the reign of his daughter Elizabeth I that the flood-gates of the new intellectual, artistic and scientific movement opened wide.

When we first went to Livorno, after the war, we were surprised to find so much of the ancient walls remaining after the heavy bombing the town had received. The Darsena (the harbour basin) lay sleepily in the shelter of the medieval walls of mellow red brick which merge into the rounded Fortezzia Vecchia, the old fort which, though split from top to bottom, was still standing. Where once the galleys found shelter after returning from the Levant or from Sluys and Southampton, now a few small pleasure boats soughed on their moorings in the morning sunshine of a winter's day. Further south is the port itself—the old Medici harbour—with the mole still there which Robert Dudley, Earl of Warwick, built for the Grand Duke of Tuscany in the early seventeenth century.

On the quay at the head of the bay our eyes were immediately drawn to the huge marble statue of this Grand Duke, Ferdinand I, a statue famous not for its representation of Ferdinand but for *I Quatro Mori*, the four larger-than-life bronze figures of captive Moors which are straining away from the base on which he stands, their wrists bound behind them by chains. They have given the statue its name, and are dominating, realistic figures in the manner of Michelangelo—and, to my mind at least, equal to his work in power—with either sharp Moorish features or flattened faces, the latter beautiful in their resignation. They are said to have been modelled from one family by the unknown sculptor, but personally I doubt it. The diarist John Evelyn visited the port of Livorno in 1644 and described it and the statue like this:

> The prime port belonging to all the Duke's territories; heretofore a very obscure town, but since Duke Ferdinand has strongly fortified it (after the modern way) drained the marshes by cutting a channel thence to Pisa navigable sixteen miles, and has raised a Mole, emulating that at Genoa, to secure the shipping, it is become a place of great receipt; it has also a place for the galleys, where they lie safe. Before the sea is an ample piazza for the market, where are the statues in copper of the four slaves, much exceeding the life for proportion and, in the judgment of most artists, one of the best pieces of modern work. Here, especially in this piazza, is such a concourse of slaves, Turcs, Moors and other nations, that the number and confusion is prodigious; some buying, others selling, others drinking, others playing, some working, others sleeping, fighting, singing, weeping, all nearly naked, and miserably chained. Here was a tent where an idle fellow might stake his liberty against a few crowns, at dice or other hazard; and, if he lost, he was immediately chained and led away to the galleys, where he was to serve a term of years, but from whence they seldom returned. . . .[1]

The man who constructed the port of Livorno and drained the marshes around Pisa was one of the most fascinating Englishmen who ever lived in Tuscany. He was Robert Dudley, Earl of Warwick, Duke of Northumberland who published in 1646 one of the greatest early works on marine navigation, *Arcano del Mare*. Guide-books, English and Italian, seem to be silent about

[1] *Evelyn's Diary*, volume 1, edited by William Bray, 1889.

him, but he is now commemorated on a plaque on the building behind *I Quatro Mori*.

He was the son and heir of Leicester, Queen Elizabeth's 'Robin'. The Queen heaped honours and possessions on her Robin, among them the Earldom of Leicester and the princely castle and estate of Kenilworth. Here he entertained her in 1575 for nineteen days with her enormous suite, at great cost. The true chatelaine of the castle was his wife Douglas, whom he had married secretly and who had been made a Lady of the Bedchamber two years before. But Douglas's happiness was about to be shattered, for it was here that Leicester renewed a previous affair with Lettice Knollys, the widowed countess of Walter Devereux, Earl of Essex, a close relative of the Queen, and he seems to have fallen uncontrollably under her spell. She became pregnant, and her father, Sir Francis Knollys, kinsman and trusted servant of the Queen, insisted on a marriage ceremony with Leicester. This soon became known to everyone except the Queen, whose wrath none dared to risk by enlightening her. When, finally, she discovered the deception she raged and confined Leicester for a time in Duke Humphrey's tower in Greenwich Park.

Robert Dudley was Leicester's rightful son and heir, by marriage to Douglas, but he came to be regarded as his 'natural' son, although Leicester visited him regularly and gave him an excellent education. He had taken him from his mother Douglas at the age of five, possible when she remarried, and Robert went to Christ Church as 'an Earl's son' in 1587. There he was placed under an outstandingly wise and stimulating tutor, Thomas Chaloner, who though only twenty-six had travelled widely, particularly in Italy.

In 1578, while commanding Her Majesty's Forces in the Low Countries, Leicester had made his will. After providing amply for his 'dear wife' Lettice, he left to Robert the bulk of his fortune and property, including Kenilworth, after the death of his own brother Ambrose; but unfortunately he referred to Robert throughout as his 'base-born son', so placating Lettice, who would otherwise have lost her position as his lawful wife and widow.

After Leicester and his brother Ambrose died Robert occupied

Kenilworth and had a place at Court. It seems that by October 1591 the young man had married Margaret Cavendish, cousin of Captain Thomas Cavendish, circumnavigator of the world, for Robert was 'forbidden the Court for kissing Mistress Cavendish in the Presence, being his wife, as is said'.[1] His step-brother, the handsome Earl of Essex, became the Queen's favourite courtier, but it is clear that she treated Leicester's son Robert gently and with interest.

The real love of Robert Dudley was ships and the sea. In a manner unusual for a nobleman at that time, he set about 'learning his trade' at Deptford, under great shipwrights, studying not only navigation but the co-ordination of naval and land forces in war. He was a child of his age, and now he had the means to fit out and equip vessels which could make a long sea voyage.

The Queen curtailed his original grandiose plans and sent him to the West Indies and Guiana. When he returned in May 1595 it was to discover that his wife Margaret had died of the plague. Her brother-in-law was Richard Hakluyt, Prebend of Westminster, who had begun to collect the records of voyages of exploration which were later to make him famous, and for him Robert Dudley wrote an account of the expedition. The experience of this voyage led to his appointment as a naval captain, commanding a 500-ton man-of-war of the Royal Navy as part of a powerful fleet intended to take the offensive against Spain. He was not yet twenty-two and it must have been a moment of great happiness, but just then news was received that Drake's West Indies expedition had failed and both Drake and Hawkins were dead.

In 1596, for his part in the capture and sacking of Cadiz, Robert received a knighthood for gallantry. He married again, this time the seventeen-year-old daughter of a wealthy merchant, and continued his studies of marine navigation, designing a new type of compass and a complicated instrument for registering the ebb and flow of the tides; and in addition wrote a book on navigation. He also set up a merchant fleet with Captain Benjamin Wood for a two-year voyage to the East, which was accompanied by two London merchants. The expedition received the Queen's commission and left at the end of 1596, Wood carrying 'A

---

[1] *Antiquities of Warwickshire*, by Sir William Dugdale, 1656.

Gracious Commendation by her Majesty to the Emperor of China'. None of the ships or the men ever returned.

The miniature of Robert painted by Nicholas Hilliard must have been done at this time. It shows a resemblance to Leicester when young, and that the father was by no means more distinguished or handsome than his son.

Dudley became involved in the Earl of Essex's disaster in Ireland. Although Essex forfeited his life, Dudley was amongst those who were pardoned by the Queen without trial or penalty. She must, it seems, have known he had no traitorous intentions; but it was a warning, and from then onwards he suffered her displeasure.

His wife Alice bore him four daughters. Possibly she was resentful on their behalf, or her own, at not being able to claim their rightful titles as legitimate descendants of Leicester. Whether or not this was the cause, Robert Dudley decided to fight to establish his legitimacy. By this time his mother, who had married again happily and had two sons, at last felt able to suffer the indignities of dredging up her secret marriage to Leicester, and in June 1604 a court action was accordingly embarked upon. But by then the old Queen had died, and when Lettice Knollys, Leicester's widow, filed a bill in the Star Chamber against Dudley for defamation, so great was her family influence at King James's corrupt court that the whole evidence was sealed up and judgment was given against Dudley.

The blatant injustice of the proceedings, and also no doubt the strain, led Robert to throw over his country and all his responsibilities there. He applied for royal permission to travel abroad for three years and left with a party which included his second cousin, the beautiful Elizabeth Southwell, maid of honour to Queen Anne, but not his wife. Great was the scandal at Court that he should leave a wife and young family, and the Queen was justifiably annoyed at the elopement of one of her maids. Especially were the gossips irate that the love affair had escaped attention; Robert, unlike Essex, had not been promiscuous.

Nor was he an intriguer like his father. Indeed his nature was normally open and it may have been frustrated rage which drove him to an impetuous course of secret action; and worthy of censure though he doubtless was, it must be said in mitigation that he and Elizabeth afterwards lived in great happiness together in Tuscany, being converted to the Catholic faith and marrying with Papal dispensation. The girl who had given up everything was more than merely beautiful. She was sweet-natured, intelligent and sympathetic, and in all their twenty-four years together as exiles at the Medici Court in Florence there was never a whisper of unfaithfulness on either side.

From England Robert had written to the Grand Duke of Tuscany, Ferdinand I, begging his protection and asking him to be allowed to establish himself in Florence. Ferdinand I was a Medici. He was a cardinal of the Church when he succeeded to the Grand Duchy, bringing with him from Rome his wonderful collection which helped to establish Florence as the centre of Renaissance art. He also encouraged a new form of music—the opera. He was an able administrator and a strong ruler, rooting out corruption in the courts of justice. When he died in 1609 he bequeathed to his son and heir, Cosimo II, not only his wealth but a powerful State envied throughout Italy and Europe for its industry and commerce. The thirty-one-year-old Cosimo had recently married the Archduchess Maria Maddalena, sixteen-year-old daughter of the Archduke Charles of Austria. She was, moreover, a sister-in-law of the powerful Philip III of Spain and her brother Ferdinand was soon to become the Holy Roman Emperor. When Cosimo died of consumption in 1621 his ten-year-old son, Ferdinand II, became Grand Duke of Tuscany with his mother, Maddalena, and his grandmother Christina, as joint Regents, advised by a Council of four. Robert Dudley was to be the valued servant of the Duchy under all of these rulers, from 1606 to 1636.

The Grand Duke Ferdinand I had obviously been impressed by his background, and abilities in the building of ships and in naval command; and he took him into his service in 1607. For the first two years the Dudleys lived at Pisa and Livorno where he was fully employed building the harbour and designing ships; and afterwards they rented a house in the Via dell'Amore in Florence. Here we find him in 1611 and 1612 acting as unofficial negotiator of a proposed marriage between the Grand Duke Cosimo's sister, Caterina, and the heir to the English throne, the

seventeen-year-old Prince Henry—a proposal which foundered
on religious differences. By the middle of December 1612,
Elizabeth presented Dudley with their fourth child and he began
to plan a palace for himself and his growing family. In April 1614
he bought from the Rucellai family a wedge-shaped piece of
ground between Via della Vigna Nuova and the Via della Spada
in Florence, with the narrow end facing Palazzo Strozzi. For
this house, in which he remained until his death thirty-five years
later, he was probably his own architect.

The palace is still there with a plaque on the wall in Via della
Vigna Nuova, erected to Dudley's memory by John Temple
Leader two hundred years later. The loggia underneath is glassed
in and is under restoration by a firm which sells fine table-linen,
P. Navoni, which has cut its name in large lettering into the
stone on the first floor, under the Rucellai crest. Looking down
the Via della Spada the fine curved sweep of the building, now
housing the American Express Bank among other offices, is
impressive. Beyond is the shell of the former Church of San
Pancrazio, where doubtless Dudley intended to be buried beside
his wife. At present there is scaffolding everywhere and the
Church's future is uncertain. The little asymmetrical Piazza of
San Pancrazio is a sorry sight, the great church window above it
broken, and birds flying in and out at will.

Dudley had another house as well—or rather the life use of it,
granted him by Cosimo II—near Quarto, and called I Rinieri.
I was shown it by Dottore Ferdinando Chiostri, of the Florence
Restoration Committee, who explained that much of the original
villa remains despite additions made by the Corsini family, who
converted it into a fine baroque house in the eighteenth century,
adding the lovely façade with its central clock. As we entered
the gardens and came round to the back of the house the long,
low proportions of the original building showed themselves to
advantage. The rooms open off a central courtyard and include
an elegant theatre which was previously the ballroom. It is
possible to imagine the house animated by the gay life of the
large Dudley family with their beautiful mother, and their
handsome talented father. Upstairs Dottore Chiostri pointed
with pride to the original beamed ceilings and assured me that
with a concentrated work force it would be possible to restore

the villa as a museum in a year or so; the work having already started in the orangery along the side of the garden. The staircases are of grey *pietra serena*, the local stone of Maiano, and I noticed in the upstairs rooms simple and elegant window seats, in the same stone with a step up and a seat at either side. The garden, with its low scalloped wall sweeping round in a semi-circle, was altered to the style of the eighteenth century by the Corsini family, who used to own all the surrounding land with its peaceful farms and *olivetti*. When industry arrived and factories were built in the twentieth century they moved away.

The plaque on the baroque façade of the house describes it in Italian as the place where Dudley for many years found 'delicious repose', and one can easily believe it. Here he must have found quiet after the noisy Florentine streets, and no doubt he entertained the Grand Ducal family (the Archduchess Maddalena was the godmother of one of his daughters). And when sorrow struck it must surely have been here that he came to mourn.

By 1621 Dudley's work on the harbour and mole at Livorno was completed, and he was able to devote more time to his Court duties, where he was Grand Chamberlain both to the Archduchess Maddalena and to her mother-in-law, the Grand Duchess Christina. This was the year in which the young Grand Duke Cosimo died, and Dudley was responsible for the funeral ceremony. He continued in the highest esteem of the ducal family and of the other important families in Florence.

In 1630, when the plague swept through Florence, one of its victims was his eldest daughter, the seventeen-year-old Anna, who was buried in San Pancrazio. Then the sun shone again when his second daughter, named Maddalena after the Archduchess, was married to the Prince of Piombina by the good offices of the Grand Duchess Christina, who no doubt helped with the dowry. But life was precarious in days when the only real defence against disease was building up a natural resistance to it, and two more heavy blows were about to strike: first Dudley's promising eldest son Cosimo, who was already Captain of the Grand Duke's bodyguard, succumbed to a fever just before his twenty-first birthday while staying at his sister's house; and then his beloved wife Elizabeth, who had borne her thirteenth child a few months before this death, fell ill. She died in the house in Via della Vigna Nuova in September 1631, at the age of forty-five, and was buried in San Pancrazio under an imposing sepulchre.

Dudley had greatly loved this courageous woman who had followed him loyally and uncomplainingly through all the vicissitudes of their exile. Life with a man of his restlessly brilliant mind and proud nature which had been fretted for years by injustice, cannot have been easy for her, and they were often short of money: no doubt Tuscany had offered her trials as well as splendours. But she had smoothed her husband's rough edges, restrained his impulsiveness and eased his path at court where she was a close friend of the Archduchess Maddalena (a foreigner like herself), and he must have missed her painfully.

The bright day was beginning to fade for him, and when 1636 saw the death of the Grand Duchess Christina who had been his friend for so long, he felt that the links he had forged were breaking and that his influence at Court was on the wane. He retired and settled down to complete and prepare for publication his great work, *Arcano del Mare*, and in 1639 he died at his country house, I Rinieri. No doubt he intended to be buried beside Elizabeth in San Pancrazio, but for some reason this was not done, and it is not known where his body lies.

The great esteem in which Dudley was held in Tuscany, and his achievements there, did not divert his mind from the loss of his possessions in England and his hope of reclaiming them; and the Grand Ducal family supported him in this hope.

Duke Ferdinand I instructed Lotti, his ambassador in London, to attempt to reinstate Dudley in the King's favour:

> Here he is known as a worthy knight and of the utmost goodwill
> ... he could not possibly entertain any idea of disloyalty or ill-faith
> towards King James or his State. ...

and again:

> It seems to us that this knight shows himself every day more
> worthy of our protection and especially of our efforts to prove in

Rome the validity of his last marriage. We will, therefore, that you do your best to elucidate the matter in his favour as far as you can for truth's sake.[1]

These attempts failed—Dudley had too many enemies at the Court of James I—and another was made through the sympathetic interest of the heir to the throne of England, Prince Henry, whose alliance with the Grand Ducal family Dudley was then attempting to negotiate. Dudley's former tutor, now Sir Thomas Chaloner, was Chamberlain of the Prince's household, and the young man's precocious intelligence had benefited greatly from his guidance. It was agreed that the Prince should help by buying Kenilworth for himself for a nominal sum, and holding it until such time as Dudley could return to England; but the Prince died of typhoid fever in November 1612, and after his death Chaloner, who himself had not long to live, lost his influence. Dudley's hopes saw an even more bitter blow in 1618: news came that Robert Sidney had been created Earl of Leicester, and Robert Rich Earl of Warwick. It was reported by Amerigo Salvetti, who had replaced Lotti as ambassador, and who regretted that it was 'to the prejudice of Sir Robert Dudley, Earl of Leicester and Warwick'—'who is at great disadvantage now because he has no one to take his affairs in hand for him'. The Archduchess Maddalena put the facts before her brother, the Holy Roman Emperor Ferdinand II who had ousted James I's Protestant son-in-law, Frederick of the Palatine, from the imperial throne. Affirming that everyone ought to possess what is his own, even while in exile, the Emperor—to the great annoyance of King James—issued letters patent recognising Dudley as the legitimate heir of his grandfather, whose attainder he put aside, thus confirming him Duke of Northumberland with the title continuing in the male line.

At one time Dudley's anger against James I was so bitter that through a friend, the merchant Andrew Tracey who lived in Florence, he informed Amerigo Salvetti that he intended to take reprisals against English Protestant shipping and English merchants coming into Livorno until he had recovered the equivalent of the value of his confiscated estates in England. This rather piratical

---

[1] The State Archives, Florence.

plan received the approval of the Papal authorities, with whom Dudley, despite bad relations between Pope Urban VIII and his master the Grand Duke, was on such good terms that he was enrolled as a member of the Roman nobility and was authorised to form an Order of Knighthood. In the end nothing came of this impetuous and ill-judged idea.

Almost equally ill-judged was Dudley's attempt to propitiate King James by sending him a tract he had written entitled 'For Bridling the Impertinence of Parliament', which also proposed methods of increasing revenue based on those of Tuscany. This was ill received, and even in the next reign, when copies were at last distributed, was regarded as a dangerous document.

In spite of his continuing resentment against his mother-country, Dudley must have gained innumerable satisfactions from the opportunities offered him by the State of his adoption. They were exactly suited to his unusual and diverse talents.

Anthony à Wood tells us:

> I have heard from some living who have visited those parts, that this . . . Robert Dudley was the chief instrument in causing the said Duke [Ferdinand I] not only to fortify it [Livorno] and make it a *scala franca*, that is a free port, but of setting up an English factory there, and of drying the fens between that and Pisa. At which time also our author induced many English merchants what were his friends to go and reside there.

The harbour and mole of Livorno were, indeed, built to Dudley's design, as was a canal and the aqueduct bringing fresh water to Pisa. He brought English shipwrights out to what might almost be called 'his' port, and introduced English shipyard practice. He also designed a whole range of ships to out-sail and out-gun those of the Turks; and his galleon the *San Giovanni Battista*, 'which carried sixty-four guns and was a rare and strong sailor of great repute and the terror of the Turks in those seas', once captured a galleon of twice her own size, and put a Turkish fleet of forty-eight galleys to flight without assistance. And a new form of oar which he invented was praised by the galley-slaves who used it as being much easier and more effective than the old.

As well as being a designer of ships and their equipment and a marine engineer, he was evidently a good administrator who could get things done. Of Livorno he wrote: 'Completed the mole at no great cost and within a period of twelve years, when similar works undertaken elsewhere cost millions of scudi, and took twice as long to finish'.

At Court, with the support of his wife, he was a trusted friend and guide, proving that in spite of his impetuous nature he must have commanded the arts of diplomacy and tact when necessary. He must also have been an ornament to great occasions: a handsome bearded man, towering above the Italians, striking in doublet and silk hose under a mantle of rich purple velvet embroidered with the Medici crest, his broad sash tied on the left over his sword, a plumed felt cap on his head, and in his hand his wand of office.

He shared the scientific interest of his masters, and almost certainly visited Galileo with Cosimo II when the Grand Duke took the genius under his protection, building a house for him at Arcetri (just to the south of Florence) after the Jesuits had declared his teaching heretical and had driven him from the University of Pisa, at which Ferdinand I had given him a professorship. Dudley himself dabbled in chemistry and medicine, inventing a powder which came to be known under the name of Dr Cronachinus of Pisa and was analysed as 'scammony, sulphuret of antimony and tartar, triturated together'. Dudley claimed to have been cured by it when he caught an attack of pleurisy while he was hunting and hawking between Livorno and Pisa, and apparently many other people used it with success.

And in addition to all this, he crowned his life's work by producing a great book. He had begun *Arcano del Mare* as a young man, and it was brought to its conclusion after he had retired from court life in his sixties. He dedicated it to 'The Most Serene Ferdinand II, Grand Duke of Tuscany, his lord', and immediately after the title page he placed the Patent of the Emperor Ferdinand confirming him in the title of Duke of Northumberland, showing how important he found this one triumph in his struggle to establish his rights.

There are five books in the work, which includes not only known facts but also imaginative schemes for the development of navigation, shipbuilding, ocean commerce and maritime power, and which demonstrates his immense knowledge of shipbuilding, warships and the sea. The final book is an original atlas of maps and charts, including a map of the Orinoco delta showing the island he had named Dudleyana. The printing seems to have been delayed by lack of money, but it was completed in 1647 by Stamperia di Francesco Onofri. Some idea of the cost, especially that of the engravings, is given by Jacopo Lucini who published a second edition twelve years after Dudley's death: 'For twelve years sequestered in a little Tuscan village, I have consumed no less than 5,000 lbs of copper in engravings to illustrate the book'.

Arcano del Mare was widely acclaimed. A former superintendent of the Map Room of the British Museum, Edward Lynham, describes it as the work of—

> by far the greatest of the early English chart-markers . . . in many ways a century before its time. It was the first sea atlas in which every chart was on Mercator's projection, the first to give the magnetic delineation of a large number of places and the first to show the prevailing winds and currents at all important harbours and anchorages. . . .
>
> The engraving is superb. Handsome compass roses, ships and little anchors are abundant, soundings are marked, the coasts are shaded inwards, an improvement, at least for charts, on the usual custom of hatching outwards. Large engravings of the surveying and navigational instruments—the best of their day—used or designed by Dudley are included, giving the work an added value.[1]

In Italy there has been almost complete silence about Dudley's work in Tuscany, due perhaps to the jealously nationalistic sentiments of native historians. Bottia's *Historia d'Italia* (published in 1832) for example, gives all the credit for the development of the port of Livorno, its status as a free port, and the draining of the marshes behind it to the Grand Dukes Cosimo II and Ferdinand II.

Nearly three hundred years after Dudley left England, John Temple Leader, Member of Parliament for Westminster from 1837 to 1847, felt the call of Tuscany and bought a little farm in

[1] *British Maps and Mapmakers*, by Edward Lynham, 1904.

the parish of San Martino at Maiano, near Florence. Learning that an adjoining farm had once belonged to a 'Duca di Berlicke', he examined documents relating to the property and found that it had belonged to a Dudley, styled Earl of Warwick and Duke of Northumberland: the son of our Robert Dudley. Mr Leader wrote a *Life of Sir Robert Dudley* (which he described as merely a chronicle of the principal events in the life) and says in the preface that he was unable to find a monument of any kind to this illustrious man, not even a gravestone. He proceeded to remedy the matter as best he could by having plaques erected to Dudley's memory on the palazzo in Via della Vigna Nuova, on Dudley's country villa at Quarto, and at Livorno on the building behind the *I Quatro Mori*. He himself remained in Tuscany and made his home in the fortress of Vincigliata above Maiano, completely restoring it to its former plan.

John Temple Leader's plaques seem a modest memorial to the most towering personality among the English in Tuscany: the one whose work contributed most to the country. Robert Dudley was an example of the complete man of his age, a man of both action and intellect. After him were to come the men of letters only, a simpler, less versatile company.

The carving by Grinling Gibbons sent by Charles II to Cosimo III as a symbol of friendship in 1682, restored in 1972 after flood damage.

Tobias Smollett, by an unkown Italian artist.

CHAPTER IV

In Search of Smollett at Livorno

THE century which followed Dudley's death, from the mid-seventeenth to the mid-eighteenth, saw extraordinary developments in both science and literature. When Robert Dudley was settling down in the Grand Duke of Tuscany's territories at Livorno and Pisa, Galileo had already conducted experiments, possibly from the Leaning Tower of Pisa, to challenge the theory of Aristotle and demonstrate that two lead balls of different weights dropped to earth at the same speed. Galileo held the chair of mathematics at Padua, where he constructed the telescope from theory, proved that the planet Jupiter was attended by four separate bodies each moving in orbit, and indicated that the earth was not stationary but moved in space. He was a man who could be witty but never chose to be tactful, and having openly announced his support for Copernican theories challenging all orthodox opinion of the time, he returned to his native Tuscany and was appointed 'Mathematician and Philosopher to the Court' of the enlightened Cosimo de Medici, as well as 'First Mathematician to the University of Pisa'. Later, after his prosecution for heresy by the Inquisition, he wrote perhaps his greatest work, *Discourses on Two New Sciences*, published in Leyden while he was working under house arrest at Arcetri. Here he enjoyed a reputation as the world's foremost scientist and was kept supplied with the finest food and wine from the palace of the reigning Duke (now Ferdinand II). In 1637 his eyesight failed completely. The following year he received a visit from John Milton, who was also to become blind, and whose sonnet on his blindness is one of the jewels of English poetry. Though the impression of Milton which has come down to many of us, largely through Dr Johnson, is that of a scholar with a reserved and gloomy nature, there seems reason to believe that he could be cheerful and courteous, and in Italy, where he lectured to the academic societies, he made lasting friendships both in Lucca and particularly in the Florentine academies.

In the year that Galileo died, 1642, another scientific genius was born, this time in England—Isaac Newton. His work carried scientific thought so far forward that more than a century was required to digest it: though contributions of enormous importance were also made by Astronomers-Royal Edmund Halley and James Bradley.

These great scientific movements affected only a very small minority of the population. The majority were more influenced by another important development with far-reaching results: the ever-widening dissemination of the printed word. A great many pamphlets and periodicals sprang up, and in England after the ending of the censorship in 1695 no less than thirty new journals appeared in addition to early forms of newspapers. In 1700 Joseph Addison's friend Steele started *The Tatler*, to which both he and Addison contributed. When this ceased some two years later *The Spectator* rose from its ashes: avoiding politics and by no means ignoring a female audience, it found its wide readership largely on account of Addison's essays. The influential Addison had set out on a tour of Italy in 1699, and during his stay in Florence as the guest of the Earl of Shrewsbury he hailed the Uffizi Gallery as the 'noblest collection of Art in the world'. He visited Florence again in 1702-03. His letter in verse, *Tour of Italy*, and his *Remarks on Italy* which followed, were read eagerly. The latter was so widely used as a guide-book that the second-hand value of the first edition became five times greater than the price of the second edition, issued in 1705.

Meanwhile novelists, playwrights and satirists were emerging, and one of the writers who shared the glory of establishing the English novel was Tobias George Smollett, born in 1721. Like another of them, the carelessly brilliant Henry Fielding, he was to die in early middle age and to die abroad—in Tuscany, where he was buried in the English cemetery at Livorno.

This cemetery, which can be entered at 63 Via Verdi (an ambulance station run by the Misericordia), sees few visitors nowadays. Enclosed between walls in the heart of the busy industrial city, it feels less lonely than one would expect in spite of being somewhat neglected, and is full of urns and sarcophagi, skulls and crossbones, broken pillars, cherubs, wreaths and medallions, most of which have suffered some damage from the elements, earthquake or war. There does not seem to be any record of the cemetery's foundation, but there is said to be at least one tomb dated 1594, when Ferdinand I gave Livorno city status. For a long time it was the only English (probably the only Protestant) cemetery in Italy. There are graves of Mr Henry Lambton, MP for Durham, who died in Pisa on November 30, 1797, Frances Horner, Countess Cowper, Countess Orford; and names such as Lockhart, Murray, Lubbock, Ross, Maclean, Stopford, Dunnett abound. It was closed in 1839. Although the British 'factory' at Livorno had ceased to exist in 1825, there were still enough British residents to justify the opening of another cemetery further afield. (The British 'factory', an exceedingly wealthy community, seems to have had the right to levy taxes on shipping entering the port. Visitors to the Tuscan coast often used its banking services—John Evelyn in 1644, for example, and Shelley in 1822.)

Smollett is commemorated by a plain grey marble monument shaped like a pyramid, bearing the inscription:

Memoriae
Tobias Smollett
Qui Liburni
Animam efflavit 16 *Sept. 1773 quidam*
Ex suis valde amicis
Civibus
Hunc Tumulum
Fecerunt

The grave is outlined with a rectangle of marble containing two neglected-looking rose bushes.

Smollett is little read nowadays except by students of English literature, but *Roderick Random*, *Peregrine Pickle*, *Humphrey Clinker* and the rest were immensely popular in the nineteenth century.

Born in Dunbartonshire in 1721, into a Scottish family of standing, he was apprenticed to a surgeon in Glasgow at the age of fifteen and came to England three years later, having already begun his writing career. In order to make a living he found he had to take the position of surgeon's mate on HMS *Cumberland*, and he served during the siege of Cartagena in 1741, returning with the fleet to Jamaica where he fell in love with a planter's daughter, Nancy Lascelles. He married her after his return to England, and her dowry must have been a lifesaver for he was able to set up as a surgeon in Downing Street and obtained his MD degree in June 1750; but it soon became evident that medicine was not his vocation. He decided he must concentrate on writing fiction. His first novel, *Roderick Random*, published in 1748, was based on his experiences on the highroad to England and on board the *Cumberland*. In a letter written to his friend Dr Alexander Carlyle (minister of the parish of Inveresk for fifty-seven years) he tells us:

> The whole was begun and finished in the compass of eight months. . . . I take the opportunity of declaring to you in all the sincerity of the most unreserved friendship that no person living is aimed at, in all the first part of the book that is, while the scene is laid in Scotland; and that (the account of the expedition to Carthagena excepted) the whole is not so much a representation of my life as that of many other needy Scotch surgeons whom I have known either personally or by report. . . .[1]

His second novel, *The Adventures of Peregrine Pickle*, was a great success both in England and France. After his third, *Ferdinand, Count Fathom* (1753), he settled in Chelsea. This novel did not make money and Smollett had to do uncongenial literary hack work, such as organising big and easily sold standard works for the booksellers. He was a generous man, but impetuous; when a Scot named Peter Gordon, who had refused to pay him a debt, wrote him an insulting letter, he forthwith set out with a witness, and had Gordon called out of his lodgings and thrashed him. Gordon brought a suit for assault with intent to murder: the case was dismissed but Smollett had to pay the costs. Dr Carlyle recalled that he and Smollett and several Scottish friends 'frequently resorted to a small tavern at the corner of Cockspur Street at the

---

[1] *Letters of Tobias Smollett*, edited by Edward S. Noyes, 1969.

Golden Ball, where we had a frugal supper and a little punch, as the finances of none of the company were in very good order. But we had rich enough conversation on literary subjects which was enlivened by Smollett's agreeable stories which he told with peculiar grace.' They were together on the night that the news of the defeat at Culloden was brought, and Smollett, who did not support the Jacobites, was nevertheless shocked and enraged at the reported atrocities perpetrated by the Duke of Cumberland's victorious soldiers. Accordingly he wrote a poem, 'The Tears of Scotland', which was circulated freely and set to music by a well-known Edinburgh musician, James Oswald:

> *Yet, when the rage of battle ceas'd,*
> *The victor's soul was not appeas'd:*
> *The naked and forlorn must feel*
> *Devouring flames and murd'ring steel.*

By 1756, when his portrait was painted by William Verelst (later he sat for Nathaniel Dance), Smollett's appearance was that of a well-to-do doctor and gentleman of the time, and he obviously lived well. He developed a friendship with John Wilkes, politician and wit, but later, when Wilkes edited *The North Briton* in reply to Smollett's editorship of *The Briton*, which was subsidised by the Tory Earl of Bute's administration, they inevitably quarrelled.

Before this, in 1756, Smollett had edited a new literary periodical entitled *The Critical Review*. In 1758 he was tried and convicted for libel on Admiral Knowles, fined £100, sentenced to three months' imprisonment in the King's Bench Prison, and obliged to give security for good conduct for seven years: a cruel blow.

Although Smollett advocated social reform, he disliked the mob. He attacked Catholics at one end of the religious scale and fanatical Protestants at the other, having moved from the Presbyterianism of his Scottish youth towards the Church of England when he settled in Chelsea. Inevitably, with his tendency to sarcasm, spleen and invective, he sometimes went beyond satire into personal abuse in his descriptions of such London personalities as David Garrick, but in his fiction he had an unusual eye for exact detail which accords with his medical training.

Deserted by Lord Bute, *The Briton* died in 1763, and Smollett began to think of gigantic undertakings such as a universal gazetteer and a translation of Voltaire in thirty-eight volumes. But he was ill, shattered by the death of his only daughter at the age of fifteen, and disgusted with things in England, and his anxious wife persuaded him to go abroad for a period, to recuperate. In June 1762, a year before he went to the Continent, he had written to his friend Dr Moore: 'I have had no attack of asthma these two months but I am extremely emaciated: and am afflicted with a leeking catarrh and cough all night without ceasing'.[1]

From Dover he and his wife set out, with his Greek and Latin classics and copies of Shakespeare, to travel through France to Nice; and from there he was transported by gondola (hugging the pirate-ridden coast in a vessel which he described as 'smaller than a felucca, rowed by four men and steered by the patron') to Genoa. At this stage he was favourably impressed by the Italians, particularly by those in Genoa, *la Superba*.

A Frenchman lays out his whole revenue upon tawdry suits of clothes or in furnishing a magnificent *repas* . . . a Genoese on the other hand keeps himself and his family at short allowance that he may save money to build palaces and churches, which remain to after-ages so many monuments of his taste, piety, and munificence; and in the meantime give employment and bread to the poor and industrious. . . .

The business then was to travel by land to Florence by the way of Pisa, which is seven posts distant from Lerici. Those who have not their own carriage must either hire chaises to perform the whole journey or travel by way of *cambiatura*, which is that of changing the chaises every post, as the custom is in England. In this case the great inconvenience arises from your being obliged to shift your baggage every post. The chaise or *calesse* of this country is a wretched machine with two wheels, as uneasy as a common cart, being indeed no other than what we should call in England a very ill-contrived one-horse chair, narrow, naked, shattered and shabby.[2]

[1] *Letters of Tobias Smollett*, edited by Edward S. Noyes, 1969.
[2] *Travels Through France and Italy*, by Tobias Smollett, 1766.

At last they arrived at Pisa, where he was glad to find himself
'housed in a very good inn . . . and was not disappointed'. He
carried letters of introduction to one of the professors at the
university, and like John Evelyn more than a century earlier was
much impressed by

the fine old city that strikes you with the same veneration you
would feel at sight of an ancient temple which bears the marks of
decay without being absolutely dilapidated. The houses are well
built, the streets open, straight and well-paved: the shops well
furnished: and the markets well supplied: there are some elegant
palaces, designed by great masters. The churches are built with
taste and tolerably ornamented. There is a beautiful wharf of
freestone on each side of the river Arno which runs through the
city, and three bridges thrown over it, of which that in the middle
is of marble, a pretty piece of architecture; but the number of
inhabitants is very inconsiderable: and this very circumstance gives
it an air of majestic solitude, which is far from being unpleasant to a
man of a contemplative turn of mind . . . The University of Pisa
is very much decayed; and except the little business occasioned by
the emperor's gallies which are built in this town,[1] I know of no
commerce it carries on; perhaps the inhabitants live on the produce
of the country which consists of corn, wine and cattle. They are
supplied with excellent water for drinking by an aqueduct consisting of above five thousand arches, begun by Cosmo and finished
by Ferdinand I, grand Dukes of Tuscany. It conveys the water
from the mountains at the distance of four miles. This noble city
formerly the capital of a flourishing and powerful republic, which
contained above one hundred and fifty thousand inhabitants
within its walls is now so desolate that grass grows in the open
streets: and the number of its people do not exceed sixteen
thousand. . . .

In the cathedral which is a large Gothic pile . . . the greatest
curiosity is that of the brass gates, designed and executed by John
of Bologna, representing, embossed in different compartments,
the history of the Old and New Testament. I was so charmed with
this work that I could have stood a whole day to examine and admire
it.[2]

---

[1] In a MS note Smollett says this is a mistake. 'No gallies have been built
here for a great many years and the dock is now converted into stables for the
Grand Duke's Horse Guards.'

Travels Through France and Italy, by Tobias Smollett, 1766.

Smollett was always conscious of his Scottish origins and had felt isolated in London, which perhaps accounted for the sharpness of his satire on the English. In 1768 he hoped through his friend David Hume, another of his Scottish contemporaries, and then Under-Secretary of State, to obtain the consulship of Leghorn (the English name for Livorno) or Nice, but without success, and this doubtless explained his increasingly jaundiced views of Europe.

Writing his *Travels Through France and Italy* in 1765, some five hundred years after Dante had deplored the attitude to money of the nobles, Smollett found it strange that

> with all their pride, however, the nobles of Florence are humble enough to enter into partnership with shopkeepers, and even to sell wine by retail. It is an undoubted fact that in every palace or great house in this city there is a little window fronting the street, provided with an iron knocker, and over it hangs an empty flask by way of a signpost. Thither you send your servant to buy a bottle of wine. He knocks at the little wicket which is opened immediately by a domestic who supplies him with what he wants and receives the money like the waiter or any other cabaret. It is pretty extraordinary that it should not be deemed a disparagement in a noble to sell half a pound of figs or a palm of ribbon or tape, or to take money for a flask of sour wine, and yet be counted infamous to match his daughter in the family of a person who has distinguished himself in any one of the learned professions.[1]

But even the misanthropic and ailing Smollett succumbed to the spell of the city. 'Florence is a noble city' he said, and he talked of her 'very elegant appearance to which the four bridges and the stone quay contribute in great measure.' 'There is a considerable number of fashionable people at Florence and many of them in good circumstances. They affect a gaiety in their dress, equipage and conversation but stand very much on their punctilio with strangers, and will not without great reluctance admit into their assemblies any lady of another country whose *noblesse* is not ascertained by a title.' Then came the sting: 'This reserve is in some measure excusable among a people who are extremely ignorant of foreign customs, and who know that in their own

---

[1] *Travels Through France and Italy*, by Tobias Smollett, 1766.

country every person, even the most insignificant, who has any pretensions to family, either inherits or assumes the title of principe, conte or marchese'.

He meditated upon the fact that

though Florence be tolerably populous there seems to be very little trade of any kind in it: but the inhabitants flatter themselves with the prospect of reaping great advantage from the residence of one of the arch-dukes for whose reception they are now repairing the palace of Pitti. I know not what the revenues of Tuscany may amount to since the succession of the princes of Lorrain, but, under the late dukes of the Medici family, they were said to produce two millions of crowns, equal to five hundred thousand pounds sterling. These arose from a very heavy tax upon land and houses, the portions of maidens and suits at law, besides the duties upon traffick, a severe *gabelle* upon the necessaries of life, and a toll upon every eatable entered into this capital. If we may believe Leti, the grand duke was then able to raise and maintain an army of forty thousand infantry and three thousand horse; with twelve gallies, two galleasses and twenty ships of war. I question if Tuscany can maintain at present above one half of such an armament. He that now commands the emperor's navy consisting of a few frigates, is an Englishman, called Acton, who was heretofore captain of a ship in our East India Company's service. He has lately embraced the Catholic religion and been created Admiral of Tuscany. There is a tolerable opera in Florence for the entertainment of the best company, though they do not seem very attentive to the musick. Italy is certainly the native country of this art; and yet I do not find the people in general either more musically inclined or better provided with ears than their neighbours. Here is also a wretched troop of comedians for the bourgeois and lower class of people; but what seems most to suit the taste of all ranks is the exhibition of church pageantry. I had occasion to see a procession where all the *noblesse* of the city attended in their coaches which filled the whole length of the great street called the *Corso*. It was the anniversary of a charitable institution in favour of poor maidens a certain number of whom are portioned every year. About two hundred of these virgins walked in procession two and two together, clothed in violet-coloured wide gowns with white veils on their heads, and made a very classical appearance. They were preceded and followed by an irregular mob of penitents in sackcloth with lighted tapers and monks carrying crucifixes, bawling

and bellowing the litanies; but the great object was a figure of the
Virgin Mary, as big as the life, standing within a gilt frame, dressed
in a gold stuff, with a large hoop, a great quantity of false jewels,
her face painted and patched, her hair frizzled and curled in the
very extremity of the fashion. Very little regard had been paid to
the image of our Saviour on the cross, but when his lady-mother
appeared on the shoulders of three or four lusty friars, the whole
populace fell upon their knees in the dirt. This extraordinary
veneration paid to the Virgin must have been derived originally
from the French who pique themselves on their gallantry to the
fair sex.[1]

This little sarcasm was nothing to his disgust at the *cicisbei* of
Florence: the last straw to a manly Northerner:

Just without one of the gates of Florence there is a triumphal arch
erected on occasion of the emperor making his public entry, when
he succeeded to the dukedom of Tuscany: and here in the summer
evenings the quality resort to take the air in their coaches. Every
carriage stops and forms a little separate *conversazione*. The ladies
sit within, and the *cicisbei* stand on the footboards, on each side of
the coach, entertaining them with their discourse. It would be no
unpleasant inquiry to trace this sort of gallantry to its original and
investigate all its progress. The Italians having been accused of
jealousy, were resolved to wipe off the reproach, and, seeking to
avoid it for the future, have run into the other extreme. I know it is
generally supposed that the custom of choosing *cicisbei* was calcu-
lated to prevent the extinction of families, which would otherwise
often happen in consequence of marriages founded upon interest,
without any mutual affection in the contracting parties. How far
this political consideration may have weighed against the jealous
and vindictive temper of the Italians I will not pretend to judge:
but certain it is, every married lady in this country has her *cicisbei*
or *serviente*, who attends her everywhere, and on all occasions:
and upon whose privileges the *husband dares not encroach without
incurring the censure and ridicule of the whole community*. For my part
I would rather be condemned for life to the gallies than exercise
the office of *cicisbeo*, exposed to the intolerable caprices and dangerous resentment of an Italian virago. I pretend not to judge the
national character from my own observation but if the portraits

[1] *Travels Through France and Italy*, by Tobias Smollett, 1766.

drawn by Goldoni in his comedies are taken from nature I would not hesitate to pronounce the Italian women the most haughty insolent capricious and revengeful females on the face of the earth. Indeed their resentments are so cruelly implacable and contain such a mixture of perfidy, that in my opinion, they are very unfit subjects for comedy, whose province it is rather to ridicule folly than to stigmatise such atrocious vice.[1]

At first Smollett settled at Pisa, but in the spring of 1770 he moved to a house outside Livorno on the slopes of Monte Nero called Il Giardino, where he remained till his death a year later. It is still there, with an enchanting view of the sea at Antignano to the south of Livorno and the wooded slopes of Monte Nero higher to the north—but alas the main coastal railway, some modern blocks of buildings and a petrol station intervene. When I visited the house I was kindly received by the present member of the noble Niccolai-Gamba family from whose ancestors Smollett leased it: a gentle, slender widow whose husband had been a colonial governor. She showed me over the long, low, well-proportioned villa, and opened the windows of Smollett's simple room on the south corner. The once well-kept gardens, she pointed out, were now much overgrown, because instead of seven gardeners she could afford only one for two days a week. In the sheltered courtyard below Smollett's bedroom at the back the climbing roses were blooming in the February sunshine. Smollett himself noted of the place: 'I am at present rusticated on the side of a mountain that overlooks the sea, in the neighbourhood of Leghorne, a most romantic and salutary situation'. And Alexander Malcolm, a travelling Scot, described it in this way when he followed in the steps of his fellow countryman:

There is none to be compared in point either of situation or elegance with the last abode of Smollett. You may hire a gig to go this distance . . . winding around the mountain . . . the place bursts upon you all at once, and certainly nothing on earth can be truly more romantic. It commands a divine view of the Mediterranean with the Islands of Gorgona and Elba on the right and left, and the snow-capped mountains of Corsica between in the distance. There is also a delightful stream which skirts the front of the house,

---

[1] Ibid.

almost as transparent as Smollett's own poetry-inspiring Severn . . . and the road for five or six miles beyond in the direction of Rome forms one of the most charming rides in the country. The apartments of the house . . . are plain but lofty, and without that air of comfort or snugness which is so essential with us. You may guess the state of my feelings, however, the feelings of a countryman and an ardent admirer of his genius, when I was shown the very bed where the poet's eyes were closed forever upon all terrestrial things, and also when the identical stadium was pointed out in which his last and most humorous work was begun and finished. The premises are now occupied by a rich bookseller of Leghorn who takes apparently a mighty pride in detailing his *Smollett's reminiscences* and who boasts with much truth, but some vanity, that the place is just such a one as any poet or philosopher might select either to live or to die in.[1]

It was a little saddening to find that local pride in the novelist has now faded. When I asked a native of Monte Nero, whose family had lived there for two or three generations, to direct me to Smollett's house, he had never heard of any such writer living or dying in the district.

Smollett had his own ideas of how to treat the illness which killed him. Writing from Nice to Dr William Hunter the anatomist, a Scot who had become very successful in London, he was sarcastic about the diagnosis made by a Dr Fizes of Montpellier: 'An old sordid scoundrel, and an old woman into the bargain. . . . He insisted upon it that I had Tubercules, which were suppurated. He prescribed Bouillons of Land Tortoise, for a fortnight, opiates at night, and then a course of Goats milk; but not a word of exercise. . . .'

Dr Fizes was probably correct in his diagnosis—and the goat's milk would not be laughed out of court by more modern opinion, whatever it might make of the land tortoise soup—but the self-willed Dr Smollett had an unwavering faith in the value of cold baths and exercise (Peregrine Pickle had Mrs Pickle's firm use of cold water to thank for his good health). Both the *Travels* and the correspondence show that he followed this spartan regime, and it may well have hastened his death.

---

[1] *Letters of an Invalid from Italy, Malta and the South of France*, by Alexander Malcolm.

When it came—of 'an acute intestinal infection', it was said—
he was attended by an Italian, Dr Gentili, whose diary is in the
Biblioteca Riccardiana in Florence. Gentili's account of Smollett's
end translates thus:

> Mr Smollett aged fifty, a man of historical talent. 1771 September,
> asthmatic, suffers from colic, chronic diarrhea, convulsions, fever.
> He has vigour, fiery temperament, will not drink. Visited for the
> first time on Saturday evening 14th September. Dr Garden on the
> 15th prescribed vesicatories. He has a scabrous condition as in skin
> disease. His parents were healthy. He died asthmatic and consump-
> tive without trying to help himself. The night of September 17th
> he expired. He had been ordered a cordial of Rhine wine with
> cane sugar. A man of matured talent enduring the blows of human
> life, but almost misanthropic. He lived eighteen years in perfect
> harmony with his wife by whom he had a daughter who wrote
> poetry. He had a very ardent and choleric temperament but was
> reflective and devoted to political and historical studies.

Just before his death Smollett completed what I believe to be
his best book, *Humphrey Clinker*. Some fifty years later a little
boy who lived at Chatham, Charles Dickens, fell voraciously
upon some novels in a collection of cheap editions brought home
by his father: they were *Roderick Random*, *Peregrine Pickle*,
Humphrey Clinker and Smollett's translation of *Gil Blas*. He was
to say 'they kept alive my fancy, and my hope of something
beyond that place and time';[1] and in 1845, when he, in his turn,
was visiting Tuscany, and arrived at Livorno, he described it as
'made illustrious by Smollett's grave'.

---

[1] *Pictures from France and Italy*, by Charles Dickens, 1846.

CHAPTER V

The Grand Tour and the Shelley Circle

ADDISON prefaced his *Remarks on Several Parts of Italy* (1705) with an observation which sums up the attitude of the educated and upper classes of England in the eighteenth century:

> There is evidently no place in the world where a man may travel with greater pleasure and advantage than in Italy. One finds something more particular in the face of the country, and more astonishing in the works of nature, than can be met with in any other part of Europe.

Dr Johnson went so far as to declare that a man 'who has not been to Italy is always conscious of an inferiority'; and although by then the puritanism of northern Europe had encouraged the feeling that the Italian people were slightly decadent, every young man of good family was sent to Italy to complete his education. These British were often self-assured and arrogant: it was Italy's past they came to study; they were satisfied with their own manners and customs, finding them superior to those of anyone else. Yet they were attracted by much of what they saw, and especially by Florence. Enclosed within the medieval walls (so unnecessarily demolished in the nineteenth century), Florence charmed the British then as it does today.

The English representative at the Court of Florence from 1740 was Sir Horace Mann, protégé of Sir Robert Walpole who was Prime Minister to George II, and friend of Walpole's son Horace. Soon after his appointment Horace Walpole went to stay with him at Casa Manetti on Via Santo Spirito where Mann continued to live for forty-six years, and the correspondence which followed between the two men is perhaps Mann's chief claim to fame. While he was in Florence Horace Walpole seems to have allowed his immense enjoyment of the social round to divert him from more cultural interests. Perhaps he saw too much of Elizabeth Grifoni, whose *cavaliere servente* he became, to allow him much time for the artistic and historic treasures he had come to study. Fifty years later he remembered nostalgically:

> The delicious nights on the Ponte di Trinita, at Florence in a linen night-gown and a straw hat, with improvisatori, and music and the coffee houses open with ices.[1]

English envoys to the Courts of Italy were not usually of high intellectual calibre, being often appointed by reason of family connection. Mann was no exception, but he was a typical cultured Englishman of the time. He was a charming host to innumerable visitors whose entertainment ruined him financially, including the great architects James Adam and his brother Robert. He had to present many of them at the Grand Ducal Court. He was conscientious in his duties which included keeping an eye on Charles Edward, the Stuart Pretender to the English throne; protecting the English traders at Livorno when they were involved with the central government of Tuscany; and accompanying the Court when it moved to Pisa. A man of taste, he made a small additional income by organising for the English copies of great paintings in public galleries and private collections. He was a kind man and went to Livorno, for instance, to visit Smollett to see if he could help in any way. The long and regular correspondence he kept up with Horace Walpole (who never returned to Tuscany but maintained a great interest in it) became a vivid source of information about the era.

In 1751 Giuseppe Baretti, friend of Dr Johnson, came to London with a very poor opinion of English tourists. He remarked that:

> the English travel to see things, not men . . . their poor curiosity will hardly extend farther than pictures and statues or carnival festivities and holy-week ceremonies. . . .

[1] *Letters*, volume 1, by Sir Horace Walpole.

In his *Account of the Manners and Customs of Italy*, in 1769, he estimated that in the preceding seventeen years more than 10,000 Englishmen had been 'running up and down Italy', and by 1785 there were said to be 40,000 on the Continent of Europe. He himself aided the influence of Italy on England by the publication of an Italian-English dictionary, as well as by three volumes of *Travels*, and other books.

Despite the superficial approach of those who came to Tuscany on the Grand Tour—Lucca, for instance, was often visited only for the purity of its speech, and Siena for its relative cheapness, without much attention being paid to their architectural and artistic treasures—Italian influence on the British was very strong.

Science, which was encouraged in Tuscany by the Grand Duke Peter Leopold, joined with art in providing a meeting-ground. Lord Holland's *Memoirs* refute the idea of Tuscan intellectual inferiority: he remembered that in Florence 'Natural philosophy . . . was the passion of the day and geology, chemistry and electricity the fashionable topics of conversation'.

George Nassau, third Earl Cowper, who sacrificed his seat in parliament and offended his father by staying on in the Florence he loved for thirty years, was one of the more pompous Englishmen who came on the Grand Tour, yet he too cemented Anglo-Tuscan friendship. As a linguist he was completely at home in Italy and his wealth allowed him to be not only a leading host in Florence but also a generous patron of the arts. In 1764 he bought the Villa Palmieri, in Via della Compora where over a century later Queen Victoria was to stay. Cowper's interests also extended to science, and he became a friend of Alessandro Bicchierai, founder member of the Accademia degli Armonici. In 1784 Mary Berry described his laboratory:

> Breakfasted at Lord Cowper's, in the cabinet, an apartment of five small rooms elegantly fitted up with the finest instruments for experiments in all the different branches of natural philosophy: one is dedicated to electricity, a second a laboratory, a third for optics, a fourth for hydraulic experiments, a fifth for air.[1]

[1] *Extracts from the Journals and Correspondence of Miss M. Berry*, volume 1, edited by T. Lewis, 1865.

Percy Bysshe Shelley, painted by Amelia Curran in 1819.

Mary Wollstonecroft Shelley, painted by R. Rothwell in 1841.

Palazzo Lanfranchi in Pisa, which Shelley rented for Byron.

The eighteenth century was marked by the colonial struggle between France and Britain, and there came to Livorno at the end of the century one of the greatest and most loved men in English history—Admiral Lord Nelson. We have seen how the new port of Livorno was constructed by Dudley. It seems somehow fitting that his initiative should later be put to good use by his own country at a critical time in her history. When war broke out with the French in 1893 Captain Horatio Nelson was given command of a sixty-four-gun man-of-war—the *Agamemnon* —and soon afterwards he blockaded Toulon. In the autumn of that year he was in Livorno, essential to the British Navy as a free and neutral port and one of its main victualling and rest centres. Many of Nelson's letters in the next seven years are date-lined 'Leghorn', 'off Leghorn' and 'Leghorn Roads'; and he received much of his mail here. Carola Oman in her superb biography of Nelson[1] writes:

> He was now fast becoming what he called 'an old Mediterranean man', well accustomed to brown shirts and scanty dinners, and he knew the free and neutral port of Leghorn as well as his native Lynn. The Tuscan sea-bathing resort, used by the Mediterranean fleet for refitting and revictualling, had not many wholesome attractions for the exile, and when a sterner Admiral succeeded Hotham, he took ruthless measures to check behaviour which had resulted in a lamentable percentage of officers and men being invalided to Ajaccio Hospital. The second-rate hotel and opera charged exorbitant prices. Nelson haunted the house of the Pollards, Levant merchants, and together with Mr Udney, British Consul, often agents for prizes taken by the fleet. He ordered his portrait in miniature from a local artist, who produced for the admiration of Mrs Horatio Nelson a curiously pursy-looking sea-captain, with fashionably curly hair.

In 1796 Napoleon and his army arrived just in time to see the British fleet evacuate the English merchants. In the following May Nelson was informed that they could safely return: but in 1799 the French finally occupied Livorno, the British Envoy (Mann had died in 1786) retired to Palermo, and the Grand Duke was expelled by the French.

---

[1] *Nelson*, by Carola Oman, 1947.

Just before Livorno finally succumbed, however, Nelson sailed in with the Bourbon King and Queen of Naples accompanied by his friends, the British Envoy at Naples, Sir William Hamilton, and his wife Emma. The King and Queen set off for Florence, followed a day later by Nelson and the Hamiltons and an English-woman, Miss Knight. The last described in her *Autobiography* how they travelled by coach to Ancona (breaking down near Florence) to take ship for Trieste and travel overland to England, thus escaping from the French Army under Napoleon, who had already occupied Lucca, by a matter of hours. Had Nelson been captured the course of English history might have been changed.

While England was at war with France, travel in Italy had to be suspended, but after the British victory at Waterloo in 1815 tourists once more crossed Europe. Three years later another great Englishman arrived in Livorno: Percy Bysshe Shelley.

'I knew that miserable man and am well acquainted with his dreadful history', wrote the poet Southey after Shelley's death, although he too had been a rebel in his youth. 'Shelley was not wicked by disposition . . . but he adopted the Devil's own philosophy.' And Lamb: 'Shelley the great Atheist has gone down by water to eternal fire!' Shelley's adherence to the Spirit of Nature rather than to God was too much for many people, even for some who knew him well. But Byron rallied to his defence: 'You were all brutally mistaken about Shelley, who was, without exception, the *best* and least selfish man I ever knew. I never knew one who was not a beast in comparison.' And Leigh Hunt: 'He was like a spirit that has darted out of its orb and found itself in another world'.

This descendant of solid, conservative parliamentary squires, who was born in Sussex in 1792 and given a sound classical grounding at Eton, was well described by his close friend and future biographer, Thomas Jefferson Hogg, whom he met when he was at University College, Oxford.

His clothes were expensive . . . but they were tumbled, rumpled, unbrushed. His gestures were abrupt, and sometimes violent, occasionally even awkward, yet more frequently gentle and grace-ful. His complexion was delicate and almost feminine . . . his hair

was long and bushy, and in fits of absence, and in the agonies . . .
of anxious thought, he often rubbed it fiercely with his hands or
passed the fingers quickly through his locks unconsciously, so that
it was singularly wild and rough . . . His features were not sym-
metrical (the mouth perhaps excepted) yet was the effect of the
whole extremely powerful. They breathed an animation, a fire, an
enthusiasm, a vivid and preternatural intelligence, that I never
met with any other countenance. Nor was the moral expression
less beautiful than the intellectual; for there was a softness, a delicacy,
a gentleness, and especially (though this will surprise many) that
air of profound religious veneration . . . But there was one physical
blemish that threatened to neutralize all his excellence . . . the
voice . . . was intolerably shrill, harsh and discordant. . . .[1]

At Oxford Shelley was both chemist and alchemist, and
wrote a novel, but the greatest influence on his thought was
Godwin's *Political Justice*: 'Government is an evil, a usurpation
upon the private judgment and individual conscience of mankind'.
Godwin's daughter Mary Wollstonecraft, became Shelley's
second wife. His first was the sixteen year-old Harriet Westbrook
whom he married in 1811, the year he was sent down from
Oxford for publishing an anonymous pamphlet entitled *The
Necessity of Atheism*, and broke with his father. After three
unhappy years with him Harriet drowned herself in the Serpentine
in Hyde Park.

Shelley married Mary Wollstonecraft in March 1818 (the
year her novel *Frankenstein* was published), and the couple left
England for Italy, with their two children William and Clara, in
1819. They were accompanied by Mary's step-sister Claire
Clairmont who had thrown herself at Byron and now had a
daughter by him, Allegra. The baby was becoming something
of an embarrassment because gossip attributed its paternity to
Shelley and it was thought time to put her in the care of her
father who was in Venice.

To avoid the heat of summer, the party went to Bagni di Lucca,
a watering place in a wooded valley above Lucca. The tide of
fashion has now receded from it, but Bagni di Lucca remains

---

[1] *Life of Shelley*, by Thomas Jefferson Hogg.

charming, embowered in shade and full of echoes of its past, touched with the faded elegance which seems to be peculiar to once-famous spas.

Its reputation as a place of healing seems to date from 1245, and in 1291 Jacopo Puccio, member of a Lucchese society called the Companions of the Baths of Corsena, bought a piece of land there for a hospital. The baths were for both men and women, and crowds gathered on the first Thursday in March, when it was believed that an angel blessed the springs. Puccio administered them until his death in 1316. In 1471 they were rebuilt and improved by Domenico Bertini, who erected the inscription in praise of their waters which can still be seen. Further improvements were made by Napoleon's sister, Elise Baciocchi. She built the road from Lucca and a house for herself which became the centre of a gay seasonal life until she was driven from her Duchy of Lucca, to be succeeded by Marie Louise, Napoleon's second wife. Shelley was transported by the beauty of Bagni di Lucca, and wrote to his friend Thomas Love Peacock:

> . . . the nights are forever serene, and we see a star in the east at sunset—I think it is Jupiter—almost as fine as Venus was last summer: but it wants a certain silver and aerial radiance, and soft yet piercing splendour, which belongs, I suppose, to the latter planet by virtue of its at once divine and female nature . . . In the middle of the day I bathe in a pool or fountain, formed in the middle of the forests by a torrent. It is surrounded on all sides by precipitous rocks, and the waterfall of the stream which forms it falls on to it on one side with perpetual dashing. Close to it, on the top of the rocks are alders, and above the great chestnut trees, whose long and pointed leaves pierce the deep blue sky in strong relief . . . My custom is to undress and sit on the rocks, reading Herodotus, until the perspiration has subsided, and then to leap from the edge of the rock into this fountain. . . .[1]

And two weeks later: 'The chestnut woods are now inexpressibly beautiful, for the chestnuts have become large, and add a new richness to the full foliage. We see here Jupiter, in the east: and Venus, I believe, as the evening star directly after sunset.'

The chestnut woods are still beautiful, and the thermal estab-

---

[1] *The Letters of Percy Bysshe Shelley*, edited by Roger Ingpen, 1913.

lishment is still in use in a quiet way. I was shown two hot springs in grottoes, said to be beneficial for rheumatic complaints among others. It is not expensive to stay there and take the treatment, and visitors interested in the history of the British in Tuscany will find other traces of it in Bagni di Lucca besides the ghosts of Shelley and his party.

A permanent resident there in about 1840 was a Mrs Henry Stisted, who published a book called *Bye-ways of Italy* in which she tells how she and others overcame the reluctance of the Papal authorities in Rome to grant permission for the building of a Protestant church. They won their point at last on condition that it 'should be called a house'; and they chose an architect from Lucca who had visited England, Signor Pardini, to design 'a small Venetian palace with Gothic windows and a porch . . . altogether chaste and handsome'. Now, although disused, it can be viewed upon application to the custodian living in an apartment at the back of the building. The large high room where services were conducted retains the wooden church benches, the altar table, the carved wooden screen behind, and the altar rails; but there are large holes in the ceiling and the custodian keeps repeating that it is dangerous. Mrs Stisted was also responsible for the Protestant cemetery which lies across the enchanting swing bridge which spans the valley for pedestrians. She was determined that her husband, who had died in Rome, should be buried in Bagni di Lucca, and according to Thomas Adolphus Trollope in his *What I Remember* (volume II), she overcame not only ecclesiastical difficulties but also those raised by the customs house (Lucca being an independent State at the time) by having him brought in by *vetturino* (a coachman) with a permit to import 'used goods'.

Nowadays a new link is being forged in Bagni di Lucca between Italy and Great Britain by the British Institute of Florence, which holds congresses there to bring together Italian and British scholars. The Institute grew from a library formed in 1917 by Edward Hutton, who wrote excellent travel books about Italy, and Lina Waterfield, daughter of Janet Ross. They wished to counteract the anti-British propaganda of the Italian socialists who were blaming Britain for dragging Italy into the war. The library was intended to be under British management, but Italians and Americans contributed as well, giving generously both money and books. It led to the formation of the Institute, which aimed to promote intellectual relations between the two countries, and soon a school of languages had been set up, and the British Government offered to take over financial responsibility until such time as the Institute could support itself. In 1923 it was given a royal charter, and it survived Mussolini's Fascists because of the apparent sympathy towards them of the then Director, Harold Goad. The years brought independence and the present Director, Ian Greenlees, has managed to raise the money to keep the Institute going. Many Italians study English there, and British students go there to learn Italian; the magnificent library now contains over forty-five thousand books; and eminent people journey from far and wide to lecture there. This library may be the nucleus of the new University of Europe which is to be established in Florence.

Their stay in Bagni di Lucca was a period of relative peace for Mary and Shelley, but it was disturbed by Claire's insistence on trying to see Allegra, whom Byron, leading a dissipated life in Venice, had placed in the care of the British Consul and his wife. It seems that Claire loved Shelley and that he found charms in her which the more intellectual Mary could not provide. He escorted her to Venice, hoping to soften Byron's intransigent attitude towards her, but while Byron was delighted to see Shelley again he would have nothing to do with Claire. However, he offered Shelley a house at Este where Claire could stay with Allegra for a month or two. Shelley thereupon wrote asking Mary to join them with the two children. 'Kiss the blue[eyed] darlings for me and don't let William forget me.'[1] Alas, the Shelleys' baby Clara developed dysentery on the long hot journey. Shelley met them at Padua and escorted them to Venice, and there the baby died. Deeply saddened he turned to poetry, and at Este composed 'Julian and Maddalo', the story of his talks with Byron as they rode together on the day of his arrival.

When Allegra was returned to Byron in mid-October, the little party travelled south to Naples, Shelley finding relief in architecture, painting and sculpture, while Mary mourned and

---

[1] *The Letters of Percy Bysshe Shelley*, edited by Roger Ingpen, 1913.

withdrew into herself. Three months in Rome began the healing processes, and Shelley returned to 'Prometheus Unbound' and began the blank verse drama, *The Cenci*.

They had, however, to face further tragedy. On June 8 Shelley wrote to Peacock: 'Yesterday after an illness of only a few days my little William died . . . It is a great exertion to me to write this and it seems to me as if, hunted by calamity as I have been, that I should never recover any cheerfulness again.'[1] Shelley did not make the casual friendships or even acquaintances of everyday life, nor did he take an interest in the Italians as living people; as Mary noted after his death, while editing his work: 'We lived in utter solitude. And such is not the nature of cheerfulness.'

After William's death the Shelleys and Claire Clairmont returned to Livorno and took the Villa Valsovona, a little way out of the town towards the hills. Mary describes it thus:

Our villa was situated in the midst of a *podere* [a small holding]; the peasants sang as they worked beneath our windows during the heats of a very hot summer, and at night the water-wheel creaked as the process of irrigation went on and the fire-flies flashed from among the hedges;—nature was bright, sunshiny, and cheerful, or diversified by storms of a majestic terror such as we had never before witnessed. At the top of the house there was a sort of terrace. There is often such in Italy, generally roofed. This one was very small yet not only roofed, but glazed: this Shelley made his study: it looked on a wide prospect of fertile country and commanded a view of the near sea. The storms that sometimes varied our day showed themselves most picturesquely as they were driven across the ocean: sometimes the dark, lurid clouds dipped towards the waves and became waterspouts that churned up the waters beneath as they were chased onward and scattered by the tempest. At other times the dazzling sunlight and heat made it almost intolerable to every other, but Shelley basked in both, and his health and spirits revived under their influence. In this airy cell he wrote the principal part of *The Cenci*.[2]

The British Consul at Livorno from 1908-22, Montgomery Carmichael, writing in 1900,

[1] Ibid.
[2] *In Tuscany*, by Montgomery Carmichael, 1901.

visited the Villa Volsovona, which is situated at the end of the Via del Fagiano, just within the Municipal wall: in Shelley's day it was far outside the town. The present proprietor courteously permitted me to ascend to the 'airy cell'. The small terrace still exists, but is no longer either roofed or glazed. The 'wide prospect of fertile country' survives undiminished. In the garden of the villa is a picturesque arbour formed by artificially training the branches of a stout elm-tree. This sheltered nook was also used by Shelley as a study. It was in the lanes of Leghorn that he heard the skylark which he immortalized.[1]

In the Second World War Livorno was almost razed by aerial bombing. Rebuilt, it engulfs the site of the little farm surrounding Shelley's villa, and the fast road carrying motor traffic to the *autostrada* runs across the end of the Via Fageano beyond the villa. New buildings occupy the site of the house, though part of its handsome entrance gates remains.

In October 1819, the Shelleys and Claire arrived in Florence to spend some four months, staying at the *pensione* of Madame Merveilleux du Plaintis, in Palazzo Marini on Via Valfonda. Their third child, a boy destined to inherit the title, was born on November 19 and christened in the English Church. They named him Percy Florence after the city, which Shelley declared to be the most beautiful he had ever seen. Among the English music students at the *pensione* who entertained the guests in the evening was a Miss Stacey, a ward of Shelley's uncle Robert Parkin, who sang and played the harp. A flirtation with her resulted in the poems 'I arise from Dreams of Thee', 'Thou art Fair and Few are Fairer', 'Good Night', 'Love's Philosophy', and 'Time Long Past'—trifles to be set to music which Shelley did not think worth publishing in his *Other Poems* with 'Prometheus Unbound'.

To Shelley conventional restraints were a tyranny alien to his nature, and he was without any sense of guilt in obeying his emotional and sexual impulses. He declared that 'the partner of my life should be one who can feel poetry and understand philosophy' and Mary fitted this role: whilst the admiration of beautiful women who were less intellectual was necessary to calm

---

[1] *In Tuscany*, by Montgomery Carmichael, 1901.

his fervent highly strung temperament. Sometimes this developed into affection as with his first wife Harriet, with Claire Clairmont and with Jane Williams who was to join the Shelleys' later, in Pisa, with her companion Edward Williams. In the case of Claire and of Jane it is probable there was a sexual affaire. Other infatuations such as that with the young Sophia Stacey in Florence and with Emilia Viviani, in Pisa, would appear to have been poetic rather than physical, like that of Petrarch for his Laura. His wife Mary doubtless understood this. His undeniable attraction for women was in no small measure due to his acceptance of them as intellectual equals as well as to his charm and innate kindness, and an apparent frailty which may have brought out a motherly tenderness in the opposite sex.

The Cascine and the Boboli Gardens behind the Pitti Palace in Florence were the Shelleys' favourite walking places. In the Cascine, he tells us, the 'Ode to the West Wind' was 'conceived and chiefly written . . . in a wood that skirts the Arno, near Florence':

> *O wild West Wind, thou breath of Autumn's being,*
> *Thou, from whose unseen presence the leaves dead*
> *Are driven, like ghosts from an enchanter fleeing,*
>
> *Yellow, and black, and pale, and hectic red,*
> *Pestilence-stricken multitudes: O thou,*
> *Who chariotest to their dark wintry bed*
>
> *The winged seeds, where they lie cold and low,*
> *Each like a corpse within its grave, until*
> *Thine azure sister of the Spring shall blow. . . .*

No deadening classroom recitation, no pedantic criticism can dim the beauty.

The Boboli Gardens, inspired 'The View from the Pitti Gardens'. The galleries absorbed the time of Mary and Shelley in the mornings, particularly the sculpture. He aimed at the influence of art on poetry in the fragment 'Medusa of Leonardo'. 'Peter Bell the Third' and the fourth Act of 'Prometheus Unbound' were written during these months of 1818-19.

The severe winter and unheated rooms then drove them to

Pisa, where they took an apartment on the Lungarno: two bedrooms, two sitting-rooms, a kitchen and servant's room near the Ponte Mezza, with a beautiful view of the river and the city. In May 1820 their friends the Gisbornes left on a visit to England carrying money to succour Shelley's insatiably impecunious father-in-law, Godwin—not the first instalment. Shelley wrote to the Gisbornes on May 26, 'Your impressions about Godwin . . . will especially interest me—you know that although I believe he is the only sincere enemy I have in the world, that added years only add to my admiration of his intellectual powers, and even the moral resources of his character.' But on June 30 he sounded more wary: 'The chief object of my writing distinctly from Mary, however is this: do not pay the money into Godwin's hands'. Shelley was making sure that the £400 he was sending would be used for payment of Godwin's debts to the landlords, who would give their signatures for it. He goes on: 'If you perceive that the money will not fulfill its object or that you cannot enforce the intended appropriation of it, I entreat you to refuse to lend it at all. You know my situation; you know Godwin's boundless and plausible sophistry. . . .'[1]

The Shelleys accepted the loan of the Gisbornes' house at Livorno probably because it would be healthier by the sea, and cheaper, but the heat must have been excessive by August, for they moved on to the Baths of San Giuliano, a summer resort four miles out of the town. The river Serchio overflowed its banks in October; they escaped by boat from an upstairs window of their house and returned to Pisa, where they were to remain for the next eighteen months.

In that year, 1820, Shelley wrote 'The Sensitive Plant', 'A Vision of the Sea', 'The Cloud', 'To a Skylark', 'Arethusa', 'Hymn to Apollo', 'Ode to Liberty', 'Hymn to Pan', 'Ode to Naples' and 'The Question'.

In July and August he added to his amazing output some poems which were more satirical and humorous than anything he had done before; and 'The Witch of Atlas' (Mary remarked in her notes on his work that it was 'peculiarly characteristic', 'wildly fanciful, full of brilliant imagery') and the satire 'Swellfoot the

---

[1] *The Letters of Percy Bysshe Shelley*, edited by Roger Ingpen, 1913.

Tyrant' alluding to the undignified trial of Queen Caroline and attacking her husband George IV, represented two further facets of his genius.

The closeness between Shelley and Claire Clairmont, which caused Mary first irritation and finally bitterness, ended in Claire's leaving Livorno for Florence on October 20 escorted by Shelley. He brought back his cousin Medwin whom, with his usual careless geniality, he had invited to share his home. But Claire's attempt to find independence by working in Florence was not a success, and she returned to Pisa after a month, just before they received a call from a professor of the University of Pisa, Francesco Pacchiani, who introduced them to a little circle in the city. He took them to visit the daughter of the Governor of Pisa, Emilia Viviani, in the convent where she was being educated until he was able to make a good marriage for her. When she was described as 'a bird in a cage' Shelley's sympathy was aroused at once, as it had been with his first wife Harriet, at her school. Medwin was present on the first visit and described the girl as resembling a piece of marble in a Grecian bust, which naturally ensured one of Shelley's 'Italian Platonics', as his wife called them. The girl relished the situation and wrote romantic letters to him, including an essay on 'True Love'. This inspired Shelley to compose 'Epipsychidion', modelled on Dante, a soul-love poem, slightly autobiographical.

In April, when Medwin was in Rome, Shelley wrote to him: 'I hear Keats is in Rome and dangerously ill. Should you happen to see him, or if you could take the trouble to call upon him, I should be very glad to know how he is, and that you would say everything that is kind from me to him and entreat to know if I can in any manner be of any service to him. . . .'[1] He had previously urged Keats to come to Italy for his health and join him at Pisa. Unknown to Shelley, Keats had died on February 23. Shelley's elegy 'Adonais', is somewhat remote—he had not known of Keats's last months and they had not been close friends—but perhaps achieved a greater poetic coherence for that very reason.

Meanwhile, Byron had formed an attachment for Teresa,

[1] Ibid.

Countess Guiccioli, and took the extraordinary liberty of asking Shelley, who had never met her, to write to her at Florence, persuading her to come to Pisa instead of going to Switzerland. She and her brother arrived, Shelley having rented on Byron's behalf the Palazzo Lanfranchi at the edge of the Lungarno. It was opposite the Tre Palazzi di Chiesa, where the Shelleys were living in apartments with two new friends, Jane and Edward Williams. It was three months before Byron at last bestirred himself and left Venice to join his beloved at Pisa. She, a young woman who knew only the formal society of Ravenna and Venice, must have found this self-contained group of English very strange; but they were sympathetic towards her anomalous position, which prevented her from mixing in the society of Pisa, and were completely unpriggish. Had not Mary lived with Shelley before he was free to marry her, and were not their friends Jane Williams (whom Teresa described as 'gentle and sweet') and Edward Williams, a half-pay officer who 'tried his hand at writing', unmarried? Mary, of whose intellectuality Teresa was afraid, thought the countess a 'nice pretty girl without pretentions, good-hearted and amiable', while to Shelley at first she seemed 'a very pretty, sentimental, innocent, superficial Italian who has sacrificed an immense fortune for the sake of Byron. . . .'[1] But his cousin Medwin was enslaved by her 'eyes large, dark and languishing [and] shaded by the longest lashes in the world . . . the most beautiful mouth and teeth imaginable . . . It is impossible to see without admiring, to hear the Guiccioli speak without being fascinated. Her amiability and gentleness show themselves in every intonation of her voice . . . Grace and elegance seem component parts of her nature.'[2] Teresa's later estimate of Medwin was far from complimentary, but then she could hardly be expected to forgive the reference to Byron's affection for her in his *Conversations with Lord Byron*, published soon after Byron's death—'without actually being in love with her'. Her spontaneous sympathy, however, went out to Shelley, of whom Byron had spoken much. He was no longer beautiful, and she described him as being 'extraordinary in his dress for he generally wore a schoolboy's jacket, never any gloves, and

---

[1] Shelley to John Gisborne, *Works*, edited by H. B. Forman.
[2] *Revised Life of Shelley*, by Thomas Medwin.

unpolished shoes', but she went on to say: 'and yet, among a thousand gentlemen he would always have seemed the most accomplished'.

When Byron arrived in Pisa in November he at once associated the Palazzo Lanfranchi, an imposing Renaissance building, with the tormentor of Count Ugolino in Dante's *Inferno*, and he described it romantically as 'a famous old feudal palazzo large enough for a garrison, with dungeons below and cells in the walls . . . There is but one place where people were evidently *walled up*';[1] and he invented a ghost. In fact the palace did not exist in Dante's time and the cellars were the warehouses of silk merchants who used to load cargo direct on to barges on the Arno. Nowadays the state archives of Pisa are housed in the building and the present Director, Prof. Dott. Bruno Casini, is proud to have as his office the well-proportioned though not vast room which was Byron's study when he wrote *Don Juan*, and delighted to point out the baroque painting on the ceiling representing Byron with the Muse of Poetry.

Earlier, in Ravenna, he and Shelley had agreed to invite Leigh Hunt (whose *Examiner* had recently closed) and his large family to Pisa to share in the launching of a new periodical, *The Liberal*. They were to arrive the following summer, and as one stands at the foot of the staircase it is impossible not to smile at the thought of Byron's bulldog tied at the top to protect his irate master's privacy against the invasions of the uncontrolled and dirty Hunt children, who were brought up on the principle of absolute freedom and who were housed on the ground floor in rooms which Shelley furnished for them at Byron's expense.

The members of the strange circle gathered in Pisa were supremely oblivious of the effect they made on the native Tuscans around them. A contemporary student at Pisa University, Francesco Domenico Guerazzi, shows Byron's fearsome European reputation:

At that time the rumour spread in Pisa that an extraordinary man had arrived there, of whom people told a hundred different tales, all contradictory and many absurd. They said that he was of royal blood, of very great wealth, of sanguine temperament, of fierce

---

[1] Byron's *Letters and Journals*, edited by R. E. Prothero.

habits, masterly in knightly exercises, possessing an evil genius, but a more than human intellect. He was said to wander through the world like Job's Satan . . . It was George Byron. I wished to see him: he appeared to me like the Vatican Apollo.[1]

The days of the Grand Tour, when British aristocrats met aristocratic Italians and moved in their high society, absorbing culture as they went, had given way to nineteenth-century travellers who were more often middle-class intellectuals with no desire for social intercourse with the Italians; but the brilliant exceptions among them such as Byron were still of sensational interest.

The other eccentrics caused less stir. Shelley, wandering about in his schoolboy clothes, reading as he went, bony and thin on account of his vegetarian diet of tea and buns; John Taafe, a pleasant, pompous Irishman admired by Shelley and Byron for his translation of Dante, if not for his horsemanship: and the newly arrived Cornish adventurer, Edward Trelawny, who had come to join Medwin and Williams. With his hawk-like nose and cold dark eyes, thick eyebrows and flowing moustaches, Trelawny might have stepped straight out of a bloodthirsty novel of high adventure.

To Shelley's consternation Byron had not brought the child Allegra with him from her convent near Ravenna. Shelley seemed to be very happy this spring in the company of his friends and of Byron—'our roots were never struck so deeply as at Pisa' he wrote—but it was on him that fell the unpleasant task of mediating tactfully between Claire, the sometimes hysterical mother, and Byron. On April 20 news reached Byron (Claire fortunately was at Lerici) that the five-year-old child had died during an epidemic of typhus, and a mood of melancholy descended on him. At the end of May he and Teresa moved for a while to the Villa Dupuy, in the suburbs of Livorno, which Leigh Hunt fresh from a cold winter in England, described later on as 'the hottest-looking house' he had ever seen, but which Teresa liked for the garden's roses, jasmine, heliotrope and tuberoses, and the view of Elba, Corsica and the Mediterranean from the large terrace. Even today the story is familiar of the

---

[1] *Memorie,* by Francesco Domenico Guerazzi.

water supply drying up in June; it infuriated Byron, who sued the villa's owner. Apparently every drop had to be fetched on the back of mules from a spring in the hills a mile away. Yet the house in which Smollett had lived, not far away, was never without water.

Mary did not give Shelley the adoring, uncritical domestic background which Teresa supplied for Byron, and he turned towards Jane Williams, with whose Edward he so much enjoyed sailing. Whether or not this was just another of the poet's flights of platonic love, Mary was unhappy and distinctly out of sympathy with his practical application of his theories on love. Yet we have his passion for Jane to thank for the mood which induced the serene poems, 'The Invitation' and 'The Recollection'.

In the spring, under Trelawny's influence, both Shelley and Byron, for whom the sea was a necessary part of living, had commissioned boats to be built at Genoa. Shelley and Williams had planned a holiday with their families at Lerici on the Gulf of Spezia, to which they departed somewhat prematurely in order to break the news of Allegra's death to Claire far from the presence of Byron.

The house at Lerici, Casa Magni, almost on the beach, though simple and with little comfort was exactly what Shelley loved. Storms buffeted it and the eerie wind excited him: and in the calm which followed there was the view of the bay with the old castle of Lerici to the west, and the Mediterranean spread before him.

The place was so remote that on hot summer evenings parents and children danced about in the water singing, and Shelley could abandon himself to nature, though the practical problems of housekeeping were not much fun for Mary, who, it seems, suffered a miscarriage early in June.

Meanwhile, on June 28, Leigh Hunt and his family arrived at Genoa on their way to Livorno. They had embarked at the Port of London in November: the old sailing vessels of the fourteenth century had surely never taken longer. Shelley promptly arrived in Livorno from Lerici, his usual kindly self, and swept them off to the ground floor of the Palazzo Lanfranchi in Pisa: he then returned to Livorno so that he and Williams could sail back in his *Ariel* to Lerici. With Trelawny, who had engaged for Shelley a young English seaman named Charles Vivian, he visited a bank and then a store. Trelawny, from the deck of Byron's boat the *Belivar*, watched them leave in hot sultry weather. There were to be many stories of what happened to their boat, which never arrived at Lerici. A squall of brief duration certainly blew up and the three occupants of the boat certainly perished. When the *Ariel* was recovered, it was evident that a vessel had struck her on the starboard quarter. In 1857 Trelawny, who was then retired in England, was sent news through his daughter in Rome that an old fisherman had made a death-bed confession of having been party to an attack on Shelley's boat to seize money.

When the *Ariel* did not return to Lerici, Mary Shelley and Jane Williams set out for Pisa to obtain news. Teresa, standing on a balcony of the Palazzo Lanfranchi in the moonlight, saw the carriage draw up, and she describes the anxious voice of Mary replying to the maid's query—'Me—Mary Shelley—pray open at once'. When Teresa got downstairs Mary stood 'white as marble' asking her *'Sapete alcuna cosa di Shelley?'* When they heard there was no news they set off immediately from Pisa for Livorno, hoping against hope that the boat might have returned there.

Two weeks after Shelley sailed from Livorno two of the bodies were found, Shelley's washed up on the beach at Viareggio and Williams's three miles away.[1] Trelawny, who had already organised search-parties, took charge—he recognised Williams's body by the boots and Shelley's by the tall slight build and the volume of Aeschylus in one pocket of his jacket and a copy of Keats's poems, borrowed from Leigh Hunt, in the other. For the moment both bodies were buried in quicklime on the shore, but by August 13 Trelawny had made arrangements with the Tuscan authorities to comply with Italian sanitary law, and to disinter and cremate the bodies. Williams's cremation took place on the beach near the place of burial, and next day, under a cloudless blue sky and overlooked by the Apuan Alps rising sheer behind the coast, Shelley's body was raised and laid upon an iron furnace which Trelawny had ordered to be made at

---

[1] Vivian's body was not washed ashore until two weeks later.

Byron in May, 1923

Both of them drawn
by Count d'Orsay.

Teresa Guiccioli
in October, 1839

Walter Savage Landor,
painted by R. Faulkner

Livorno. When the fire was kindled Shelley's three friends—Byron, Hunt and Trelawny—administered the ancient Greek rites, salt, frankincense, oil and wine.

A statue of Shelley stands in the square at Viareggio—Piazza di Shelley. Honour came to the poet in death if not in life, and on the 150th anniversary of his death, in July 1972, a wreath was dropped on the sea, and the Casa Magni at Lerici was renamed Casa Shelley: it is to become a cultural centre.

The village is at the head of the bay, with Lerici a little way to the south, almost adjoining it. On a brilliantly fine Sunday at the end of May 1972, it was crowded with families enjoying the sun and the sandy beach. The house which Shelley and Mary rented for the summer with the Williamses, the former Casa Magni, stands almost in the centre of the busy front, differentiated from the rest by a projecting arched terrace on the ground floor, the rooms above having quite large windows and the second floor very small ones, as if for nurseries or servants. When I visited it, it was washed a weather-stained white, in contrast with the rest of the houses with their pinks and creamy yellows. It stood empty.

In a little café where the ice-cream was mixed with fresh fruits and was better than any I have tasted, I enquired of the owner if Shelley's house was empty. Yes, Signora, it is always empty. It must belong to some rich people! A monument, he exclaimed, as if suddenly finding the way to describe it. The plaque on the façade states dramatically that in this house Mary Shelley and Jane Williams waited tearfully and anxiously for PERCY BYSSHE SHELLEY, and at either end of the house are plaques with these quotations in English:

> I still inhabit this Divine Bay reading dramas and sailing and listening to the most enchanting music—Shelley.

> A lonely house close by the soft and sublime scenery of the Bay of Lerici—Shelley. San Terenzo, Maggio, 1833

Today there is a Bar Shelley and further on towards Lerici a Hotel Byron. Then the place must have been very small and almost wild. On the coast further south, at the seaside resort of Forte dei Marmi (which also has a Hotel Byron), a strong wind from the sea was blowing the sand, but here the little bay was protected. To this day there is a *Coppa Byron*—a Byron cup, the prize for the winner of the swimming contest from Porto Venere to Lerici. As we walked round under the ruins of the small castle the spray was beating on the rocks, and one could imagine the storms which Shelley loved as they beat upon his house.

Mary returned to England towards the end of August 1823, earned her living by her writings, and with determination and a good deal of self-sacrifice educated her son Percy Florence at Harrow and afterwards at Cambridge. Eventually Shelley's father made her a small allowance, on condition that she did not proceed with a biography of her husband. In 1838, by which time her health had deteriorated, she published Shelley's works with notes.

When Sir Timothy Shelley died in 1844, Percy inherited the baronetcy (Harriet's son having died in 1826), together with an income which released his mother from all money troubles. She enjoyed a social life in her own right as an author and as the daughter of celebrated parents. From Trelawny she received a proposal of marriage to which she haughtily replied:

> My name will never be Trelawny. I am not so young as I was when you first knew me but I am as proud. I must have the entire affection, devotion and above all the solicitous protection of any one who would win me. You belong to women-kind in general, and Mary Shelley will never be yours.[1]

She died at her home in Chester Square, London, in 1851, only fifty-four years of age.

[1] *Life and Letters of Mary Wollstonecraft Shelley*, by Mrs Julian Marshall, 1889.

CHAPTER VI

Byron and his Friends

Now I have 'lived' among the Italians; not Florenced and Romed and Galleried and Conversationed it for months, and then home again —but been of their families and friendships and feuds, and loves and councils, in a part of Italy least known to foreigners; and have been amongst them of all classes, from the Conte to the Contandino.

So Byron wrote to his publisher John Murray on September 23, 1820, explaining his involvement with Italy while deriding the superficiality of the Grand Tour.[1]

He left England in 1816, never to return, and watching his ship depart his Whig friend, Hobhouse, involuntarily pronounced a benediction: 'God bless him for a gallant spirit and a kind one'. English society had ostracised him for outraging its conventions— the conventions of a licentious age, be it added. He had flaunted his vices in the face of a public which had accepted him as the greatest poet of his day from the moment when he published *Childe Harold* in 1812.

If, like Shelley, he had rejected England because of his intellectual beliefs, he might have found fulfilment in Italy, since he became genuinely interested in the people and involved in their political struggles. But he was there because he was basically a rebel against his own deep approval of English conventions, which he was unable to shake off whatever gestures he made. It extended to religion, and was later to be exemplified when he preferred that his natural daughter, Allegra, should be brought up as a Catholic rather than live with her mother Claire Clairmont in the household of the brilliant and affectionate but atheistic Shelley.

In Italy he was to find Teresa Guiccioli; a woman 'with talent enough to be able to understand and value mine, but not sufficient

[1] *Letters and Journals of Byron*, volume II, ed. Thomas Moore, 1833.

to be able to shine herself', as he explained later to Lady Blessington with his superbly intelligent and devastating frankness. 'All men with pretensions desire this though few, if any, have the courage to avow it.'[1] The adoration which she gave him released the full development of his powers in *Don Juan*. She was a lively young woman with a strong will, married to an eccentric and devious husband some forty years older than herself, and she fell headlong in love with the thirty-one-year-old poet, no matter if by then his hair was already turning grey and his figure had become slack. With the determination and un-questioning assurance of an educated girl from a loving and affectionate family, she set out to capture him within the framework of the conventions of her society, as a *cavaliere servente*. Despite the diversions of a life of dissipation in Venice, he was lonely and unfulfilled, and Teresa may have reminded him of his half-sister Augusta Leigh, the only woman for whom he had ever experienced a deep enough passion to bring forth real tenderness, although this incestuous relationship had emphasised his conviction of doom. He had said to his wife at the beginning of their married life, with characteristic cruelty, 'I ask nothing of a woman but to make me laugh. I can make Augusta laugh about anything. No one makes me happy except Augusta.'[2]

But if in many ways Teresa may have reminded him of Augusta, she was very different in her determination and courage, and Byron was to learn how completely disinterested her love would remain. The romantic, novelettish affair which they conducted in Venice, revelling in lovers' letters, secret meetings, and languorous gondola excursions, gave way to an enforced separation while Teresa stayed in one of her husband's estates on the Po. Byron then sat down to write for her the romantic 'Stanzas on the Po':

> River that rollest by the ancient walls
> where dwells the Lady of my love. . . .

When she returned to her home in Ravenna he followed her, throwing discretion to the winds; for in the quiet provincial town

---

[1] *Conversations of Lord Byron with Lady Blessington*, 1834.
[2] Lady Byron's Journal, quoted in *Byron*, by André Maurois, 1936.

where her husband and family lived their every movement would be noted. However mockingly he might write to his friends in England about it, this passion was something new to Byron. 'I am a foreigner in Italy,' he wrote to her, 'and still more a foreigner in Ravenna, and naturally little versed in the customs of the country'—'If I lose you what will become of me? . . . Until now the fruits of my journey have been rather bitter—but if you are pleased, I do not regret what I am suffering—for I am suffering for your sake. . . . If trouble arises there is only one adequate remedy, that is, to go away together and—for this a great Love is necessary—and some courage. Have you enough? I can already anticipate your answer. It will be long and divinely written—but it will end in a negative. I kiss you from my heart ten million times.'[1] Where was the assured and cynical lover that he painted in letters for English consumption?

We know what Smollett thought about the Italian convention of the *cicisbeo*, which allowed the wife in upper-class circles to remain with her husband and have the consolation of a companion of the opposite sex of her own choosing, without disturbing the proprieties of family life, since it was accepted that the husband would discreetly keep a mistress. But Byron was not talking about formalised love. When Teresa accompanied her husband on a visit and he was left alone in Bologna, he wrote to John Murray:

I have to do with a woman rendered perfectly disinterested by her situation in life, and young and amiable and pretty—in short as good and at least as attentive as anything of the sex can be, with all the advantages and disadvantages of being scarcely twenty years old and only two out of her Romagnolo convent at Faenza. But I feel—and I feel it bitterly—that a man should not consume his life at the side, and on the bosom of a woman, and a stranger; that even the recompense, and it is much, is not enough, and that this Cicisbean existence is to be condemned. But I have neither the strength of mind to break my chain nor the insensibility which would deaden its weight. I cannot tell what will become of me— to leave, or to be left would at present drive me quite out of my senses; and yet to what have I conducted myself?[2]

[1] Quoted from *The Last Attachment*, by Iris Origo, 1949.
[2] *The Letters of Lord Byron*, selected by R. G. Howarth, 1933.

He wandered lonely through her rooms reading her favourite novel, *Corinne*: 'In that word—beautiful in all languages, but most so in yours—*Amor mio*—is comprised my existence here and hereafter'.[1]

While Byron submitted himself unwillingly to his love for Teresa he became involved with the Carbonari in Ravenna (of which Teresa's father, Count Ruggero Gamba, and her brother Pietro were leading figures). This was the most important of the secret societies ready to fight for constitutional government and to throw off the rule of Austria. To Byron, despite his hatred of oppression, it was somewhat of a game: the conspiratorial meetings, the pistol practice during evening rides. But he allowed the rooms lent to him in the Palazzo Guiccioli by Teresa's husband to be used to store arms, so the police kept a close watch on his movements.

A new stage was reached in his relationship with Teresa when the Pope granted her a separation from her husband on condition that she returned to her father's home. In winter this was in Ravenna, in summer at Filetto, fifteen miles south-west of Ravenna. Hers was an affectionate family and there she was visited freely by Byron. Count Gamba and his son Pietro, as revolutionaries against Austria, were both ordered peremptorily into exile in February 1821; and the authorities thereby hoped also to get rid of the troublesome English milord. Teresa remained in Ravenna until threats by her husband that she must either return to him or enter a nunnery forced her to join her exiled family.

In August Byron invited Shelley to visit him 'alone' in Ravenna —he wished to discuss the upbringing of his illegitimate child Allegra without the presence of her mother, Claire, who now irritated him beyond words.

In the six months preceding Shelley's visit, Byron had finished the fifth canto of *Don Juan*, made an English rendering from Dante's *Inferno*, and written three tragedies, *Marino Faliero*, *Sardanapalus* and *The Two Foscari*, two light satires, and a brilliant essay in 'poetic diatribe', *The Vision of Judgment*. Shelley, to whom jealousy was alien, and whose own work remained un-

[1] *The Letters of Lord Byron*, selected by R. G. Howarth, 1933.

recognised, fell into a state of near-hero worship which was perhaps damaging to his own genius. 'He has written three more cantos of *Don Juan*—I have yet only heard the fifth and I think that every word of it is pregnant with immortality.'[1]

The effects of Teresa upon Byron were whole-heartedly approved by Shelley. He thought him 'greatly improved in every respect—in genius, in temper, in moral issues, in health, in happiness'. It was now that Byron imposed on Shelley's kindness to the extent of making him persuade Teresa, strangers though they were to each other, to come to Pisa instead of going to Switzerland, as she was intending. Moreover, Byron suggested that he would need a large unfurnished house of distinction and that Shelley's sister-in-law, the mother of Allegra, must not be near to bother him.

The five-year-old Allegra had been sent to the convent of Bagnacavallo, twelve miles from Ravenna. The Shelleys thought that by his own standards Byron was doing his best for the child. They and her mother were under the mistaken impression that when he moved to Pisa to join Teresa he would bring Allegra with him.

He was reluctant, however, to leave Palazzo Guiccioli in Ravenna. The life seemed to suit him and he had put down some roots for the first time since he had left his home at Newstead, near Nottingham, having entered into the family life of the Gambas as well as ventured on to the political scene. Selfishly he kept putting off his departure for Pisa, the first passionate stage of his love affair having passed into a companionable feeling, so that he felt no dominating urge to be with his beloved. The kindly Shelley had meanwhile not only rented the Palazzo Lanfranchi on his behalf, but was offering to teach Teresa English to help fill in the lonely void when she would be among strangers. We know she was impressed by Shelley when she met him: 'his countenance is full of goodness and talent'. Byron replied, tersely and cynically—even cruelly—'You do not know the horrible things that are said about Shelley and me—and if you are not careful the English in Florence and Pisa will say that, *being tired of you*, I handed you on to him.'[2]

[1] *The Letters of Percy Bysshe Shelley*, edited by Roger Ingpen, 1913.
[2] *Byron and Shelley*, by John Buxton, 1968.

The move to Pisa was not without its trials. Byron who was so generous in big things, had become mean in small ones. He made a great fuss about the carriage of his furniture from Ravenna to Pisa, saying that the charges of the Ravenna carriers were so exorbitant that he must engage the Pisa carriers. Lady Blessington, for one, was unimpressed by some of this furniture, but her own novels do not incline one to put much faith in her taste. Of Byron's bed, when she saw it later in Genoa, she wrote: 'The most gaudily vulgar thing I ever saw; the curtains in the worst taste and the cornice having his family motto of "Credo Byron" surmounted by baronial coronets. His carriage and his liveries were in the same bad taste, having an affectation of finery.'[1] Their owner was restless and uncertain and wrote to Tom Moore: 'I wanted to go to Greece lately (as everything seems up here) with her [Teresa's] brother who is a very fine fellow (I have seen him put to the proof)'.[2] All the same he settled for Pisa for the time being, and on September 23 four carts left Ravenna with his furniture, books, saddles, dogs and even Teresa's 'nerve lotion'. He wrote thoughtfully before leaving: 'Man is born *passionate* of body, but with an innate though secret tendency to the love of Good in his Mainspring of Mind.'[3]

Through all this Teresa was awaiting him anxiously. As Shelley wrote him, 'The Countess is very patient, though sometimes she seems apprehensive that you will *never* leave Ravenna.'

As we saw earlier, the Palazzo Lanfranchi suited Byron—his sense of style must have been satisfied by its elegant Renaissance simplicity and his sense of romantic fantasy by the underground cellars which were really nothing more thrilling than the warehouses of silk merchants. Shelley had taken an apartment on the other side of the Arno about a hundred yards away, in a much less imposing building which was to suffer bomb damage in the Second World War. These were happy times for Byron and Shelley, and here Shelley was the leader.

Trelawny, the colourful Cornish adventurer (who had sought out Shelley after making the acquaintance of his cousin Medwin),

[1] *An Idler in Italy*, by Countess Blessington, 1839.
[2] *The Letters of Lord Byron*, selected by R. G. Howarth, 1933.
[3] *Letters and Journals of Byron*, edited by R. E. Prothero.

whose tough masculinity was protective of Shelley's delicate personality, was prepared to be circumspect about Byron. On his first visit to the Palazzo Lanfranchi he recalls that, escorted by Shelley, he

> ascended a gigantic staircase, passed thro' a spacious apartment and entered a smaller room containing books and a billiard table. The bull-dog Moretto growled. His master appeared, quick of step and only slightly obviously lame—very pale but fresh, vigorous, animated, not a stain or furrow on his transparent skin. Well-proportioned body, curly hair. Blue velvet cap and braided tartan jacket which he explained was of the Gordon tartan his mother's and loose nankeen trousers. Obviously extremely shy, air of flippancy to conceal it. Once he had begun to talk as he played billiards he impressed by his mental veracity and wonderful memory. Gay and friendly towards Shelley and deferential in questions of literary judgment, provocative and slightly teasing in worldly matters.[1]

Others were observing Byron besides Trelawny. The spies of the Austrian Chancellor Metternich were still keeping watch on the mysterious, rich, revolutionary English milord. Unfortunately, after two or three months at Pisa an incident occurred after the regular evening ride into the country of the Shelley-Byron party, at which pistol shooting practice would take place, a habit which justified their surveillance by the police. A local sergeant-major, Masi, riding back to Pisa after dining in the country, found the road blocked by Byron, Teresa's brother Pietro Gamba, Shelley, Trelawny, the Irishman John Taafe, a Captain Hay, their servants and Teresa in her carriage. As he pushed through them the somewhat unsure rider Taafe lost his hat as his horse shied, and he called out that he had been insulted. Byron mistook the non-commissioned Masi for an officer and challenged him to a duel, and as they approached the gates of the city with voices raised an attempt was made to arrest Byron. Shelley fell from his horse, struck by the flat of a sword, and Captain Hay was wounded in the nose. Byron spurred on his horse to reach his palazzo and there called his steward, and in the noisy confusion one of the Gamba servants stabbed the

---

[1] *Records of Shelley, Byron and the Author*, by E. J. Trelawny, 1878.

sergeant-major. Fortunately he recovered, and the indulgent governor of the city did not take too serious a view of the matter, though legal proceedings were protracted. Meanwhile, however, it was indicated to the Gambas that their presence in the city was unwelcome. Teresa's father and brother then moved to a villa taken by Byron at Monte Nero, outside Livorno. The poet himself lingered with Teresa in Pisa, having settled into a routine in which he worked through the night and rose after noon, breakfasting often on a 'cup of strong green tea, without milk or sugar' and the raw yolk of an egg. It appears that even his conversation, except when stimulated by Shelley, had become somewhat routine: he was still interested in the snobbish beau-monde and always asking questions or making reflections about Society.

It is from Leigh Hunt that we get the best picture of Byron at this period. Shelley, it will be recalled, had enthusiastically persuaded Hunt to travel by sea to Livorno with his wife and large family, so that he could become the editor of a new radical paper they were planning. Byron financed the voyage. For Byron this interest in a radical journal which he hoped would become important perhaps compensated for his lack of action since leaving Ravenna.

Leigh Hunt was a brilliant editor and an equally brilliant writer; some of his less enviable characteristics were satirised by Dickens in Mr Skimpole, in *Bleak House*. He became editor of *The Examiner*, owned by his brother John, and both were sent to prison in 1813 when Leigh Hunt attacked the Prince Regent as 'a fat Adonis of fifty'. It was then that Tom Moore brought Lord Byron to meet the audacious editor, while Shelley began his friendship with him when he sent his congratulations from Oxford. Hunt's circle was a distinguished one, including Hazlitt and Lamb as well as Keats, Southey and Coleridge. In his autobiography Hunt was rueful but charming about his long, long winter sea voyage to Livorno. Shelley had told him airily to put his music and books on board a vessel and he would have no more trouble. 'I believe if he had recommended a balloon I should have been inclined to try it.' The actuality must have been a nightmare for Hunt, his wife and his six children, some of them very young.

He was a curious and vivid observer of the personalities and the scene he now encountered:

In the harbour of Leghorn I found Mr Trelawny . . . He was standing with his knight errant aspect, dark, handsome and moustachioed, in Lord Byron's boat the *Bolivar*, of which he had taken charge for his lordship. In a day or two I went to see my noble acquaintance, who was in what the Italians call Villeggiatura at Monte Nero; that is to say enjoying a country house for the season. . . .

Upon seeing Lord Byron I hardly knew him he was grown so fat; and he was longer in recognizing me, I had grown so thin. He took me into an inner room and introduced me to Madame Guiccioli, then very young as well as handsome, who was in a state of great agitation. Her face was flushed, her eyes lit up, and her hair (which she wore hanging loose) streaming as if in disorder. The Conte Pietro, her brother, came in presently, also in a state of agitation, and having his arm in a sling. I then learned that a quarrel having taken place among the servants, the young Count had interfered, and been stabbed . . . though the stab was not much, the inflictor of it threatened more, and was at that minute keeping watch outside, with the avowed intention of assaulting the first person that issued forth. . . . He had a red cap on like a sansculotte, and a most sinister aspect. . . .

How long things had continued in this state I cannot say; but the hour was come when Lord Byron and his friend took their evening drive, and the thing was to be put an end to somehow. A servant had been despatched for the police and was not returned.

At length we set out, the lady earnestly entreating his lordship to keep back, and all of us uniting to keep in advance of Conte Pietro, who was exasperated.

It was a curious moment for a stranger from England . . . Everything was new, foreign and vehement . . . Nobody, however, could have put a better face on the matter than Lord Byron did—composed and endeavouring to compose; and as to myself I was so occupied with the whole scene that I had not time to be frightened. Forth we issue at the house door, all squeezing to have the honour of being first, when a termination is put to the tragedy by the man's throwing himself on a bench, extending his arms and bursting into tears. His cap was half over his eyes; his face gaunt, ugly and unshaved, his appearance altogether more squalid and miserable than any Englishman would conceive it possible to find in such an establishment. This blessed figure reclined weeping and wailing, and asking pardon for his offence; and to crown all, he requested Lord Byron to kiss him.

The noble lord conceived such an excess of charity superfluous. He pardoned him but said he must not think of remaining in his service; upon which the man renewed his weeping and wailing, and continued kissing his hand. I was then struck with the footing on which the gentry and their servants are with each other in Italy, and the good-nature with which the strongest exhibitions of anger can be followed up. . . . Conte Pietro who was full of good qualities . . . accepted the man's hand, and even shook it heartily; and Madame Guiccioli . . . speedily accorded him her grace also, seeing my lord had forgiven him. The man was all penitence and wailing but he was obliged to quit. The police would have forced him if he had not been dismissed. . . .

We occupied the ground-floor of his Lordship's house, the Casa Lanfranchi, on the river Arno, which runs through the city. Divided tenancies of this kind are common in Italy, where few houses are in possession of one family.[1]

Hunt's description of Byron at Pisa, and of the town itself, are fascinating.

Our manner of life was this. Lord Byron who used to sit up at night writing *Don Juan* (which he did under the influence of gin and water), rose late in the morning. He breakfasted; read; lounged about, singing an air, generally out of Rossini; then took a bath, and was dressed; and coming downstairs was heard, still singing, in the courtyard out of which the garden ascended by a few steps, at the back of the house. The servants at the same time brought out two or three chairs. My study, a little room in a corner, with an orange tree at the window, looked down upon this courtyard. I was generally at my writing when he came down and either acknowledged his presence by getting up and saying something from the window, or he called out 'Leontius'. The garden was small and square, but plentifully stocked with oranges and other shrubs; and being well watered, it looked very green and refreshing under the Italian sky. The lady . . . her appearance might have reminded an English spectator of Chaucer's heroine—

> *Yclothed was she, fresh for to devise.*
> *Her yellow hair was braided in a tress*
> *Behind her back, a yarde long, I guess:*

[1] *Autobiography of Leigh Hunt*, edited by J. E. Morpurgo.

And in the garden (as the sun uprist)
She walketh up and down where as her list
(The Knightes Tale) . . .

Let the reader imagine a small white city, with a tower leaning at one end of it, trees on either side, and blue mountains for the background; and he may fancy he sees Pisa, as the traveller sees it in coming from Leghorn. Add to this, in summer-time fields of corn on all sides, bordered with hedgerow trees and the festoons of vines of which he had so often read, hanging from tree to tree and he may judge of the impression made upon an admirer of Italy, who is in Tuscany for the first time.

In entering the city, the impression is not injured. What looked white in the distance remains as pure and fair on closer acquaintance. You cross a bridge and cast your eye up the whole extent of the city one way, Arno the river, the river Arno of Dante, Petrarch and Boccaccio, winding through the middle of it under two more bridges; and fair, elegent houses of good size bordering the white pavement on either side. This is the Lung'Arno or street 'Along the Arno'. The mountains in which you fancy you see the marble veins (for it is from these that the marble of Carrara comes) tower away beautifully at the further end, and owing to the clear atmosphere, seem to be much nearer than they are. The Arno which is about as wide perhaps as the Isis at Oxford is sandy-coloured, and in the summer time shrunken; but still it is the river of the great Tuscan writers, the visible possessor of the name we have all heard a thousand times; and we feel what a true thing is that which is called ideal.

The first novelty that strikes you . . . is the singular fairness and new look of houses that have been standing hundreds of years. This is owing to the dryness of the Italian atmosphere. Antiquity refuses to look ancient in Italy. . . .

The ground floors of all the great houses in Pisa, as in other Italian cities, have iron bars at the windows. They were for security in time of trouble. The look is at first very gloomy and prison-like, but you get used to it. The bars are round and painted white, and the interstices are large; and if the windows look towards a garden, and are bordered with shrubs and ivy, as those at the back were in the Casa Lanfranchi, the imagination makes a compromise with their prison-like appearance, and persuades itself they are but comforts in times of war, and trellises during a peace establishment. All the floors are made for separate families, it having been the

93

custom in Italy from time immemorial for fathers and mothers, sons and daughters-in-law, or *vice versa*, with as many other relations as might be 'agreeable', to live under the same roof. . . .

After Shelley's death . . . we remained but three months at Pisa . . . We then went to Genoa where we received the first number of the periodical work the *Liberal*, which Lord Byron had invited me to set up and in which Shelley was to have assisted. He did assist; for his beautiful translation of the *May Day Night* from Goethe, appeared in the first number.[1]

After the tragedy Byron and his party, the Hunts and Mary Shelley moved on from Pisa to Genoa to look at the first number of Hunt's journal; but *The Liberal* did not survive after the first few issues.

Byron and Mary Shelley were by no means naturally easy together, but he coped as well as he could with her grief. He made available to her copying work which would bring in some income, and pleaded unsuccessfully on her behalf with her father-in-law, the inflexible Sir Timothy Shelley.

Byron then suggested that Mary should return to England, offering to pay the cost, since he felt that as the daughter of Godwin she would have a better chance there of pursuing her profession of woman of letters. He was co-executor with Thomas Love Peacock of Shelley's estate, and he took his responsibilities seriously; but Mary, who went to live in the Hunts unruly household in Genoa, procrastinated and stayed to await the birth of Marianne Hunt's seventh child. The rest of her life has been touched on earlier in this book.

Byron must already have been in ill health, but he continued to ride every day and made a new circle of friends in Genoa, including the celebrated Lady Blessington, her rich, good-natured husband, formerly Lord Mountjoy, and their inseparable companion, the most elegant of dandies, Count D'Orsay. Teresa was naturally jealous of this good-looking woman of the world who drew interesting men to her side wherever she settled, but in reality Lady Blessington was only supplying to Byron gossip and companionship and conjuring up the fashionable world which he had renounced but by no means forgotten.

[1] *Autobiography of Leigh Hunt*, edited by J. E. Morpurgo.

So while Lady Blessington was enjoying the company of one of the most talked-about and talented Englishmen of his day, and while he was glad to break his routine of work, exercise and vegetarian diet in talk with her, his adoring Teresa was fuming. On May 17, 1823, he wrote to Lady Hardy that his new friendship was causing 'a bit of domestic trouble . . . Mde. la Comptesse G. was seized with a furious fit of Italian jealousy and was as unreasonable and perverse as can well be imagined'. Nevertheless his feelings for Teresa were sufficiently deep to make him agree when she demanded that her brother Pietro accompany him on all future visits to the Blessingtons.

It was in this month, May, that Byron learned he had been elected a member of the Greek Committee, composed of Liberals like Jeremy Bentham, Douglas Kinnaird and Byron's friend Hobhouse. When he made up his mind to go to Greece, Byron invited Count Pietro Gamba to accompany him, but he could not bring himself to break the news to Teresa. She tells us[1] that

> one day when he was sitting beside her on the terrace which looked out over the bay he said, looking at her sadly. 'I have not even got a portrait of you which is like you. A miniaturist has been recommended to me; will you sit to him for me?', but he lacked the courage to confess his plan of going to Greece, and finally her brother had to break the news to her. They went first to Leghorn, then to Greece, Trelawny being of the party.

The story of Byron in Greece and of his death at Missolonghi is so well-known that we will leave him here, as he departs from Tuscany, giving the last word to Teresa's brother, Pietro. From Missolonghi, on April 20, 1824, he wrote to Hobhouse:

> You will already know that my Lord was struck down by an unforeseen epileptic fit only two months ago. His health, however, seemed to have improved and it appeared that the fit had left not the slightest trace. Yet he was always debilitate, both as an effect of the infirmity and because of the severe abstinence which he maintained with the object of preventing a relapse.
>
> On the 10th of this month he was caught in a violent rain while

---

[1] Quoted from *The Last Attachment*, by Iris Origo.

riding on horseback, according to his custom, outside the city. There followed a feverish chill. The symptoms were inflammatory —It looked for a while as if he might overcome it if he had submitted to the advice of his doctors who ordered him to be bled. He would not have it and the fever increased. Then he submitted and three or four bleedings were performed and leeches applied etc. but it was too late. . . .

What an end to his marvellous faculties, which had already borne a strain above human endurance. He died on the 19th April at half past six in the evening.[1]

Teresa was left in an unenviable position on Byron's death. During his lifetime she had refused to accept any money from him. Her father was still in exile, and her return to her strange and violent husband lasted for only five months. After a second separation she settled in Rome and saw mostly English people, despite her imperfect English. Eight years after Byron's death she left for England, accompanied by her younger brother Vincenzo, and visited John Murray and Byron's half-sister Augusta, with whom he had never allowed her to correspond. What passed between them was never known. They both expressed satisfaction, but they never met again. Teresa, who could be affected and silly, living on Byron memories, was shrewd enough not to allow herself to be exploited by Lady Blessington. In the end Teresa found peace with a witty and generous French nobleman, the Marquis de Boissey, whom with great pomp she married in the chapel of the Luxembourg in 1847 when she was forty-seven and he forty-nine.

Thirty-four years after Byron's death, when Teresa had read Byron's published letters, which might well have disillusioned her with their flippancy, she wrote in fierce anger to John Murray, Junior, about the unpleasant book by Leigh Hunt; and surprisingly, confounded her critics with the greatest generosity and wisdom: 'Since the last word on Lord Byron (not as a poet, but as a moral and social being) is far from having been said, I hope that, as you may imagine—it will be done, after my death. Whatever the consequences may be to my reputation is unimportant, so long as none of the documents and letters are lost,

[1] *Byron's Last Journey to Greece*, by Pietro Gamba, 1825.

Villa Gherardescha, where Landor found 'the best water, the best
air, and the best oil in the world'.

Villino Trollope, on Piazza Independenza, Florence, to which the
Trollopes moved after Thomas Adolphus married in 1848.

Frances Trollope
painted by
A. Hervieu

Thomas Adolphus and Anthony Trollope in Florence.

which can reveal in its true light the great and kind heart of Lord Byron.'[1]

She then wrote *Vie de Byron en Italie* and put it away with Byron's letters at the villa her husband had bought for her at Settimbello, near Florence, where she spent the last seven years of life after his death. As her biographer Iris Origo, who was the first to be allowed to examine her papers by her descendant Count Gamba, describes it:

> The pleasant spacious villa, with its orangery and its little chapel stands on a slight rise above the Pistoiese plain, shaded by a few great trees. The salon is still adorned by somewhat pretentious frescoes of the grand chateaux of the Marquis de Boissey. The chapel contains Teresa's tomb. In this villa—until in the last war, they were moved elsewhere for safe keeping—remained Teresa's box of relics and all her papers bequeathed by her with the villa and all it contained . . . The bookshelves, to this day still hold her books— her annotated copies of Moore, Medwin, Lady Blessington, Leigh Hunt, and Byron's complete works . . . Here it was that she finished the 'Vie de Lord Byron' which she had begun many years before; and here, an old lady now, at last, but still proud of her long ringlets *à l'anglaise* and her plump little white hands—she would draw out her letters and 'relics' and go back to the past. There they all lay—Byron's letters to her, her own letters to him . . . So much passion and ecstasy and pain. What was now left of it all?

[1] Quoted from *The Last Attachment,* by Iris Origo, 1949.

CHAPTER VII

Walter Savage Landor

If we could find a man exempt by nature from vices and infirmities, we should find one not worth knowing: he would be void of tenderness and compassion. What allowances then could his best friends expect from him in their frailties?

Boccaccio to Petrarch, *Imaginary Conversations.*

IN 1818 Walter Savage Landor departed for Tuscany at the age of forty-three, with his wife and their first-born child. It was to remain his home, with one long interval of unwilling exile, until his death in Florence in 1864 at the age of eighty-nine. He was a larger-than-life figure of enormous vitality; great in physical stature and intellectual resource, in unyielding principle and in loyalty of friendship. A complicated figure, too, as he himself realised; a boisterously fascinating conversationalist with his own 'vices and infirmities' including an ungovernable temper with which he tried the patience of the Florentines to its limits; yet one who showed gentleness and courtesy to women and children and had a compelling affection for animals.

He settled first at Pisa in September 1818, but did not like it.

Pisa has the advantage of a river, 200 feet wide, running through its principal street, but it is infested with English and Irish moschitos. I pay a guinea a week for my lodgings without linen and plate, and everything is a third dearer than Genoa except game.[1]

Among the English 'infesting' the city was Shelley, whom he regarded as almost the greatest living poet and prose writer, but he allowed himself to be deterred from seeking out the poet by scandalous rumours about his private life. He lived to regret this

---

[1] Quoted from *Savage Landor*, by Malcolm Elwin, 1941.

missed opportunity, writing that Shelley's 'generosity and charity went far beyond those of any man (I believe) at present in existence'.

It is difficult to understand his attitude to Shelley's private life, since his own had not been blameless. Born, like Shelley, into the landed gentry, and heir to a large estate, he was expelled from Rugby and afterwards rusticated from Oxford for shooting at a don from his window. Thereafter he fell in love with a Welsh girl, Nancy Jones, with whom he lived openly for two years and who bore him a daughter who died.

He and Shelley were rebels with much in common: both expelled from university, both Greek scholars, both geniuses who could fascinate by their conversation. Landor's rebellion against authority, however, was not on behalf of an idealistic order of society. He was an individualist fighting, within the current framework of society, against mediocrity, oppression, cruelty, inflexible bureaucracy. But he lacked some element of stability or co-ordination which prevented his following either a political or an academic career, though his talents would have fitted him for either, and this waywardness also prevented him from conducting his financial and domestic affairs successfully.

In 1802, as a young man of seventeen, he had visited Paris after the Peace of Amiens as a private tourist. Although the Tory newspapers had reported the plundering of Italy's pictures and other art treasures by Napoleon he saw that there was much exaggeration about 'the spoils of Italy'. And he found that the pillaging of great houses by the mob had also been much exaggerated—'the religious houses alone have suffered by the revolution and these in general not much'. At the same time he realised that Fox had been wrong in talking of government by 'the will of the people'—it was purely a military dictatorship.

He stood within a few yards of Napoleon:

> His countenance is not of that fierce cast which you see in the prints, and which perhaps it may assume in battle. He seems melancholy and reserved, but not morose or proud . . . He rode a little white horse, about the size of my father's, and cantered up and down six or eight lines of military. . .[1]

---

[1] 'Landor's Last Years in Italy', by Kate Field, *Atlantic Monthly*, 1868.

Sixty years later in Florence he reminisced with a well-known American journalist, Kate Field, telling her that Buonoparte 'was exceedingly handsome then, with a rich olive complexion and oval face, youthful as a girl's . . . near him rode Murat, mounted upon a gold-clad charger; and very handsome he was too, but cox-combical'.

It was in about April 1808 that he had met Southey, and their friendship lasted until Southey's death. Southey, though over-rated as a poet by Landor, was one of the most genuinely kind and disinterested men of letters of the period: and writing to the woman who became his second wife, Caroline Bowles, he could still say of Landor sixteen years later:

> Differing as I do from him in constitutional temper, and in some serious opinions, he is yet of all men living the one with whom I feel the most sympathy in heart and mind.[1]

Landor's mistress at this earlier time, about whom he confided in Southey, was Jane Swifte, a lovely warm-hearted Irish girl who was a married woman and a mother. To her he addressed the love poems in *Ianthe*, and he continued to love her all his life. When she left him he, lacking direction in his life, went off to fight for Spain, which was in revolt against the rule of Napoleon's brother Joseph. An unsatisfactory armistice after months of mishandling aroused protest in England, and the weak conduct of affairs ended with the disaster of the retreat of Corunna under Sir John Moore. Landor had left Spain before this, disgusted with the bungling at Cintra, and he joined in a violent criticism of John Hookham Frere, the British minister in Spain. His experiences and feelings were embodied in a play, *Count Julian*, which did not have a great success.

Landor had quarrelled with his father about his inheritance and choice of a profession. When the father died in 1805 Landor duly inherited a fortune, and bought an estate, Llanthony Abbey in Monmouthshire. He spent enormous sums in trying to make it a model one. This did not impress the tenants and he became embroiled in a series of lawsuits with them and with neighbours.

[1] *Correspondence of Robert Southey with Caroline Bowles*, edited by Edward Dowden.

All his life he needed beauty in a woman and at Bath he met a girl of sufficient grace to make him want to marry her. To his mother he wrote:

> The name of my intended bride is Julia Thuillier. She has no pretensions of any kind, and her want of fortune was the very thing which determined me to marry her. I shall be sorry to leave Bath entirely but when I have completed my house I must remain there.[1]

They were married quietly in 1811 after four months' courtship. Southey said they were 'without passion, hoping that affection would grow out of esteem'.

The conduct of his affairs had been in the hands of a near-scoundrel, and the first architect he employed on building the house at Llanthony was so incompetent that the building fell down: when poor Landor arrived with his bride it was but half finished. By August 1813 his creditors and debtors and lawsuits made life so difficult that, as he said to Southey, 'I can never be happy here or comfortable, or at peace'. He sold out and departed, burning with injustice at the English law which had upheld his enemies.

In April 1821, he went to Tuscany to look for a house, writing to his mother, with whom he had become reconciled after the birth of his son and heir three years before:

> Julia is thin and weak, but is without any particular complaint, and is recommended to change the air for the summer as Pisa lies low, and is abandoned by all the inhabitants in the warm season.[2]

His first home in Florence was the Palace of the Medici on Borgo degli'Albizzi, and he was soon on bad terms with the British Minister's secretary, Dawkins. Lord Burghersh, the Minister, tried to pour oil on the troubled waters but Landor was not appeased. He settled down to live within his income, thanks to the cheapness of living in Italy, and enjoyed entertaining a

---

[1] Quoted from *Savage Landor*, by Malcolm Elwin, 1941.
[2] Ibid.

few friends, though, as he said in 1823, there were 'few foreigners who do not come to see me'. Two years later: 'Here in Florence I have two or three friends, a manageable number, and some dozens who call on me, but whom I cannot receive'.

At this time his closest friend was Francis Hare, seven years younger than he was and also an eldest son, the heir to a large inheritance and a man of brilliant mind. On the death of his father Hare, as a Regency buck, spent so much and lost so much on horses that after three years he had to retire to live a more modest life in Italy. This didn't prevent his engaging in amorous dalliance. The two friends must have been an extraordinary sight when engaged in conversation and argument, Landor aggressive, Hare loftily omniscient. As their friend Seymour Kirkup recalled:

> It was a constant struggle of competition and display between them, both often wrong, although men of strong memory. They used to have great disputes mostly on questions of history. . . . Hare was often astounded at being corrected. He was thought infallible; and I remember our consul-general at Rome calling him a monster of learning.[1]

One of Hare's practical jokes was to enter a confessional box and relate such a fantasy of crime and vice that the priest stopped his ears with his fingers and rushed in horror from the church. Landor's booming laugh must have rung out at this tale.

Seymour Kirkup, who was two years younger than Hare, lived mostly in Florence from 1816 till his death at ninety-two in 1880. He was a painter whom Leigh Hunt criticised for not having ability or the spur of financial necessity to develop his art to the full. 'A man of more cordial generosity, with greater delicacy in showing it, I never met with,'[2] Hunt declared. Kirkup and Landor became friends in 1824, and in Landor's last unhappy years he was still a faithful friend.

A friend common to both was Charles Armitage Brown, who had written the libretto of an opera produced at Drury Lane and shared a house with Keats at Hampstead—Brown was a

---

[1] Quoted from *Savage Landor*, by Malcolm Elwin, 1941.
[2] *Autobiography of Leigh Hunt*, edited by J. E. Morpurgo.

good friend to Keats in the poet's most tragic years. He was bald
and stout and hearty and humorous, loving wine, women and
food. He had been a friend of Leigh Hunt's at Hampstead, and
in 1823, when Hunt and his family went to live at Maiano near
Florence, he introduced them to Landor. Later, in 1838, Brown
dedicated a book, *Shakespeare's Autobiographical Poems*, to Landor
as the best lover of Shakespeare and the best living writer of
English.

At his first meeting with Landor, Leigh Hunt produced a
hair which Byron had given him as allegedly from the head of
Lucrezia Borgia, and in 1825 he published the verse Landor
wrote about it:

> *Borgia, thou once wert almost too august,*
> *And high for adoration—now thou'rt dust!*
> *All that remains of thee these plaits infold*
> *Calm hair, meand'ring with pellucid gold!*

Hunt called Landor 'a stormy mountain-pine that should produce lilies' and remarked he had never met such great delicacy
of imagination combined with such a vehement nature.

Landor refused to meet Byron because he disapproved of his
derision of Wordsworth and Southey and of his private morality.
Byron was stung to take revenge in his *Vision of Judgment*; later,
in the eleventh canto of *Don Juan*, he included Landor among
the greatest living poets:

> *Some persons think that Coleridge hath the sway;*
> *And Wordsworth has supporters, two or three;*
> *And that deep-mouth'd Boeotian 'Savage Landor'*
> *Has taken for a swan rogue Southey's gander.*

Landor then satirised Byron as the wicked Lord Rochester's
bastard Mr George Nelly: 'Whenever he wrote a bad poem,
he supported his sinking fame by some signal act of profligacy,
an elegy by a seduction, a heroic by an adultery, a tragedy by a
divorce'. But hearing of Byron's death in the cause of Greek
freedom Landor was sorry and added a footnote to his second
edition saying he would not have written a syllable against him
had he known of this.

When Landor's poetic muse deserted him Southey gave him the idea of writing dialogues. He had written a couple some twenty years before, so he took up the idea again and in them, employed his twin gifts of biographer and dramatist in bringing two characters to life in a single scene. *The Imaginary Conversations* remains his finest work, the first series being published in 1824 and supplementary volumes in 1826 and 1828.

After the inevitable quarrel with the landlord, Landor left the Palazzo Medici and in September 1825 took a three years' lease of the Villa Castiglione, in the hills a few miles from the city out of the Porta San Niccolo; he ascribed the move to his wife's health and to his own 'tendency to melancholy'. Certainly his life became animated when—as Kirkup relates—there were people like a certain old marquis around:

> The marquis enjoyed no very good name, and this had exasperated Landor the more. Mrs Landor was sitting in the drawing-room the day after, where I and some others were, when the marquis came strutting in without removing his hat. But he had scarcely advanced three steps from the door when Landor walked up to him quickly and knocked his hat off, then took him by the arm and turned him out. You should have heard Landor's shout of laughter at his own anger when it was all over, inextinguishable laughter which none of us could resist.

To Landor the Florentines were 'beyond all others a treacherous tricking mercenary race', though he hardly knew them except for his servants, with whom he had constant difficulties, doubtless because he was an eccentric master. Yet the Tuscans 'twenty miles from Florence were some of the best people I have ever yet conversed with . . . the country folks are frank, hospitable, courteous, laborious, disinterested and eager to assist one another. I have sat among them by the hour . . . and at the first time of seeing me, the whole family has told me its most intimate concerns.' With all his intelligence he could not discern that the difference was in himself—that with these simple people he was natural; with the more sophisticated he was critical, expecting too much and possibly looking for slights.

Pictures became his lifelong hobby. He judged them by historical value and originality rather than by execution, buying paintings and sending them as presents to members of his family or friends who admired them. Monckton Milnes, who saw his collection in 1833 at Florence, wrote: 'Landor anticipated the public taste in the admiration of the early Italian schools; thus amid some pretenders to high birth and dignity his walls presented a genuine company of such masters as Masaccio, Ghirlandaio, Gozzoli, Filippo Lippi and Fra Angelico'. But his favourite was Raphael, whom he regarded as the greatest painter: 'I delight in Titian, I love Coreggio, I wonder at the vastness of Michael-Angelo. I admire, love and wonder and then fall down, before Raffael'; and after him Pietro Perugino and Frate Bartolommeo. His friend Middleton annoyed him by not buying a Raphael for £500. 'It is worth £2,000 and will bring it e're long!' He was the only private collector to own a Cimabue. He offered 'about one hundred pictures, from the restoration of painting in Italy to 1500' to his brother Henry because his wife had thrown them haphazardly into a closet: they had been in the children's rooms and she gave as her reason for putting them away that they might fall down on the children's heads!

But pictures and second-hand books were hobbies. All his deepest feeling was concentrated on his children, three boys and a girl. He brought them up in such an impractical manner, however, stifling them with affection and unable to bear any separation from them, that in later life they shrank away and cruelly rejected him.

Long before this he had become a celebrated exile. Hazlitt, arriving in Florence in March 1825, was warned that he would need to be introduced to Landor by the right person, and Hazlitt replied (according to Kirkup) 'he would beard the lion in his den', and he walked up to his house 'one winter's morning in nankeen shorts and white stockings; was made much of by the royal animal; and often returned—at night; for Landor was much out in the day in all weathers'.

That autumn Shelley's friend Thomas Jefferson Hogg called while Francis Hare was with Landor. Landor took to Hogg, and Hogg made him laugh his great genial laugh when he told him how Shelley had been so absorbed in Landor's *Gebir* at Oxford one day that he, Hogg, had taken the book and flung it out of the window in order to gain Shelley's attention; uselessly, however, for as soon as a servant brought it back Shelley resumed reading.

A visit to Rome in the New Year of 1826 after the appearance of the first two editions of *Imaginary Conversations* seems to have brought home unmistakably to Landor that he was regarded as a man of achievement and genius and that he could afford to be gracious rather than being wary of affront. He remained difficult of access though enjoying some social life: Lady Blessington, who spent the spring there, did not meet him although she knew his friends well. However, in June of the following year she wrote in her diary

> Made the acquaintance of Walter Savage Landor, ten days ago, and have seen him nearly every day since. . . . His avoidance of general society though courted to enter it, his dignified reserve when brought in contact with those he disapproves and his fearless courage in following the dictates of a lofty mind, had somehow or other given the erroneous impression that his manners were, if not abrupt, at least singular. This is not the case . . . the politeness of Landor is grave and respectful, without his ever losing sight of what is due to himself . . . It is not often that a man, so profoundly erudite as Landor, preserves this racy originality, which . . . gives colour to all that he has acquired. He reads of the ancients, thinks, lives with and dreams of them, has imbued his thoughts with their lofty aspirations and noble contempt of what is unworthy.[1]

To Lady Blessington, an Irishwoman whose 'past' did not allow of her reception in the drawing-rooms of London society, but who, nevertheless, having married the wealthy Lord Mountjoy, could afford to entertain and travel in the most lavish manner, came many of the most interesting men of the day, and while she might be said to have been a lion-hunter of Landor they nevertheless remained friends and she extended to him a most disinterested kindness to the end of her days. For his part Landor was the defender of Lady Blessington, her genial husband, and the delightful dandy Count D'Orsay,[2] who made up as it were

[1] *Literary Life and Correspondence of The Countess of Blessington*, by R. R. Madden.

[2] Michael Sadleir in *Blessington d'Orsay* has a plausible theory that D'Orsay was impotent: 'Combined with his peculiar type of physical beauty—the build and stature of an athlete, the face of a woman—it explains his popularity with men, his lack of appeal to women'.

a *ménage à trois*, though whether D'Orsay was Lady Blessington's lover or not no one has ever proved.

Landor, writing to his mother after their first meeting, declared:

> Lady Blessington is without exception, the most elegant and best-informed woman I ever conversed with; but, as she is accused of some incorrectness in early life, the ladies (at least the English ladies) do not visit her. In France she enjoys the first society and admits *only* the first. Never was there a woman more generous or more high minded.[1]

Twenty-five years later, on D'Orsay's death he wrote that, with many foibles and grave faults, 'the Count' was generous and sincere. 'Neither spirits nor wit ever failed him, and he was ready at all times to lay down his life for a friend.'

In 1827 Landor told his sister Ellen: 'I am always at the Blessingtons from eight to eleven, I mean when I am in Florence. At present I do not go over to them more than once or twice a week, the distance being three good miles.'

The summer heat of Florence did not suit his wife and family and the lease of his most recent abode at Castiglione was running out; so he went to look at a cottage at San Domenico di Fiesole with a new friend, Joseph Ablett. Landor wanted him to become his neighbour, but Ablett was making enquiries about the Villa Gherardesca near by, and in fact he generously bought it for Landor, asking only that he repay the money if ever he found himself rich enough, and if not his heirs could see to it.

Landor moved there in the autumn of 1829. Exuberantly he declared: 'I have not had a moment's illness since I resided here, nor have the children. I have the best water, the best air, and the best oil in the world.' Yet nothing he engaged in ever seemed to go smoothly. An enormous planting project which he started must have used up far more than his share of the vital, jealously guarded water supply. His neighbour below, on the steep slope up to Fiesole, a retired French diplomat, naturally complained when the supply was reduced and Landor with his uncontrollable impetuosity unreasonably challenged him to a duel; but once more

---

[1] *Savage Landor*, by Malcolm Elwin, 1941.

a friend came to his aid and Kirkup, with tact, was able to prevent the engagement. All the same, the matter, which could have been talked over reasonably, went to court and Landor settled in 1842 for £200 or £300.

In 1971 I was invited by the owners to visit Villa Gherardesca. They bought the villa from an American who converted Landor's house for modern use, and now live in a charming converted farmhouse on the property because the villa itself is a Catholic home for foundlings. The Villa Palmieri is near by, where Boccaccio's ladies and gentlemen, escaping the plague in Florence, whiled away the time telling the stories which make up the *Decameron*. The view over Florence from the Villa Gherardesca is magnificent and, as always, it has a charming long terrace with a stone balustrade from which to view it. The villa itself is not too grand: none of the rooms is large enough to have held a dance in, as the owner pointed out, but they are high and well-proportioned. It is a larger house than Smollett's at Antignano outside Livorno, but then Landor had a family of four children to house. The room from which Landor is said literally to have thrown out his cook in a fit of anger after a bad meal, is not very high above the terrace, and since there were flower beds below in Landor's day, the cook must have had a soft fall; we know this because when somebody told him that the man had injured himself, all Landor did was to express concern for his violets! Above the dining-room was his study with its wonderful view over Florence. Only one of the original floors of mosaic marble remain. The staircase is of the grey stone of the region, with shallow steps, like those at Byron's Palazzo Lanfranchi at Pisa, but it is a little difficult to imagine it all as it was in Landor's day: in a contemporary picture of the exterior the lines seem much softened. The *suora* in charge of the home, who showed us round, was young and efficient-looking, and no private home or luxury hotel I have ever visited was so perfectly kept and so well-equipped as this home with only forty-eight children. It was simply furnished, with delightful small dormitories and lots of dolls decorating the almost elegant beds. The kitchens on the lower floor, on the garden side of the house, were the most modern I have ever seen.

The garden must have been beautiful in Landor's time: did he not assure his sisters that if they came to visit him their bedrooms would be perfumed by the profusion of flowers under their windows? But one could almost hear his explosion of rage and sense his ensuing attack on the authorities had he seen the new modern houses springing up beside the villa.

The third volume of *Imaginary Conversations* was so critical of the Florentines as to arouse the anger of the authorities of the capital of Tuscany, and one could hardly blame them:

Salamon: Certainly no race of men upon earth was ever so unwarlike, so indifferent to the national dignity and to personal honour, as the Florentines are now: yet in former days a certain pride, arising from a resemblance in their government to that of Athens, excited a vivifying desire of approximation where no danger or loss accompanied it; and Genius was no less confident of his security than of his power. Look from the window. That cottage on the declivity was Dante's: that square and large mansion with a circular garden before it elevated artificially, was the first scene of Boccaccio's *Decameron*. A boy might stand at an equal distance between them, and break the window of each with his sling. What idle fabricator of crazy systems will tell me that Climate is the creator of Genius?

Alfieri: Since the destruction of the Republic, Florence has produced only one great man, Galileo, and abandoned him to every indignity that fanaticism and despotism could invent. Extraordinary men, like the stones that are formed in the higher regions of the air, fall upon the earth only to be broken and cast into the furnace. The precursor of Newton lived in the deserts of the moral world, drank water, and ate locusts and wild honey. It was fortunate that his head also was not lopped off: had a singer asked it, instead of a dancer, it would have been.

Later, when he made furious criticisms of the administration after his house was burgled, he was ordered to leave Florence. But unknown to him two friends interceded with the Grand Duke of Tuscany, who rescinded the expulsion. Landor meanwhile was writing to Southey:

I resolved to pitch my tent in the midst of them; and have now bought a villa belonging to the Count Gherardescha of the family of C. Ugolino, and upon the spot where Boccaccio led his women to bathe when he had left the first scene of their story-telling. Here I shall pass my life, long or short, no matter, but God grant without pain and sickness, and with only such friends and such enemies as I enjoy at present.

He appeared to overlook his unhappy marriage, with its differences between an eccentric husband and a frustrated wife who, in a strange country, found it impossible to share his interests and friendships. It is more than possible that the beginning of the break-up of the marriage was hastened by the arrival in Florence in October 1829 of 'Ianthe' whom we have already met as Jane Swifte. As he explained in a letter to his sister Ellen:

Perhaps tho you may never have heard that the dearest of all the friends I ever had or ever shall have, Mrs Swifte, accepted the Count de Molande, for her second husband. I have advised her to accept him, as adding a fresh splendour to her lovely daughters, and very sure to conduce to their more desirable establishment in life. Her fortune, from several relations, is become very large and she has no ambition. I doubt whether she will do what I think advisable.[1]

Her son tells how Landor came to breakfast every other day, and apparently there were gay visits to his home by Ianthe's children—something which Landor must have delighted in. She helped him plan his garden and even tempted him to attend both the Grand Duke's ball and Burghersh's opera ball.

His sisters sent him grass seed from England lacking which (as today) made the great difficulty in creating a lawn in Tuscany. He wrote to them and invoked 'Ianthe' without naming her:

I have four mimosas ready to place round my intended tomb, and a friend who is coming to plant them.

> Lo! where the four mimosas blend their shade,
> In calm repose at last is Landor laid;
> For ere he slept he saw them planted here
> By her his soul had ever held most dear,
> And he had lived enough when he had dried her tear.[2]

[1] Quoted from *Savage Landor*, by Malcolm Elwin, 1941.
[2] Ibid.

Ianthe made him so happy that he began to write poetry again —it was always the passion of his life.

It was probably at this time that his wife Julia first locked her bedroom door against him, of which he complained later. Unknown to Landor, she already had a lover, a young Irishman named MacCarthy, who had been a secretary to a nobleman and was now introduced into the Landor household as temporary tutor to one of the boys. Whatever criticism is made of Julia, she was devoted to her children, and never wished them to go to England with Landor when he threatened a separation, perhaps fearing they would remain there. The acrimonious state of the Landors' relations was revealed by Armitage Brown, who came to their home for a farewell dinner before leaving for England at the end of March 1835, when Julia made a scene in front of him:

> I am ashamed to write down the words, but to hear them was painful . . . I am afraid my patience would have left me in a tenth part of the time; but you, Landor, to my astonishment sat with a composed countenance, never once making use of an uncivil expression.[1]

Three months later a saddened and solitary Landor wrote to Southey:

> It was not willingly that I left Tuscany and my children. There was but one spot upon earth on which I had fixed my heart and four objects on which my affection rested. That they might not hear every day such language as no decent person should ever hear once, nor despise both parents, I left the only delight of my existence.[2]

First he went from Fiesole to Florence, then to Bagni di Lucca for the summer, where he wrote *Pericles and Aspasia*. At Bagni he wrote to his brother Henry, saying 'she swore she never would' give up the children; then in melancholy resignation:

[1] Written by Armitage Brown at Landor's request to convince his relatives of Julia's behaviour.
[2] Quoted from *Savage Landor*, by Malcolm Elwin, 1941.

On Thursday . . . I will go to London . . . Never will I venture into Tuscany nor see her face again if I can help it. I have written to Johnstone the banker to devise some means of conveying the children to me without her, and not to furnish her with means of molesting me. I suspect at last she will keep my children from me, and the winter will whiten my bones among the Alps.[1]

In London Lady Blessington, writing that 'quiet and friendship await you' and thanking him for a copy of *Pericles and Aspasia*, persuaded him to stay at Gore House. Here he was lionised, and he must have enjoyed it. He had been throwing himself into work, and among his publications was *High Life and Low Life in Italy*. Meanwhile Charles Dickens was invited by Lady Blessington for her house-warming party (May 1836) in her search for literary friends to entertain Landor. Landor had met John Forster, who made a point of knowing every writer in London, and had introduced him to Lady Blessington. Forster was to become literary executor and biographer both of Landor and Dickens, although he had not known Landor before the old lion was sixty, and was thirty-seven years his junior. This placed him at a disadvantage, since Landor was not likely to confide in a young man about his private life, as he did to his old friend Southey for instance. In a letter of 1838 to Lady Blessington Landor wrote:

I heard from Florence not long ago, but nothing from that quarter (his wife) is likely to give me pleasure or composure. I wish I could utterly forget all connected with it. But the waves of oblivion dash against my Tuscan terraces and the spray reaches my family, and blinds the eyes that should be turned towards me, for other waters fill my heart with bitterness.[2]

In 1840 Forster took Dickens to visit Landor in Bath, and it became an annual habit for them to drive down from London for his birthday. On one occasion a young lady whose presence gave pleasure to the ageing Landor, Eliza Lynn (afterwards Mrs Lynn Lynton) was present and reported that Dickens, now a literary success, was gay and charming, and the conversation between

[1] Quoted from *Savage Landor*, by Malcolm Elwin, 1941.
[2] Ibid.

Elizabeth
Barrett Browning

*Both portraits were
painted in 1858
by M. Gordigiani.*

Robert Browning

The Brownings' salon in the
Casa Guido, Florence,
painted by George Mignaty
in 1861

him and Landor so stimulating that Dickens was inspired to get to work on the character of Little Nell in *The Old Curiosity Shop* and she became Landor's favourite fictional character. Landor thought that 'upon her Juliet might for a moment have turned her eyes from Romeo and that Desdemona might have taken her hairbreadth escapes to heart', so interesting and pathetic did she seem to him.

The following year Dickens's fourth child and second son was born, and he asked Landor to be his godfather, saying to him that 'it would give the child something to boast of, to be called Walter Landor and that to call him so would do my own heart good'; at the end of the year there were celebrations when Landor came to London for the christening. In 1843 he had been cheered by the visit for six months of his son Walter escorting his sister Julia, but they insisted on returning to their mother at Fiesole as soon as the time was up, and he realised that he would have to live without his children, although the white pomeranian dog which Julia left with her father helped to console him—he never liked to be without a dog. In the event, for twelve years Pomero and his master were inseparable. If Pomero went off for a ramble Landor would scour the streets for him and refuse to eat until he found him—the dog's death in 1856 was a terrible blow.

In 1846 his *Collected Works* were published and were well received. Browning wrote to Elizabeth:

I called on Forster this morning; he says Landor is in high delight at the congratulatory letters he has received—so you must write, dearest, and add the queen-rose to his garland. F—— talks about some 500 copies—or did he say 300?—being sold already . . . so there is hope for Landor's lovers.

As the years went by Landor suffered the loss of his great friend Lady Blessington in 1849, and two years later his beloved Ianthe. He was still living in Bath when he was immortalised by Dickens as Boythorn in *Bleak House*.

In 1845, during his visit to Italy, Dickens drove out from Florence to visit his friend's home at Fiesole, asking the coachman which was the villa of the Landor family. The story is recorded by Forster:

'He was a dull dog, and pointed to Boccaccio's. I didn't believe him . . . I went up to the convent which is on a height and was leaning over a dwarf wall basking in the noble view over a vast range of hill and valley, when a little peasant girl came up and began to point out the localities. *Ecco la villa Landora!* was one of the first half-dozen sentences she spoke. My heart swelled as Landor's would have done when I looked down upon it, nestling among its olive-trees and vines, and with its upper windows (there are five above the door) open to the setting sun. Over the centre of these there is another storey set upon the housetop like a tower; and all Italy, except its sea, is melted down into the glowing landscape it commands. I plucked a leaf of ivy from the convent-garden as I looked; and here it is. For Landor. With my love.' So wrote Mr Dickens to me from Florence on the 2nd April 1845; and when I turned over Landor's papers in the same month after an interval of exactly twenty years, the ivy leaf was found carefully enclosed with the letter in which I had sent it. Dickens had asked him before leaving what he would most wish to have in remembrance of Italy. 'An ivy-leaf from Fiesole,' said Landor.[1]

When he was past his eighty-third birthday Landor told Forster: 'I think I will go and die in Italy, but not in my old home'. Apparently he had no intention of returning to the villa at Fiesole, but had decided upon Nervi, and he therefore directed his remaining pictures and books to Genoa. On receiving an account of his health from his niece, his sons feared the publicity and scandal if he died among strangers and they asked him to come home, more or less as an 'invalid lodger'.

Twenty-three years of resentment had passed since he and his wife Julia had met. Landor found her grey-haired and haggard—he presumed from the low sort of life she had led. She saw before her a forlorn shabbily dressed old man of eighty-three, that same man who had gone out of her life a proud straight giant, young for his sixty years. He was not surprised to discover that neither she nor the family were received socially. One of his sons kept the cook as his mistress and had children by her, and

---

[1] Quoted from *Savage Landor*, by Malcolm Elwin, 1941.

Julia at the age of thirty, in 1850, had given birth to an illegitimate daughter.

Landor, who had settled his property in England on his eldest son, was still too proud to be treated as a dependent by his family, and when, after a week, Walter let him know that he no longer owned the house, he wrote to Forster asking if his brother Henry could provide him with the money to live alone in lodgings. Before anything was done he left the villa for Florence, but without money he was forced to return. In a letter to a friend he depicted the humiliations inflicted on him and how he left the house again. He started at noon on a hot June day with scarcely any money in his pocket and was on the point of collapse, after dragging himself to Florence on foot, when by a fortunate chance he met Browning, who took charge.

Nothing would induce Landor to return to Fiesole this time— 'any two rooms with simple board', he said, would be preferable to that. It was then that his past kindness in Bath to a friend, the American painter William Wetmore Story, was reciprocated. It began when Landor wrote to him:

> My friends the Brownings tell me that you are residing in Siena. This is a great inducement for me to take a house for a year in that city. My family are in possession of the most charming villa and grounds within two miles of Florence which I very imprudently gave entirely up to them with a large income, reserving for myself extremely little, so I am constrained to be economical.

Whereupon Story invited him to be his guest till he settled on somewhere to live. Browning accompanied him to Siena, and Story's daughter afterwards recalled how 'the feeling of pity that swelled in my heart as I looked on this old gentleman, and recalled what my father had said of him . . . "a master of the noblest English", and at Bath "altogether most brilliant and entertaining".' Story remarked 'it was the case of old Lear over again'.

Landor remained their guest a month and it was a happy interlude, particularly as Robert and Elizabeth Browning arrived to spend the month of August near by. All of them must have felt for Landor when Robert produced a rough linen bag containing the clothes he had left at his home at Fiesole. Apparently his wife had taken them to Browning to deliver in a manner 'all butter and honey save an occasional wasp's sting . . . when she occasionally designated our friend as "the old Brute!" '

Forster, who had received word from Browning, had hastened to get in touch with Landor's brothers on behalf of the old man, having previously believed that he was well treated at Fiesole and was only complaining like an old man losing his mind a little. Browning had found him so much better in health for the peace at the Storys' that with great kindness he immediately took a cottage near his own villa at Siena for the old man, who wrote to Forster telling him of Browning's kindness—

> who made me the voluntary offer of the money I wanted, and who insists on managing my affairs here, and paying for my lodgings and sustenance. Never was such generosity and such solicitude as this incomparable man has shown on my behalf.

When Landor's brothers realised what had happened at Fiesole they agreed to make an allowance of £250 a year with £50 held for special expenses; and one of them, Henry, was so angry with the way the children had behaved he revoked a legacy of £2000 intended for his niece Julia. Fortunately Landor was so malleable with Browning's gentle tactful handling that he agreed that Browning should administer the money. In the winter of 1859 Landor and the Brownings moved to Florence, where Landor was installed in the Via Nunziata, not far from the Brownings' Casa Guidi.

The following year Landor went again to Siena with the Brownings during the heat of the summer. Apparently he was witty as of old and Elizabeth Browning found herself irresistibly amused by his exuberance. He wanted to give his watch—for lack of money—to start a fund for Garibaldi, but Robert persuaded him of the impracticability of the scheme. Accordingly he wrote an imaginary conversation between *Savonarola and the Prior of San Marco*, the Italian version being published in Florence in 1859 as a pamphlet in aid of the Tuscans wounded in the rising against Austria. He sent the English version to Mrs Lynn Linton, who had it published in the *London Review*, and two other dialogues featuring Garibaldi appeared in *The Athenaeum*. He was unquenchable in his vitality, interested in politics, in everything. When told that Pope Pius IX was dying, having erysipelas in his legs, he retorted: 'He has been on his last legs for some time, but depend upon it they are legs that will last—the Devil is always good to his own, you know!' And on another occasion: 'How surprised St Peter would be to return to earth and find his apostolic successors living in such a grand house as the Vatican. Ah! they are jolly fishermen!'

There was to be no third summer at Siena. On June 29, 1861, Elizabeth Browning died, leaving her husband desolate. Landor, who never became a garrulous old man, wrote to Robert with the delicacy of deep personal feeling:

> My dear Browning: Of all your friends who lament your irreparable loss, no one grieves more deeply than I do. I will not say more, I can say nothing more true. Let these few lines, if they can be of small or no comfort to you at least manifest the affection of your affectionate
>
> W. LANDOR.[1]

Soon Browning left Florence, and because he could not bear to see again the places where he had been so happy with his adored Elizabeth he never returned. Landor began to fail now, and a letter on Italian politics in *The Times* on June 26, 1862, expressing his disappointment that Garibaldi had handed over the fruits of victory to King Victor Emanuel, was his last public foray. He had a slight stroke and prepared himself for the end, being persuaded to abandon his project of being buried, as he and Ianthe had planned, at Fiesole, beside the mimosas, and agreeing to interment in Florence, where he lies in the English cemetery.

In one of his dialogues the painter Filippo Lippi expresses his longing to return to his native Tuscany, and however insufferable the old man must have seemed to the Tuscans, however critical, his own desire to be back was deep:

> I often wished myself away, thinking of my friends in Florence, of music, of painting, of our *villegiatura* at the vintage time . . .

---

[1] Quoted from *Savage Landor*, by Malcolm Elwin, 1941.

Beautiful scenes on which Heaven smiles eternally, how often has my heart ached for you! He who hath lived in the country can enjoy no distant one. He breathes here another air; he lives more life; a brighter sun invigorates his studies, and serener stars influence his repose.

Yet in *High and Low Life in Italy* he surely forfeits whatever sympathy any contemporary Italian might have had for him.

My Dear Mr Drew,—You very goodnaturedly ask me how I can possibly leave so long together all the comforts and conveniences of England. Indeed in the beginning one feels awkward; but the Italians, I do assure you, have learned the use of carpets, and many have fireplaces in one, two and even three rooms. Altho' they are so economical that they always strip off at home the dresses they wear in the streets, yet they are not afraid of rotting their carpets by spitting on them most prodigally . . .

But in everything Italian there always is something mean and shabby. At the entrance of their palaces in the cities, the flask, and a little square door by the side of an immense one, show you that for five pence you may partake of the marchese's hospitality; at the entrance of their villas you meet the contadina's children covered with vermin who occupy a large part of them, among oil-jars, barrels, bags, baskets and bunches of rotten grapes suspended from the beams. In the midst of these you generally smell salt ling and goat's milk cheese as solid as the best of them and sometimes tame pigeons fly down from this open storehouse and cover with dust the dawbing they have given. At present it (Florence) is I fear the filthiest capital in Europe; and I can speak from experience that it is impossible to walk thro the market with dry feet unless you go upon stilts, or with dry shirts unless you go in a jacket. So long as the taxes are paid, the lower orders may do, or omit to do, what they please. Excessive filthiness sweeps away excessive population, and serves for moral restraint.

It is by no means a fair picture. As Giuliana Artom Treves so aptly concludes in her delicious chapter of *The Golden Ring*[1] headed 'I am Walter Savage Landor':

It is obvious that Landor never knew the historian of the Florentine

[1] Translated by Sylvia Sprigge, 1956.

State, Gino Capponi, nor the whole circle of Capponi's friends who played their part in the struggle for the unity of Italy. We feel sorry for Landor; by the word 'Italians', he must have meant the traders with whom he was always quarrelling, the picture-dealers who were always taking him in, and perhaps the aristocracy whom he parodied in his satires. It was characteristic of him (and not only of him) to engage in a theoretical love of liberty while harbouring a concrete antipathy towards those about to be liberated. Nevertheless, even after his return to England in 1835, he followed Italian affairs with passionate concern.

The Society of 'Friends of Italy' had been founded in England under Mazzinian inspiration in 1851 and Landor's is among the names on the founder's committee. Italy was ever the background and the argument of most of his works. Their landscape is our Tuscan countryside and the atmosphere of them is the pure Italian air of our Renaissance.

For the rest, Landor gave his personal belongings to his friends, knowing his sons would appropriate everything like vultures. Walter and his brother Charles were now visiting him daily, knowing the end must be near, and undressing him and putting him to bed. But he was not yet ready to 'go over Jordan'. Swinburne visited him, having been a hero-worshipper since boyhood: he fell on his knees and begged Landor's blessing but the 'hero' was gravely embarrassed. On the next visit, however, Swinburne found him 'as alert, brilliant and altogether delicious as I suppose others may have found him twenty years since'.

He died on September 17, 1864, and only Walter and Charles followed him to the grave. He had requested but a simple slab inscribed with his name and dates (1775-1864)). He lies in the charming raised oval cemetery[1] not far from Elizabeth Browning's grave above the roar of the traffic of the Piazza Donatella, at peace at last.

> *I strove with none, for none was worth my strife;*
> *Nature I loved, and, next to nature, Art;*
> *I warmed both hands before the fire of Life;*
> *It sinks and I am ready to depart.*
>
> (Dying Speech of an Old Philosopher.)

[1] For details of the cemetery see page 141.

CHAPTER VIII

Ouida

*Where lies the secret spell of Florence?—a spell that
strengthens, and does not fade with time?*

*It is a strange sweet subtle charm that makes those who
love her at all, love her with a passionate, close-clinging
faith in her as the fairest thing that men have ever builded
where she lies amidst her lily-whitened meadows.*

*Perhaps it is because her story is so old, and her beauty
is so young. . . .*

*The past is so close to you in Florence. You touch it at
every step. It is not the dead past that men bury and then
forget. It is an unquenchable thing; beautiful and full of
lustre, even in the tomb, like the gold from the sepulchres
of the Etruscan kings that shines on the breast of some fair
living woman, undimmed by the dust and the length of the
ages.*

Pascarel, Ouida

FLORENCE certainly cast its secret spell on Ouida (Louisa Ramé,
who took her own childhood mispronunciation of her first name
as her nom-de-plume). It kept her there for twenty-three years,
and even then she was to leave it unwillingly. In her first Italian
novel, *Pascarel,* she describes her arrival there with exhilaration:

> The beauty of the past in Florence is like the beauty of the great
> Duomo. About the Duomo there is stir and strife at all times;
> crowds come and go; men buy and sell; lads laugh and fight;
> piles of fruit blaze gold and crimson; metal pails clash down on the
> stones with the shrillest clangour, on the steps boys play at dominoes,
> and women give their children food, and many maskers grin in
> carnival fooleries; but there in their midst is the Duomo all un-
> harmed and undegraded, a poem and a prayer in one, its marbles
> shining in the upper air . . . Other, though not many, cities have
> histories as noble, treasuries as vast; but no other city has them
> living and ever-present in her midst.

'What manner of woman can Ouida be?' Max Beerbohm asked when he came to her defence in his essay on her.[1] Despite the slight ridiculousness which attaches to her work she had an interesting, incisive mind and she made lasting friendships with some of the distinguished people of her time: Richard and Isabel Burton, Robert Edward, son of the novelist Bulwer Lytton, Lord Curzon, Wilfred Scawen Blunt, Lady Paget.

I confess that I knew little of this prolific novelist until the appearance of an article in *The Sunday Times Magazine* by Elizabeth Jenkins. I found that Ouida had led an extravagant life, giving parties at the then new and fashionable Langham Hotel and dressing in clothes by Worth which were a little too dramatic for the small plain woman who wore them and who drove out in a satin-lined carriage. She was crazy about dogs, she was rich, arrogant, eccentric. Always over-emphatic, she wrote, 'Byron's must ever remain the most ideal, the most splendid, the most varied life which ever incarnated in itself the genius of man and the gift of the gods'. Sometimes she seems to have indulged a fantasy that she was a female version of the poet.

Despite all her busy social life Ouida never ceased to write and work at enormous pressure. She found it a natural thing to do, but in order to live in style it was also necessary. She was the breadwinner of the family. Her French father, Louis Ramé, had been an attractive though scarcely handsome man of somewhat mysterious occupation. He was probably a Bonapartist agent, having been, it is said, a friend of Napoleon III when he lived in London before becoming Emperor of the French. Ouida had much to thank her father for: despite his absences he taught her history, French, mathematics, some science and a great deal about liberalism. Hers was a happy middle-class background at Bury St Edmunds, and the studious child of fourteen wrote a history of England.

In 1857, when she was eighteen, Ouida, her mother, her grandmother and her adored dog, Beausire, settled in London. She showed not the slightest attachment thereafter to the country-side of her happy childhood, and indeed found the inhabitants of Bury St Edmunds 'so dull they are driven to ring their own

---

[1] *More*, by Max Beerbohm.

doorbells lest they should rust from disuse'. Colour and animation she had to have, and she found it easy to impart it to her earliest fiction. Luck came to her aid with this first novel. Their doctor, a neighbour, Dr Francis Ainsworth, was a cousin of Harrison Ainsworth, the historical novelist who was then editing *Bentley's Miscellany*. By 1861 he was serialising in it her first full-length novel, *Granville de Vigne*. It was a good time for a romantic novelist to begin: great was the stimulus given to novel reading in the fifties and sixties by the one-guinea a year subscription list of Mr Mudie.

In London Ouida was the family's sole breadwinner, as her father had disappeared. Triumphantly, at the age of twenty-eight, she published her most successful novel *Under Two Flags*, the book which one always associates with her name and which has been reprinted even within the last two years. She must have been gathering the material for it from her fashionable parties, decorously presided over by her mother at the Langham Hotel, where she was now living. The novel made famous the most famous of all the Ouida absurdities, her version of the guards officer:

> On the softest of sofas, half-dressed, and having half an hour before splashed like a water-dog out of the bath, as big as a small pond, in the dressing chamber beyond was the Hon. Bertie himself, second son of Viscount Royallieu, known generally in the Brigades as the 'Beauty'. The appellative gained at Eton was in no way undeserved. When the smoke cleared away that was circling round him out of a great meerschaum-bowl, it showed a face of as much delicacy and brilliancy as a woman's, handsome, thoroughbred, languid, nonchalant, with a certain latent recklessness under the impassive calm of habit, and a singular softness given to the large dark hazel eyes by the unusual length of the lashes over them.

Absurd, yes, but stylishly absurd, likeably absurd with a period flavour which some have found authentic—Norman Douglas, for instance, who had corresponded with Ouida and who admired her:

> Those guardsmen who drench their beards in scent and breakfasted off caviare and chocolate and sparkling Moselle—they

certainly seem fantastic. They really were fantastic. They did drench themselves and their beards in scent. The language and habits of those martial heroes are authenticated in the records of their day; glance, for instance, into back numbers of *Punch*. The fact is we were all ludicrous formerly. The characters of Dickens, to say nothing of Cruikshank's pictures of them: can such beings ever have walked the earth?

Ouida was never without a dog. Beausire was succeeded by Sulla, a superb Newfoundland who gave a domestic touch to the candle-lit, flower-filled room at the Langham Hotel when the novelist gave one of her parties. In her next novel *Idalia*, she gave a rather raffishly idealised version of them:

> The access of vivacity and abandon which a considerable amount of wine drunk and the introduction of tobacco invariably produce, flowed into the conversation; its gaiety grew very gay, and though there was still nothing that was licentious, there was a tone in it not customary before women of rank; the anecdotes had a Breda aroma, the epigrams had a Jockey-club flavour, the equivoques were fitted for a little gilded supper cabinet in the Maison Dorée.

No more compelling pair attended those parties than Sir Richard Burton, the explorer, and his devoutly Catholic wife, Isabel. Lesley Blanch[1] tells us: 'Perhaps more than anyone else Ouida pierced the mystery of Burton's personality and saw, behind the mask, the face, and behind it all, again, the soul of this strange man,' and she adds that it was probably the burning of his journals by his widow, rather than her destruction of his translation of the erotic *Scented Garden*, that Ouida had in mind when she wrote: 'I never spoke or wrote to her after that irreparable act'.

With the adaptation of *Idalia* for the St James's Theatre in 1867, with Charles Wyndham, Henry Irving and the beautiful Miss Herbert in the main parts, Ouida must have felt herself at the peak of success. But she had already exhausted herself in writing no fewer than forty-seven books and she suffered from bronchitis; she travelled south towards the sun to some of the places she had described so imaginatively and with such gallant perseverance; for gallant and indomitable she was, even if her

---

[1] *The Wilder Shores of Love*, 1954.

enthusiasm sometimes swept her over the line which separates the eager from the eccentric. Perhaps her greatest adoration was innocently given to the singer Mario (whom she was later to describe as Correze in *Moths*). On the last night of his performance in *La Favorita* she threw on to the stage a bouquet of flowers containing an ivory cigar-case inscribed with an adapted quotation from Dante:

> *Pietosi dissero gli Dei*
> *Oda la Terra una volta la musica*
> *Del Ciel, e labbre toccaro di Mario!*[1]

So Ouida came to the land of Dante, where she was welcomed as a famous writer and, moreover, like Byron before her, a rich and eccentric one.

The leading salon in Florence was that of a Scottish woman, Emilie, married to the Russian writer and explorer, Pierre de Tchaiatcheff, and she and Ouida became close friends. And there was also Lady Orford, who seemed to have walked straight out of the eighteenth century and who was portrayed wittily, magnificently, by Ouida in *Friendship*:

The Marchioness of Cardiff loved to call herself an old woman but she had kept three things of youth in her—a fair skin, a frank laugh, and a fresh heart. She was a woman of the world to the tips of her fingers; she had had a life of storm and a life of pleasure; she turned night into day, she thought no romance worth reading save Balzac's and Fielding's, she did not mind how wicked you were if only you were never dull. She was majestic and still handsome and looked like an empress when she put on her diamonds and sailed down a *salon*. On the other hand she would laugh till she cried; she would do an enormity of good and always conceal it; she honoured unworldliness when she saw it, though she regarded it as a kind of magnificent dementia; and, with all her sharpness of sight, the veriest imposter that ever whined of his misery could woo tears to her eyes and money from her purse. She always wintered in Rome and never lived with Lord Cardiff. He and she

[1]   *Thus the Gods pitying said:*
      The earth for once must hear
      The music of our sphere,
      And they touched the lips of . . . Mario!

were both people who were delightful to everybody else but not to each other. She was a Tory of the old school and Legitimist of the first water; she believed in Divine Right and never could see why the Reform Bill had been necessary. Nevertheless Voltaire was her prophet, and Rochefoucauld her breviary; and though she saw no salvation outside the *Almanach de Gotha*, her quick wit almost drove her at times near the wind of Democracy. Anomalies are always amusing and Lady Cardiff was one of the most amusing women in Europe.

Ouida joined the circle of some of the great Italian families, and from the Marchese Farinola she rented the Villa Farinola at Scandicci, about three miles south-west of Florence, which she furnished expensively. It faced south to the Val di Pesa and dated from the eleventh century. Since the English, unlike the Italians, always seem to this day to choose a house for its view rather than for its architecture or amenities, to someone like Ouida, who loved beauty in nature and romantic ruins, it must have seemed perfection, particularly as her garden was a formal Italian garden, with box hedges and lemons; and the lawns sloping from the terrace were limited only by a low stone wall beyond which the rounded hills clad in olive groves and vineyards stretched to the horizon.

In summer she worked in a vast cool room that had once been animated by grand balls, and here all was severity—a round table, an old ottoman and for ornament only a large portrait of Mario. The hair which Lady Orford had advised her to powder if she wished it to retain its auburn colour was now braided, where before it hung loose. She chose her own fashions and stuck to them. In winter she would receive visitors before a blazing log fire, dressed in black velvet with winter flowers at her throat, and she wrote at a beautiful Venetian writing-table.

She may have first seen the villa earlier than 1874, for there are echoes of it in *Pascarel* (which Wilfred Scawen Blunt thought the finest description of Garibaldi's Italy in English literature).

The villa was high up on the mountain side—vast, dusky, crumbling, desolate without, as all such places are, and within full of that harmless charm of freedom, space, antiquity, and stillness that does no less perpetually belong to them. Where these old villas stand on their pale olive slopes, those who are strange to them see only the peeling plaster, the discoloured stones, the desolate courts, the grass-grown flags, the broken statues, the straying vines, the look of loneliness and of decay.

But those who know them well, love them and learn otherwise; learn the infinite charm of those vast silent halls, of those endless echoing corridors and cloisters, of those wide wind-swept sun-bathed chambers, of those shadowy loggie, where the rose-flow of the oleander burns in the dimness of the arches . . . of that sense of infinite solitude, of infinite light, and stillness, and calm. . . .

The delights of an Italian garden are countless. It is not like any other garden in the world. It is at once more formal and more wild, at once greener with more abundant youth and venerable with more antique age. It holds Boccaccio between its walls, all Petrarca in its leaves, all Raffaelle in its skies.

The old broken marble statues, whence the water dripped and fed the water-lily; the great lemon-trees in pots big enough to drown a boy, the golden globes among their emerald leaves; the magnolias, like trees cast in bronze . . . high walls, vine-hung and topped by pines and cypresses; low walls with crowds of geraniums on their parapets, and the mountains and the fields beyond them; marble basins hidden in creepers where the frogs dozed all day long; sounds of convent bells and of chapel chimes; . . . and through the huge unglazed windows sight of the green vines with the bullocks in the harvest carts beneath them or of some hilly sunlit road with a mule-team coming down it, or of a blue high hill with its pine trees black against the sky, and on its slopes the yellow corn and misty olive.

In 1973 the Villa Farinola at Scandicci proved to be very difficult to find. Eventually it was identified in Alto Scandicci under another name: the *Pensionato Villa Consolata* at 20 Via Bagnese, run by the sisters of the Order of the Consolata as a home for about one hundred old people, with a morning school for children in another part of it. It stands very imposing and elegant, on a small hill with gardens and vines terraced down to the road, the whole encircled by a wall. Where Ouida would have looked across the fields there were now modern villas.

We went up the steps into a hall and turned left into a superb baroque-style room of great height and handsome proportions, where some of the old people were playing cards. In the centre of the high curved ceiling was a baroque fresco rather like the one in Byron's study in Palazzo Lanfranchi at Pisa. Below this a slender ironwork balcony encircled the entire room, with its big doorways edged in warm-toned marble opening into what must have been the large bedrooms. The original grey stone circular staircase has been entirely boxed in. The floor of the *salone* retains its original red tiles except in the centre, where a pattern in coloured marbles had replaced them. Round the room, on ledges in the walls, are what appear to be stucco busts, and the entire room looks as if it had been recently redecorated in pale cream. This was the ballroom in which Ouida sometimes worked.

Highly coloured entertainments and excursions in Florence must have seemed far more exciting than correct Henley, Goodwood and Ascot. They included the Comte de Talleyrand's fancy dress ball, the guests at which were expected to attend dressed as their most distinguished ancestors; the 'Corso' hunt, at which Ouida and everyone else wore a pink coat and ate a huge dinner afterwards at Doney's; a visit to San Rossore Grand Ducal park to see the last of the camels at Pisa; an expedition to Milan to see Garibaldi make one of his last public appearances, which must have been more exciting than anything else to the romantic, politically orientated Ouida; and, last but not least, Queen Victoria's visits to Florence in 1889 and 1893, when her fourth son, Prince Leopold, became one of Ouida's admirers.

Then, like lightning, Cupid's arrow struck the vital young woman (she was still only thirty-two) whose affection until then had been shared only by her mother and her dogs.

The Marchese della Stufa was a neighbour of hers who lived at the picturesque old villa of Castagnolo at Scandicci, and he might have been a knight in shining armour out of one of her novels—a Prince Charming, and one who shared her romantic loyalty to the Bonapartes. When Bonaparte came to Italy the father of the Marchese had considered him an Italian and believed that he taught the idea of political unity. Since 1450 the forebears of the Marchese had lived in the same beautiful house, and he himself was interested in the country, in its cattle and plants and beauty. He was more than an agriculturalist; he was a courtier, and at this time was gentleman-in-waiting to King Umberto. Other interests had taken him, four years previously, to Burma, with an Englishman, Dr Clement, to study the possibility of building a railway from Mandalay to Rangoon, and he was fascinated by such inventions as the first petrol-driven engine and the washing machine. He was undoubtedly attracted to Ouida. He found her conversation and ideas interesting and they often walked and drove together; and since the friendship continued for more than ten years it could hardly be described as merely an infatuation.

The courteous della Stufa, dressed in knickerbockers and carrying Ouida's paintbox, used to escort her on painting expeditions. She would wear a grey poplin suit with sweeping skirts and a large fashionable hat of black velvet tied beneath the chin—she must have felt that she was living the part of one of her own heroines. The Marchese was unmarried, so it was all perfectly proper, and indeed she might reasonably have assumed that he would propose. It was presumably a passionate platonic romance, and it may have inspired *Pascarel*, which is in effect dedicated to Florence.

Thus the Villa Farinola saw the blossoming of the only real love of her life. It ended in ashes because she discovered that the Marchese had a past and had previously been *cicisbeo* or *cavaliere servente* to a formidable and beautiful English woman, Janet Ross, whose husband was a banker in Florence.

Augustus Hare has a relevant note in his journal:

I am writing from the old country place of the Lotteria della Stufa. It is reached by driving from Florence through the low vineyarded country for five miles. Then on the left under the hills one sees what looks like a great old barrack, grimy, mossy and deserted. This is the villa. All outside is decay, but when you enter, there are charming old halls and chambers, connected by open arches, and filled with picture, china, books and beautiful old carved furniture. A terrace lined with immense vases of lilies and tulips opens on a garden with vine-shaded pergolas and huge orange trees in tubs; and beyond are the wooded hills. The presiding genius of the place is Mrs Ross (Janet Duff Gordon) who has redeemed lands, planted vineyards, introduced new plans for pressing the grapes—whose heart and soul are in the work here.[1]

Lina Waterfield, the niece of Janet Ross, whose aunt shares

---

[1] *The Story of My Life*, volume IV, by Augustus Hare.

Ouida -
perhaps more as she wished to be than as she was.

Villa Farinola, Scandicci, the setting of Ouida's Florentine heyday.

Ouida's tomb in Bagni di Lucca. The effigy by Giuseppe Norfini
imitates the style of della Quercia's memorial to
Ilaria del Cassetto in the Duomo at Lucca.

with Nelly Erichsen the authorship of some well-researched and fascinating books on Florence and Tuscany in the series published in 1900 by Dent, gives in *Castle in Italy* a portrait of her aunt and of Ouida which explains the situation:

Uncle Henry (Ross), who did not care for balls and found riding in the Cascine exceedingly tame, longed for a place in the country where he could indulge in his great desire to grow orchids. . . . In the autumn of 1870 Rome opened her gates to King Victor Emmanuel and much of the social glory of Florence departed. Just at this time a tempting offer was made to them; Marchese Lottaringa della Stufa, who was Chamberlain at the court, suggested that they should live in his villa of Castagnolo, a few miles out of Florence in the lower valley of the Arno. They were to repair the old house and see to the running of the farm while he would come and stay whenever he could leave his court duties in Rome. Janet . . . could now use her energies and exercise her love of command in teaching the peasants new ways of growing vines, no easy task to the Tuscan peasant who insists upon farming as his forebears farmed in the days of Virgil. She was soon known as a keen agriculturalist. . . .

As he (Henry Ross) had been dazzled by her good looks and vivacity from the first moment he saw her at Esher, he continued to be amused by her waywardness and refrained from checking her.

Marchese della Stufa came periodically from Rome and appeared to be content to be a visitor in his own house. For a whole year all was peace and contentment but in the winter of 1871 a stormy petrel arrived in Florence in the person of Ouida, the most popular novelist of the day and a woman of remarkable social brilliance. She came with a letter of introduction to Janet from her father Alexander who used to go to Ouida's famous parties at the Langham Hotel, where he said a notice was written in the hall, 'Morals and umbrellas to be left at the door.' Ouida liked to startle people more by her words than by deeds. Full of contradictions, she had the reputation of disliking women, or at least of being bored by them, but she made friends at once with Janet Ross, whose masculine qualities and plain-speaking attracted her. . . . Ouida dressed according to the heroine she was in process of creating, sometimes in trailing damasks of brilliant colours or else in simple dimity like the Tuscan peasants whose lives she lived in imagination.

Soon Mrs Ross and Ouida were known to be not friends but enemies. Ouida continued to live and entertain very expensively at Farinola, with grand receptions and food from Doney's, but however social she chose to be, and however affected, she never ceased to write prodigiously. Then in 1877, at a time when Mrs Ross was in England and her beloved was taking up his duties at the court in Rome, Ouida decided to pocket her pride and follow him. She was accepted everywhere in Rome and admired by the royal family, and it seems that the King himself suspected that della Stufa could do worse than marry the lady. She tore herself away to finish *Ariadne* at Farinola, longing the while for della Stufa's return from Rome; she then made the discovery that for the last two weeks he and Mrs Ross had been at the Villa Castagnolo. It was too much. She was not too proud to show her hurt and she published a novel, *Friendship*, in which she made no attempt to hide the identity of the trio of chief characters, Janet Ross being Lady Joan Challoner, della Stufa her lover, Prince Ioris, and herself the rather pallid heroine suffering from tuberculosis, Etoile, Countess d'Avesnes. The best one can say of the story is that it has not worn well.

Nearly all her friends tried to dissuade her from publishing it, but once the deed was done they remained loyal; and society in Florence consequently divided into two opposing camps. The strange thing is that despite the furore and some talk of action for libel the Marchese remained on the friendliest terms with Ouida for the next three years. Out of her despair and resentment came her next novel and one of her best-known, *Moths*. Its inspiration, the now-ageing singer Mario, had a magnificent villa in Florence, and she herself explained the title in these disillusioned words:

The moths will eat all that fine delicate feeling away, little by little; the moths of the world will eat the unselfishness first, and then the innocence, and then the honesty, and then the decency, no one will see them eating, no one will see the havoc being wrought, but little by little the fine fabric will go, and in its place will be dust.

It is sad that Ouida, despite her real and sympathetic interest in the Tuscan peasants, with whom she spent a good deal of time while living at Scandicci, and despite her belief that the Italian people suffered 'far more than the Irish and say nothing', continued to live artificially in a sort of vulgar splendour, still dressed, often outrageously, by Worth, and increasingly losing touch with reality as she acted out her idea of a liberal-minded *grande dame*. Her dogs were her closest friends. They were allowed the freedom of the villa and her guests were expected to share her adulation of them. Through her love for dogs she did make a great friendship with the family of the Cavaliere Tassinari, who had been Grand Chamberlain to the Duke of Tuscany. They were very kind to her and like her friends the Pagets, the de Noailles and the Storys (it will be remembered that William Wetmore Story, a warm-hearted American sculptor, befriended Walter Savage Landor) stood by her after the publication of *Friendship* and its repercussions. But she broke off her friendship with Story with capricious suddenness because he offended her by shutting up his dogs in his stable yard when ordered to do so by the commune because of a mad dog running loose in the area. The garden of Villa Farinola now contained a dogs' cemetery.

Whatever her emotional sufferings she continued to write furiously and to interest herself greatly in English politics. In 1876 there arrived in Florence a man who absorbed her attention, Robert Lytton, an attractive and cultured ex-Viceroy of India whose literary pen-name was Owen Meredith. She gave a magnificent dinner-party for him and twenty friends, and in the following year when she received an invitation to visit him in England at Knebworth she accepted with alacrity, spending money which she did not have—her most lucrative days as a writer were over—on a whole new wardrobe from Worth for the occasion. She did not take her mother with her, and as her friend Lady Paget unkindly wrote:

> In the evening I came here to Knebworth. I had promised dear Lytton to chaperone him in the train, for Ouida had insisted on his coming to London to fetch her and he fears her love much more than her hate. Lord Salisbury, the Prime Minister, described by Disraeli as 'a great master of jibes and flouts and jeers' . . . got into the carriage where I was sitting with Sir Ashley Eden and said he did not wish to know Ouida. At that moment she appeared, be-furred and be-velveted on Lytton's arm. Nobody volunteered an introduction and I felt she must never know she had missed this

long-coveted opportunity of making Lord Salisbury's acquaintance
. . . I therefore tried to prevent her overhearing his conversation
with Lytton as much as possible . . . when Lord Salisbury got out at
Hatfield he shook hands with us and Ouida asked 'And who was
that?' Lord Lytton turned to me in the most disgracefully comic
way and said, opening his green eyes very wide: 'yes, who was
that?' I said 'I know his face' and Sir Ashley Eden added 'I think
some local man.'[1]

Obviously she was coming to be regarded as a wildly eccentric
figure, and it did nothing for her reputation when it was discovered that she had called on Lady Salisbury to inform her
that the one man for the Paris Embassy was Robert Lytton.

On this visit to England she entertained in her usual lavish
way at the Langham Hotel, and when she left she had to be
helped to pay the bill by her friend Lady Dorothy Nevill.

There began the long sad path to an old age of poverty and
misery. Ouida adored trees and had prevented the gardener from
pruning, and the Marchese Farinola eventually had her forcibly
ejected from his villa. She moved into Florence and took rooms
in the Palazzo Magnani Ferroni (now Palazzo Amerighi) in the
Via di Serragli, but she could not meet her debts and her furniture
was seized by her creditors, her manuscripts were auctioned, her
correspondence disappeared. From hotel to hotel, with her
faithful maid Gori, Ouida and her elderly mother moved, until
she came to rest at the Villa della Corona, Bellosguardo, which
she described as 'a beautiful old place . . . for seven centuries a
monastery, until it was secularized by the Great Napoleon'.
This is now the Burns Murdoch villa. She continued to write
novels and letters, and in 1880 she was much affected by the
death of Richard Burton at Trieste. She had written: 'To women
Burton had an unpardonable fault: he loved his wife . . . their
marriage was romantic and clandestine; a love marriage in the
most absolute sense of the words, not wise on either side, but on
each impassioned'.

Ouida's morale was raised by a two-day visit paid her by
Lord Lytton, but soon afterwards he died of a heart attack, aged

[1] *Embassies of Other Days*, volume II, by Walpurga Lady Paget, 1923.

sixty, while sitting at his desk in Paris. Della Stufa died of cancer of the throat; Mario was dead too. The men she had admired and felt close to had all gone now.

She and her mother moved to a smaller villa, La Campora, and on September 10, 1893, her mother died. Ouida almost lost her reason, refusing at first to have the body buried. Troubles mounted. She was evicted by the *carabinieri* for failure to pay her rent and simultaneously she was further embarrassed when five Florentine banks failed.

Ouida moved to Lucca after twenty-three years in her beloved Florence; and there, unable to get rooms because of her dogs, she and her maid moved into the Villa Massoni in Saint Allessio in 1895. 'This place is very lovely; it is three miles from Lucca, with very fine trees, and gets the sea breeze. But it is quite out of the world—my world. Perhaps so much the better.' With four storeys and twenty-five rooms the villa was, of course, far too large for her and her maid.

After Oscar Wilde's trial in 1895 she wrote a comment to a friend which showed intelligence and humanity; 'I am most grieved for his mother, a talented and devoted woman who has had nothing but sorrow all her life. It may be very immoral of me but I do not think the law should meddle with these offences. The publicity caused does much more harm than the offence itself.' But then she was something more than a concoctor of fervid fiction—her opinions and her pen were sharp. At this time she wrote in *Views and Opinions*:

English genius has suffered greatly from the pressure of middle-class English opinion. It made George Eliot a hypocrite; it made Tennyson a chanter of odes; it put in chains even the bold spirit of Browning; and it has kept mute within the soul much noble verse which would have had rapture and passion in its cadences.

I have said e'er now often, and I shall say it as long as I have power to say anything, that with the private life of the man or woman of genius the world has nothing to do.

When Queen Victoria died in 1902 Ouida did not share the universal regret. Acidly she wrote: 'At least [Edward VII] is a man of the world and he won't publish silly books in bad English'.

Because she had paid the rent of the Villa Massoni for eight years in advance she was living in poverty. The owner, Madame Grosfils, the wife of the Belgian Consul at Lucca, asked Montgomery Carmichael the British Consul there—he had been very kind to Ouida—to explain that she would like her to release the villa. At length she agreed to leave on November 17, 1903. Foolishly, the owner sent her sons to take possession: they broke in and seized her paintings, china, books, manuscripts, letters and other belongings and then sat down to a drinking session until 2 a.m., when they fell asleep. At 7 a.m. they packed Ouida, her maid and her dogs into a vehicle going to Viareggio. She was weak from hunger, having given her food to her dogs. But impoverished and old though she was, she refused to be dissuaded by Carmichael from taking legal action against the Grosfils. Intellectually, too, she was undaunted, and after she met D'Annunzio she wrote an essay on him which went right to the heart of the talent of a young scholar and poet who 'at present is absorbed in the sensual ecstasies of early manhood, and the fumes of voluptuous delights obscure his sight to much else which surrounds him, and which finds him callous and negligent of it'.

D'Annunzio was to become a man of action, and Ouida had a special admiration for such men, including another poet, Wilfred Scawen Blunt:

> There are few men of our time more interesting than the man who bears this name. Fresh with English air and dark with desert suns, passionately liberal in thought and nobly independent in opinion, spending his winters on the shores of the Nile . . . the friend of the Arab, the champion of the dumb, and the standard-bearer of all lost causes.

And Blunt's diary of April 21, 1900, records in turn:

> I went with Cockerell to call on Ouida at her villa at S. Alessio . . . Our driver did not know the house or who we wanted, until he suggested 'The lady with the many dogs' . . . It proved to be a nice old villa with a high garden wall, and an eighteenth-century iron gate, towards which, from inside, seven or eight dogs, poodles and nondescripts, came at us open-mouthed . . . The bell was

answered at last by a portly man-cook in cap and apron . . . We
were shown into a front hall and there found the lady of the house,
seated at a small table . . . a little old lady, dressed in white, who
rose to meet us and to reprove her dogs, still yelping at us in
chorus . . . I had been prepared, by the violence of some of her
writings . . . to find her a person somewhat loud and masculine;
but Ouida proved the reverse of this. In face she is much more
French than English . . . with a high forehead, rather prominent
blue eyes, dulled and watery with age, almost white hair, and that
milk-and-roses complexion which old people sometimes get, and
which gives them a beautified look. It was difficult to understand
her capable of such a malevolence as her novel *Friendship*. She
can never have been a sensual woman, whatever passions she may
have revealed in her writings. Her conversation is good, intellectual,
without being affected or the talk of a blue-stocking; it gives one
the impression of a woman who thought out her ideas and has the
courage of her opinions. We talked about the inhumanity of modern
Europe, especially modern England, and the rage for slaughter
which is its chief feature. Also about Italy and Crispi, who is her
bête-noire there, as Chamberlain is in England. She talks English
perfectly, as she says she does French and Italian, and she complained to us of the slipshod writing of the day. It was evidently a
pleasure to her to talk and to find us such good listeners. With
Cockerell she was immensely taken, and was curious to know who
he could be, for I had not introduced him . . .

At the end of a couple of hours we moved to go but she would
have detained us and made us promise to come again. She cannot
go now to England on her dogs' account, and indeed these mono-
polise her life. Altogether she is a pathetic figure, condemned to
solitude, not by choice but by necessity, and regretting the cheerful
society of Florence . . . I fancy imposed on her by poverty and her
pen. 'The world' she said, 'takes it's revenge on us, for having
despised it.'

We both left her with feelings of respect, almost of affection,
certainly sympathy.[1]

She became a great friend of Sir Sydney Cockerell, who will
be remembered for the transformation he wrought in the
Fitzwilliam Museum at Cambridge and for his numerous friendships with writers and artists.

[1] Wilfred Scawen Blunt, *My Diaries (1888-1900)*, 1919.

She won her legal case at Lucca against the Grosfils and mother and one son were sentenced to ten months in prison and ordered to pay Ouida costs. The parents took the case to the appeal court at Lucca and, having lost, to the court of cassation at Rome, but lost again. The prison sentence was commuted by a royal act of clemency to a fine and the boys were allowed to leave the country for Belgium. The civil action for damages and recovery went on long after Ouida's death.

Ouida next took a small villa at Camaiore at the foot of the Apuan Alps, an attractive ancient town of narrow streets and eighteenth-century houses, but though she continued on her novel *Helianthus* she was ailing. Owing to a temporary edict about muzzling dogs in the town she hired a carriage and returned to Viareggio. In the summer she lived in the mountains at Mazzarosa on the way to Lucca. Her eyesight was deteriorating and she went blind with a glaucoma in one eye. The *Daily Mail* published an appeal by Marie Corelli on her behalf, and the *Daily Mirror* published a picture of a poor miserable old woman reading in a garden—which turned out to be a fake. Ill as she was, Ouida was furious and she wired the editor of the *Daily Mail* 'Absolutely forbid any mention of me'. Meanwhile Lady Paget, unknown to her, had successfully asked the Prime Minister, Sir Henry Campbell-Bannerman, to grant her a Civil List pension of £150 a year.

It all ended during the severe winter of 1909 on January 25, in her poor lodgings at 70 Via Zanardelli in Viareggio: there she died of pneumonia at the age of sixty-nine, cared for to the last by the faithful Gori. She was buried three days later at Bagni di Lucca, which she had disliked, having been ill there with bronchitis in her straitened days. Mr Montgomery Carmichael, the English Consul who witnessed her death certificate, is thought to have paid for the effigy, which imitates the style of della Quercia's effigy of 1406 in the Duomo at Lucca of Ilaria del Cassetto with her feet resting on a little dog. It was by Giuseppe Norfini, and it has recently been cleaned by the efforts of the Director of the British Institute in Florence, Ian Greenlees, who raised the necessary £50 through *The Times Literary Supplement*.

CHAPTER IX

The Brownings

Now comes the period of the British who made their homes in Tuscany and who really loved and cared about the Italian people: the period when the middle classes were on the march. In part this was a result of the industrial revolution in England, in part because the defeat of Napoleon and the Peace of Vienna had opened the travel routes across Europe once more. George Hillard, an American, described England wittily in 1853 in *Six Months in Italy* as 'loved by its people with such pugnacious patriotism, while they are always running away from its taxes, its dull climate, its sea-coal fires, and the grim exclusiveness of its society'. One hundred and twenty years later, though we have abandoned sea-coal fires and society is freer, his remarks still have validity. And fifty years after Hillard, Augustus Hare, in *Cities of Northern Italy*, warned against the insular superiority of his countrymen:

> Another thing which is necessary—most necessary—to the pleasure of Italian travel, is not to go forth in a spirit of antagonism to the inhabitants, and with the impression that life in Italy is to be a prolonged struggle against extortion and uncivility. . . .
>
> A traveller will be cheated oftener in a week's tour of England than in a year's residence in Italy.

Samuel Rogers, whose poem 'Italy', published in 1830 with etchings by Turner, inspired Ruskin to a love of the country, described the prevailing atmosphere in England in a note to the poem:

> Ours is a nation of travellers . . . None want an excuse. If rich, they go to enjoy; if poor, to retrench; if sick, to recover; if studious to learn; if learned, to relax from their studies.

Among those who went to Italy for reasons of health and the relative cheapness of living was Elizabeth Barrett Browning, after her romantic elopement with and marriage to Robert, a poet six years her junior whose talent was at that time far less appreciated than her own.

From Pisa, to whose mild climate they had come to spend the winter, she wrote to her friend, Mr Horne, on December 4, 1846:

> We are left to ourselves in a house built by Vasari and within sight of the Leaning Tower and the Duomo, to enjoy a most absolute seclusion and plan the work for it. I am very happy and very well . . . We have heard a mass . . . in the Camp Santo and achieved a cure pilgrimage to the Lanfranchi Palace to walk in the footsteps of Byron and Shelley. . . . This city is very beautiful and full of repose—'asleep in the sun'—as Dickens said.[1]

Her husband attached a triumphant note: 'She is getting better every day—strong, better wonderfully and beyond all our hopes'.

The story of their romantic attachment is well known, but perhaps it is not so widely appreciated that this really courageous man expected to spend the rest of his life tied to a wife who was bed-ridden; and that when he discovered that the doctors had made her an opium addict through continual prescription for every symptom, he set about systematically reducing the dose and restoring her to normal life. When they met she was taking forty drops of laudanum a day, her dose of 1·6 grains being well above the average for relieving pain, which was $\frac{3}{4}$ grain. Having a well-integrated personality she seems to have felt no side-effects and not even suffered from headaches. Laudanum was taken much as aspirin might be today, and there was no moral censure attached to it.

From Pisa the Brownings moved on to Florence, which they loved and made their home until her death in 1861, fifteen years later, during which time they were never separated. They finally settled in Casa Guidi near the Grand Ducal Palace—the Pitti—where everything from fashionable receptions to political demon-

---

[1] *Letters of Elizabeth Barrett Browning to R. H. Horne*, volume II, edited by T. Townshend and S. R. Mayer, 1887.

strations took place. An American friend who visited them in 1847 gives a vivid impression of the couple: Elizabeth

> seated at the tea-table in the great room of the palace . . . a very slight woman with very long curls drooping forward almost across the eyes, hanging down to the bosom, and quite concealing the pale small face, from which the piercing enquiring eyes looked sensitively at the stranger . . . in a few moments they were pleasantly chatting, whilst the husband strode up and down the room, joining in the conversation with a vigour, humour, eagerness and affluence of curious lore, which, with his trenchant thought and subtle sympathy made him one of the most charming and inspiring of companions.[1]

Robert's whole life was devoted to his 'Ba' as he called her. They were complementary. Her fragility was offset by his robust health and energy, her idealistic enthusiasms for the rebirth of Italy—the *Risorgimento*—were balanced by his more moderate liberalism; and in his devotion there was no sacrifice of his intellectual integrity. He strongly disapproved of her interest in spiritualism and mediums, and after her death published the lampooning poem 'Mr Sludge the Medium'. Doubtless he made sacrifices, for he was a sociable man voluntarily limiting himself to the extent of his wife's physical capacities; but no one was ever made aware of them, and the depth and fulfilment of their love have never been disproved.

Logically Elizabeth was a republican. Nevertheless, because Tuscany became her home and the suffering of its people became her sufferings, she welcomed Napoleon III: she felt he would free Italy, and Tuscany especially, where she was shocked by the weakness of the Grand Duke Leopold's resistance. 'He is made of the stuff of princes—faithless and ignoble', she wrote in her disillusionment.

In 1848 she wrote *Casa Guidi Windows*, intending to call it at first *A Meditation in Tuscany*. It was a record of her reactions to political events and was written in two parts: the first with impetuous optimism, and the second part three years later, in 1848, when an Austrian tyranny had been established. The

---

[1] *Elizabeth Barrett Browning*, by John H. Ingram, 1892.

revolutionaries were on the run and Garibaldi in hiding. She wrote of Mazzini, who spent his exile in London, befriended by one of Elizabeth's heroes, Carlyle:

> Mazzini is the truest hero and patriot and he has not wisdom. He can die for her [Italy] but never will cause her to live. That is my view of Mazzini . . . While I was writing these last sentences I heard the nurse calling me 'Signora! Signora! Ecco i Tedeschi!' The Austrians had arrived. We ran out on the terrace together.[1]

At the end of 1858 the unity of Italy and its freedom seemed assured, and Elizabeth confessed in a letter:

> I have been living and dying for Italy . . . You don't know how vivid these things are to us which serve for conversation at London dinner parties.[2]

Ten years before this Elizabeth, after suffering several miscarriages, had given birth to a healthy son in Florence. He was a golden-haired boy, Penini, whom she spoiled, not unnaturally, and whom, to her husband's silent disapproval, she dressed effeminately in embroidered trousers. (Robert banished them only a few days after her death.) After the baby's birth they spent a working holiday at Bagni di Lucca, where, as in Florence, they were the centre of a happy intellectual circle. Twice they paid visits to England, but they regarded Florence as their home. Elizabeth worked hard and yet was strong enough to join in expeditions, walking up the hill to Bellosguardo to visit her friend Isa Blagden. Penini grew up speaking Italian, and in September 1859, when they holidayed at Siena, his mother wrote: 'Penini has been very happy here, made friends with the *contadini*, has helped to keep the sheep . . . and to pick the grapes at the vintage'.

During their second summer at Siena she received the news of the death of the Italian patriot and prime minister of Piedmont, Cavour. She collapsed and was taken back to Florence. According to their neighbour and friend at Siena, William Wetmore Story,

---

[1] *Letters of Elizabeth Barrett Browning to R. H. Horne*, volume II, edited by T. Townshend and S. R. Mayer, 1887.
[2] Ibid.

this 'had greatly affected her. She had wept many tears for him and been a real mourner. This agitation undoubtedly weakened her, and perhaps was the last feather that broke her down.' Apparently she contracted a chill which turned to bronchitis; she died in Robert's arms in Casa Guidi on June 29, 1861, having previously 'laughed with pleasure and *youth*, and I believe in some perfectly gracious way allowed by God suffered no pain whatever'. So Robert wrote to her brother George.

> She was buried yesterday—with the shops in the street shut, a crowd of people following sobbing, another crowd of Italians, Americans and English crying like children at the cemetery, for they knew who she was—the greatest English poet of the day, writer of the sublimest poem ever penned by woman, and Italy's truest and dearest of friends, as the morning and evening papers told them.[1]

On a sunlit autumn day in 1972 I visited Elizabeth's grave in the English Cemetery in the Piazza Donatella. As in Livorno and Bagni di Lucca, I was expecting to find a little cemetery tucked away and perhaps difficult to locate. Instead, after driving round the 'viale' or ring road, clockwise, as a friend had advised, I came quite suddenly on a large oval piazza. There it was in the centre, elevated high above the road, outlined by an ample walk of old paving stones edged by laurel hedges, which separated this oasis of peace from the continuously moving round-the-city traffic. I rang at the gates and was admitted through a dignified arched entrance-lodge where the custodian lived; and before me a sloping path led up towards a central column. Just before it on the left I found a simple tomb resting on slightly baroque pillars —Elizabeth Barrett Browning's grave. One had the impression that although Florence has changed so much in the past century Elizabeth lies happily within her beloved city. Her devoted friend, Isa Blagden, is buried near by, and so is the writer with whose views she so strongly disagreed (although she showed him kindness); Walter Savage Landor.

It fell to the American admirers of the Brownings who formed

---

[1] *Letters of The Brownings to George Barrett*, edited by Landis, 1958.

the New York Browning Society, to raise the money between 1970 and 1972 to buy the apartment in Casa Guidi, above the door of which the municipality of Florence had placed a plaque. When it became obvious that their efforts would be successful, the Browning Institute was formed with a membership of scholars and laymen, whose responsibility it would be to restore the rooms and the furnishing of the salon (of which there is a painting by George Mignaty done very soon after Elizabeth's death). Although Browning himself never returned to the house, his son Pen, who had been born there, bought the palazzo at the turn of the century from the Guidi family, restoring as many of his parents' furnishings as he could find; but on his death in 1912 they were returned to London and sold by auction, and the house itself was bought by an American, Mrs Ellen Laura Centaro. The Browning Institute will therefore have difficulty in finding the original furnishings, but will do so as far as possible and use copies where necessary. Eventually the apartment will be open to the public and there will be publications and a library with facilities for study.

It was a cold afternoon in early March when I obtained admission to see the apartment between the hours of four and five, when it is open to visitors. The echoing rooms were completely empty and a charming young man took me round explaining how they had been used by the Brownings. I could visualise Elizabeth seated in a low armchair by a window with her faithful dog Flush at her feet, at a writing-table strewn with papers, writing perhaps *Casa Guidi Windows* or *Aurora Leigh*, her novel in verse, which she considered her most mature work; and Robert working at a high desk, seated on a stool, preparing *Men and Women*, which included some of his best poems.

I went out on to the stone terrace with cherubs at either end— in Elizabeth's day it was filled with orange trees and myrtle. The vast wall of the side of San Felice church was oppressive to me, and I could not imagine the Brownings having much exercise on the narrow balcony, but Elizabeth obviously adored it. Writing to her sister Arabel she said:

The eight windows which are very large opening from ceiling to floor, open on a sort of balcony terrace . . . not quite a terrace yet no ordinary balcony either . . . which is built out from the house, giving an antique and picturesque appearance to the exterior. And you may suppose what a pleasure it is to have such a place to walk up and down in, when we are not inclined to go into the streets. Opposite is the gray wall of a church, San Felice, and we walk on the balcony listening to the organ and choir. Nothing can be much more delightful after all.[1]

Soon after Elizabeth's death Robert left Florence, and though he lived until 1889, he could never bear to return to the city in which they had found such happiness together. Among his possessions which fell under the auctioneer's hammer in 1913 was a carefully wrapped, feather-weight object—a flower plucked from Shelley's grave.

[1] Letter in the Berg Collection of the New York Public Library.

CHAPTER X

The Trollopes

AN astonishing literary family living in Florence at the same time as the Brownings was that of the Trollopes. Four of them, in addition to the famous Anthony, were writers: his mother Fanny, his elder brother Thomas Adolphus, and Thomas's two wives, Theodosia, and Frances Eleanor. Their combined output of work was prodigious.

Frances, or Fanny, Trollope settled in Florence in 1843 and remained until her death twenty years later. She had begun writing some eleven years before, at the age of fifty, in order to save the family from financial ruin. An earlier effort to support them by emigrating to America where she set up an oriental-type bazaar in Cincinnati, had failed, but it resulted in *The Domestic Manners of the Americans*, a book which made her widely known.

During her first visit to Italy in 1841 she had fallen in love with Bagni di Lucca, finding it not only beautiful but fifteen degrees less hot than Florence in July of that year. By August, she assures us, the three villages composing the resort were absolutely full, and a gay social life could be enjoyed by all. There was the lower village where the river Lima was bridged, called Ponte a Serraglio, and above it Bagni alla Villa, or The Villa, where stood the grand-ducal house; and a third part at the thermal establishment near the hot-springs, called the Bagni Caldi. She tells us that the hospitable Grand Duke gave a ball every week, and was 'adored throughout his English Colony'.[1]

In addition a ball was held at the Casino on Mondays, and she enjoyed French plays at the theatre and was impressed by recitations from Dante. Outings were usually picnics in the chestnut-covered mountains which Shelley had so much enjoyed, whose paths had to be ascended by mule.

[1] *Visit to Italy*, volume I, by Mrs F. Trollope, 1842.

HORAM NESCITIS

Memorial to Florence Nightingale
in the Cloisters at Santa Croce
(*immediately on the right as you enter the cloisters*).

Queen Victoria's
continental travelling coach.

Thomas Adolphus made his home with his mother when she settled in Florence. They were received into literary and social circles, becoming the centre of an international group including many Italians, with whom they found themselves in natural sympathy. To the delight of both mother and son, Charles Dickens and his wife turned up one day: they had been his admirers 'from the early days of Pickwick', they told him, and a warm friendship developed between the two men. Trollope wrote:

> Of course we had much and frequent talk about Italy and I may say that our ideas and opinions, and especially feelings on that subject, were always, I think, in unison . . .
>
> I was for several years a frequent contributor to *Household Words*, for the most part consisting of what I considered tit-bits from the byways of Italian history, which the persevering plough of my reading turned up from time to time.[1]

Tom, as he was called, was a fluent and prolific writer and Tuscany was not only his home but his chief interest. In 1848, already in middle age, he fell in love with and married Theodosia Garrow, a young woman of twenty-three, fifteen years his junior, who shared this interest in Italy. She had been a poet at thirteen, and when Elizabeth Barrett Browning heard that Landor hailed her as a new Sappho she wrote acidly:

> Theodosia Garrow I have seen face to face, once or twice. She is very clever—very accomplished, with talents and tastes of various kinds, a musician and linguist in most modern languages, and a writer of fluent graceful melodious verses . . . but more intense than Sappho! more intense than intensity itself! to think of that![2]

No doubt the bride's background gave the English colony, who had thought Tom too attached to his mother ever to marry, a great deal to chatter about. Her father, Joseph Garrow, was the son of a British Officer who had married a high-caste Indian lady. Her mother was a Jewish widow of musical talent who was no longer young when Theodosia was born. The girl's health, like that of Elizabeth Barrett, was always fragile. However, after

---

[1] *What I Remember*, volume II, by T. A. Trollope, 1887.
[2] *Letters of Elizabeth Barrett Browning*, edited by F. C. Kenyon.

five years of marriage she had a daughter, a child named Beatrice, always called Bice.

The newly-weds moved to a house known as Villino Trollope on the corner of Piazza Indipendenza, and Via v. Salvagnoli, where they were joined by Fanny Trollope and by Theodosia's father. Theodosia wrote continuously, becoming surrounded by sincerely liberal people who loved Italy. Her writings were considered by the Florentines to have actively helped the cause of Italian freedom and a plaque was eventually erected to her memory on this house, a few years after that on Casa Guidi to Elizabeth Browning.

As well as Dickens and the Brownings, the Trollopes numbered among their friends G. H. Lewes and George Eliot, Owen Meredith (Lord Lytton), Professor Pasquale Villari (the Florentine historian), Garibaldi and his English friend Colonel Peard. In 1861 a long letter from Peard to Theodosia ended with a significant assessment of Garibaldi:

> Poor Garibaldi is made a tool of by a set of designing intriguers, who will sacrifice him at any moment. He is too honest to see or believe of dishonesty in others. He has no judgment of character.[1]

The revolutionary hero himself arrived on Tom's lawn early one morning, through the friendship of Jessie White Mario, an Englishwoman who followed him as a nurse on all his campaigns. In describing him approvingly Trollope noted that one of Garibaldi's assests was a voice 'of great range; sweet yet manly, and with a suggestion of stored-up power which harmonised with the man'. No doubt this contributed to the unexpected and unprecedented warmth of his reception in London on a visit in 1864, when he was lionised by society, and adored by the ordinary people, much to the annoyance of Queen Victoria.

While continuing to work diligently on Italian studies and in addition to several novels, and writing for newspapers, Thomas Adolphus produced: *The Girlhood of Catherine de Medici*, *A Decade of Italian Women*, *Filippo Strozzi*, *Paul the Pope and Paul the Friar*, *The Life of Pius IX*, the *Papal Conclaves* and his great work *The History of the Commonwealth of Florence*. This happy

[1] *What I Remember*, volume II, by T. A. Trollope.

and extraordinarily industrious life was clouded by the death of his mother in 1863, and of Theodosia two years later after seventeen years of marriage. It had been a successful one, although he wrote rather pathetically in *What I Remember*, looking back in old age, that while Theodosia's worship of their child had been natural, he had felt that after the birth he came second in his wife's heart. Now she was laid beside his mother in the English Cemetery in Florence, near to the grave of Elizabeth Barrett Browning, and he was left with the twelve-year-old Bice.

Tom had been both the eldest and the favourite child of Fanny Trollope, who had probably been selfish in keeping him near her throughout her life; but she had suffered great trials. A warm, impulsive not very intellectual woman, she had been married to a cold rational man who brought disaster on the family, and she had lost six children. Browning apparently found her vulgar, but the somewhat rarified atmosphere at Casa Guidi probably set high standards. According to Tom his mother put aside her deep sorrow and anxieties, and simply concentrated on living. Once she had started writing she never stopped, producing in all one hundred and fifteen volumes. It was at first a means of making a living, and later, when sheer necessity no longer drove her to it, a way of gaining freedom to travel.

Perhaps the least attractive thing about Fanny Trollope was her neglect of her fourth and only other surviving son, Anthony, who was born in 1815 five years after Thomas Adolphus. He developed his life and his fame as a novelist completely separately from the Florentine household, although he and his wife Rosa paid three visits. When Tom was widowed he came to his aid by introducing to the household a pleasant, serious, energetic friend, Frances Eleanor Ternan, to look after Tom's little daughter, hoping that she might become the wife of the now eligible widower.

Tom found Villino Trollope unbearable after the death of Theodosia, and bought a property outside the city called Ricorboli. The house was in need of restoration and he confesses to the acquisition of ten beautiful marble columns from the choir of the Duomo of Florence, which had lain in the crypt since their removal from the church after the murder of the Medici in the Pazzi Plot in 1478. Tom was deaf, but Robert Browning still thought he was eligible enough 'to throw his handkerchief to anybody in Florence', as he wrote to their mutual friend, Isa Blagden. However, some eighteen months later Anthony's match-making bore fruit and the marriage with Frances Eleanor took place. She too became a writer and novelist. She collaborated with him in *Homes and Haunts of Italian Poets*, and established a friendship with her step-daughter Bice, but there was great sadness when in 1881 Bice died in childbirth scarcely a year after marrying Charles Stuart Wortley.

Thomas Adolphus and his wife then moved on to Rome, where they lived until 1886 when they returned to England. He died six years later at the age of eighty-two. Frances Eleanor wrote a biography of her late mother-in-law, Fanny Trollope, which was published in 1895.

By the time Thomas Adolphus Trollope died, the coming and going of the British in Tuscany had been greatly accelerated by the railway, and by 1910 the British Consul in Florence knew of no less than 35,000 British residents in the region. Some had been drawn to Florence when for a few heady years (1865-71) it was the capital of newly united Italy and there was a resident British Ambassador there. Many others came to paint, or to study painting, largely as a result of John Ruskin's influence. He made several Tuscan tours and his *Mornings in Florence*, together with his Oxford lectures, gave people a new way of seeing Italy which we still share.

Of the visiting painters, Turner was the most important. He made five tours of north and central Italy and put them to memorable use: indeed, they inspired him to alter his style, developing his brilliant use of colour and his almost mystical treatment of light. His Italian sketch books are in the British Museum. Ruskin, of course, recognized his genius and not only wrote about him but bought his work. In a letter to his father from Pisa, in 1845. he declared 'I should be sorry to lose *any* of my drawings for oils, or for anything in the world but what Turner is now doing or has done within two years, of watercolour from his own sketches.' (It is one of these important and beautiful watercolours which is reproduced on the jacket of this book.)

To Florence came Walter Scott, William Wordsworth, William Makepeace Thackeray, Alfred Austin, Tennyson, Matthew Arnold, Algernon Swinburne, Thomas Hardy—and innumerable writers whose names are now forgotten but who were inspired to write books, often charming, about life in Tuscany. The cost of living there was low, labour was plentiful, and then as now the English people who set up house there found so much pleasure in designing their gardens and so on that they were moved to record their experiences. And in addition to the painters and writers, famous or obscure, there were the scientists. What an occasion it must have been when many of them gathered at the Accademia del Cimento (the natural science museum) to watch Sir Humphrey Davy and his brilliant assistant Michael Faraday use the great burning glass of the Grand Duke, to accomplish the combustion of a diamond in 1814!

A particularly distinguished Anglo-Tuscan of the nineteenth century was Florence Nightingale. She was not a visitor, but was born in Florence in Via Colombaia near the Porta Romano in 1820, and it was because of her subsequent fame that the city's name became what it had not been before: a common name for girls.

Another English visitor's name ought to be better known than it is, because of all those who came to Tuscany in the nineteenth century, he probably made the greatest contribution to the understanding of the region. This was George Dennis, a self-educated scholar and archaeologist born in 1814. For six years, from 1842, without any of the financial or academic support available for such work today, he devoted himself to piercing the mysteries of the Etruscan civilisation. Away from the towns the country was wild and almost depopulated as a result of malaria, but with one companion, Samuel Ainsley, he investigated the story of the *Cities and Cemeteries of Etruria*, as he called the book he was to write. He received little recognition at the time or immediately afterwards, and his only public memorial is a plaque at Ferento, erected by the Department of Antiquities of the Italian Ministry of Public Works. But a hundred and thirty years later his book is still the most comprehensive work on Etruscology. In spite of this it went out of print in the Everyman edition in 1907; but now Dennis Rhodes, a bibliographer at the British Museum, has published a book about him.

CHAPTER XI

Queen Victoria

WHEN Queen Victoria first visited Tuscany she was sixty-nine: a stout little figure dressed in black with white stockings and elastic-sided boots, accompanied on outings by an Indian and a Highlander—not John Brown, who had been dead for many years by then. She made three visits in the spring of 1889, 1893 and 1894, under the title of Madame la Comtesse de Balmoral.

She travelled in the grand manner, her special coach attached to the trans-continental train, with a luxurious drawing-room and a sleeping compartment for herself and her daugher, Princess Beatrice, who was allowed to marry Prince Henry of Battenberg in 1885 provided she remained her mother's constant companion. The Queen was superstitious enough to refuse to cross the Channel on a Friday. A speed limit of thirty-five miles an hour was observed, reduced to twenty-five at night, and the train was halted between eight and nine in the morning to allow the Queen to dress, and at meal times. Her entourage numbered some eighty people, including her private secretary, Sir Henry Ponsonby. Each morning word would be sent ahead and the train halted at a station to take on hot shaving water for the gentlemen.

The visit to Florence did not mean that the Queen escaped work. The Queen's Messengers arrived constantly carrying state papers to which she attended every morning. On one occasion a Messenger arrived in Florence after the Queen and her suite had retired to bed, and not wishing to cause a disturbance he crept round the Villa Palmieri where the Queen was staying, trying to find the window of a servant. Unfortunately he hit upon the window of the Queen's bedroom and caused an uproar, with half-clad footmen surrounding him within minutes.

The Villa Palmieri was lent to the Queen for her first two visits to Florence in 1889 and 1893 by the Countess of Crawford and Balcarres, and these visits were preceded by the painting and decorating of the villa, the connecting of a special water supply, and the installation of that most novel of instruments of communication, a telephone. The narrow road leading to the villa had to be widened to allow carriages to pass, and whereas before it was unlit, now there were street lamps so that members of the royal party could return from evening engagements in safety.

Even on an unusually cold spring day in 1973 when I visited the villa, the view over the whole city of Florence from the terrace was stupendous, and there is an inner courtyard which must have provided the Queen with alternative sheltered positions out of doors. Owing to a family bereavement many of the rooms were closed when I was there, but the Italian owner, knowing my interest, produced from a lacquered box a copy of the charming letter of thanks which Victoria had written to her host Lord Crawford, who had copied it in his own hand to remain in the villa, accompanying it with a page from a contemporary newspaper containing a picture of the elderly Queen in Florence.

In 1894 the Villa Fabricotti, in the Via Vittorio Emmanuele, on the little hill of Montughi, was provided for her use. Built on the site of an earlier villa, as recently as 1864, it was chiefly attractive to the Queen for the view from her rooms on the first floor. When I saw it after my visit to Palmieri it had a sad neglected air, and the notice on the firmly locked gates showed that it has become a youth hostel.

Queen Victoria seems to have liked Florence. She would arrive at the railway station beaming with pleasure, and before leaving she always received the mayor and city council in order to thank them for all the kindness she had received in their city. In 1894, accompanied by Princess Beatrice and her husband, as well as her large suite, she was welcomed by the Duke of Aosta on behalf of his uncle, King Umberto. Sir Clare Ford, the British Ambassador to Rome, awaited her, and after the usual greetings and the presentation of a bouquet, the carriages were entered and the procession moved off. The Queen's Indian attendant and her Highlanders attracted the most attention, and preceded by municipal guards and outriders and escorted by a detachment of *carabinieri*, she drove out of the city gate under a triumphal arch of flowers spelling the word WELCOME. There were crowds everywhere, and Victoria, despite her age and the distance she had travelled, showed no signs of fatigue.

Each afternoon she would drive out in a donkey carriage to visit places of interest. In 1893 she witnessed the ancient Florentine ceremony of the *Scoppio del Carro* (the Flight of the Dove) on Easter Saturday. A cart laden with flowers and drawn by two white oxen, carrying fireworks, entered the Piazza del Duomo. A firework dove was ignited from a candle on the high altar of the cathedral and 'flew' along a wire, out through the central west door to the cart in the piazza. It set off the fireworks and the choir sang '*Gloria in excelsis*' followed by the pealing of bells.

The only stir caused during the Queen's visits appears to have been an objection to her servants and dressers occupying a loggia adjoining that of the Queen of Serbia. Matters of protocol are always important in the entertaining of royalty, and were even more so then: at one luncheon given at the Pitti Palace there were not enough kings to go round and the King of Italy had to take in both Queen Victoria and the Empress of Brazil, one on either arm.

On her first visit Victoria expressed disapproval at the lack of finesse of Signor Crispi, the Prime Minister. According to her diary:

> Villa Palmieri, Florence. April 5. At eleven received the King and Queen of Italy, who arrived at Florence yesterday evening. The King is aged and grown grey, the Queen is as charming as ever. To my astonishment Signor Crispi, the present very radical Prime Minister, came into my room and remained there, which was very embarrassing. After the usual presentations of ladies and gentlemen the King and Queen left. I then went out into the garden for a little. At four, drove with Beatrice, accompanied by the ladies and gentlemen, to the Palazzo Pitti, to pay my visit to the King and Queen who received me at the private entrance and took me to their rooms. They were most kind and amiable, making excuses for Crispi's behaviour this morning—the King saying that he was a very clever man but had no manners.[1]

---

[1] Quoted from *Queen Victoria Travels*, by David Duff, 1970.

Later, on April 6: 'The King talked very pleasantly and sensibly. Signor Crispi came in, with whom I had some conversation. He has no savoir faire whatever'. She seemed, however, to enjoy a visit from the Archbishop of Florence—'who came purposely with a message of welcome from the Pope'. Did he, I wondered, use the beautiful chapel which the present owner of Palmieri showed to me? The Queen not only visited the galleries and churches of Florence and its surroundings but made trips along the Siena railway line as far as Poggibonsi, taking her sketchbook with her.

In her book *In a Tuscan Garden*, Georgina Grahame, who had settled in Tuscany, renting a villa in the grounds of a large house, tells us she was agog at the news of Queen Victoria's visit to her landlord and neighbour to see his collection, 'of which the library is the leading feature'. She was requested on this particular Saturday afternoon in the spring of 1893

to kindly refrain from taking her guests across the park, as they were expecting the English Queen to tea! Just then our landlord had a large family party in the house, and as very short notice of the royal visit had been given all the servants were beside themselves. I sent our gardener out to sweep and tidy up the avenue, and then we ran up our flag and just below the creeper-clad *berceau* hung out some fine old brocades on the fragment of wall over-looking the avenue and were all very smart indeed when Her Majesty and suite drove by . . . a stalwart Highland gillie behind . . . The young Grand Duchess, Alice of Hesse, sat opposite her august grandmother and laughed and nodded up to us in most friendly fashion. . . . Out of this visit of Queen Victoria grew three urgent requests from her that our landlord would let his villa for her occupation the following spring. But to our great joy, he was not to be persuaded so to do . . . we would have had to give up our house for the suite, and I never could have fancied it again. . . . He is an old man and an Austrian subject and may with great reason have felt that if the Queen of England, coming so often to Italy as she did, wished to have a pied à terre there, she could easily purchase one or avail herself of that offered by her 'good friend and brother' King Umberto. . . . The sentiment of royalty conferring honour on a residence by occupying it does not prevail abroad to the extent it does in England, and I know the remark was made here that, had the Commendatore allowed himself to be persuaded to turn out, her Majesty would have had what was termed the 'corragio' to present him with her photograph by way of recompense.

But though the Florentines, with their age-old concern for money, smiled at what the Queen's Scottish subjects might have called her 'canny' habits, they approved of her regality and her charm.

Florence was also to give pleasure to Queen Victoria's future granddaughter-in-law, Princess May of Teck, who was to become Queen Mary when George V came to the throne. Perhaps too much pleasure, the old Queen worried. Six years before her own first visit she wrote a warning to May's mother, Princess Mary Adelaide: 'It was with much regret that I heard you were gone to Florence for living in a town full of attractions and temptations to expense, made me very anxious . . .'.

The warning might well have been appropriate to Mary Adelaide, a flighty and sociable princess incapable of understanding the most elementary rules of family finance, but for Princess May she need not have feared. The shy, grave, graceful sixteen-year-old had suffered greatly from the humiliation of the family's financial failure and never forgot the lesson that one should live within one's income. She was depressed by Florence to begin with, being homesick and finding the narrow streets between the fortress-like walls of the palazzi gloomy in winter; but she disciplined herself to take advantage of the city's art treasures and was soon writing to a friend that she spent all her afternoons at museums where she learnt so much more than 'going out to tea and gossip'. At first the Tecks stayed at Paoli's Hotel on the Lungarno, but in 1884 a Miss Light lent them a villa called I Cedri, a few miles outside the Porta San Niccolo, which had an English garden. By then May was enjoying herself, and had begun to form the taste and appreciation of beautiful objects which remained with her all her life.

Another woman connected with Queen Victoria, although in a way which she could only deplore, was to end by making Florence her home. 'The Hon. Mrs George Keppel, a gracious figure of the Edwardian age and a link with the intimate circle of the Court in those days, died in Florence on Thursday' began

The Times obituary notice on September 15, 1947, discreetly avoiding overt mention of her position as mistress of Queen Victoria's son Edward from 1898 until his death in 1910.

Edward VII met Alice Keppel when he was fifty-eight and still Prince of Wales, a man whose chief enemy was boredom owing to his mother's reluctance to let him play his rightful part in affairs of State. Alice was twenty-nine, the attractive wife of a handsome Army colonel who was a younger brother of the Earl of Albemarle. Though not an intellectual she was intelligent, and so infallibly discreet that politicians were able to use her influence on the King in minor matters without anxiety.

Queen Alexandra sent for Mrs Keppel to say goodbye to King Edward when he was dying, as she did for all his closest friends. It was, as has often been said, a noble-hearted gesture inspired by generosity rather than indifference; for although Princess Alice of Battenberg who had stayed at Sandringham when the Keppels were guests thought that her aunt welcomed the liaison, a letter from the future King George V to his wife suggests otherwise. He was at Cowes Regatta with his parents, on the royal yacht *Britannia*, and wrote: 'Alas, Mrs K. arrives tomorrow and stops here in a yacht, I am afraid that peace and quiet will not remain'.

Harold Acton, in his second book of autobiography, *More Memoirs of an Aesthete*, published in 1970, remarks that despite the decline in the numbers of British residents in Florence since 1932 owing to the fall in the value of the pound, Mrs Keppel, who had bought her house, L'Ombrellino on Bellosguardo in 1925, still 'came and went with the seasons'. He ascribes her success to 'her generous heart', and it is generally agreed that she was witty without ever being malicious. She had won the confidence of the King's banking friends and no doubt benefited from their advice. Acton found her house gloomy, despite its view over Florence, but thought her taste in furnishing and in 'titled guests' compensatory.

Osbert Sitwell wrote to *The Times* after her death:

Those who knew her will never forget her personality, her tall, striking figure, the bold comprehending eye and direct look, her deep voice and the fun of talking to her, the sense of largeness in

her character and in all she said and did . . . The outbreak of war
with Italy in 1940, and the consequent loss of her home, had been a
sorrow and worry to her, and it will be a comfort to her friends
to know that she and her family were once more established there
before her death.

Derek Patmore visited her at L'Ombrellino when she was
approaching eighty and found that 'although an invalid her vital
personality, her wit and her natural grace as an Edwardian great
lady gave vivacity and life to the house she loved so well . . .
these rooms had a peculiar charm, for Mrs Keppel had not
attempted to furnish them in the Italian style but with her own
fine English furniture, with tapestries from France and superb
examples of Chinese art which she herself had brought back from
her travels in China. This happy blending of English taste with
Florentine *décor* seemed to me to symbolise the close links which
have long united this Italian city with the cultured Anglo-Saxon
world.'[1]

I visited the house on an early autumn morning. It is a classical
villa with rooms on either side opening from the central room,
which runs from front to back, and with perhaps the finest view
of any villa outside Florence, especially from the paved terrace.
Mrs Keppel had two daughters, and the elder, Mrs Violet
Trefusis (born four years before her mother's meeting with
Edward, and the reckless partner with Vita Sackville-West in an
extraordinary lesbian love affair), had died in the villa a few months
earlier. When I visited it the house was for sale.

---

[1] *Italian Pageant*, by Derek Patmore, 1949.

CHAPTER XII

D. H. Lawrence

*Lawrence has loved Italy as much as any English poet ever
did, and he got from it more than most.*

Catherine Carswell

IN an essay called 'Flowery Tuscany', written in 1926-27, D. H.
Lawrence leads us into the countryside he loved:

Tuscany is especially flowery, being wetter than Sicily and more
homely than the Roman hills. Tuscany manages to remain so
remote, and secretly smiling to itself in its many sleeves. There are
so many hills popping up, and they take no notice of one another
. . . though the land has been under cultivation these thousands
of years. But the intensive culture of vine and olive and wheat,
by the ceaseless industry of naked human hands and winter-shod
feet, and slow-stepping soft-eyed oxen does not devastate a country
. . . it is a work of many many centuries. It is the gentle sensitive
sculpture of all the landscape. And it is the achieving of the peculiar
Italian beauty which is so exquisitely natural, because, man feeling
his way sensitively to the fruitfulness of the earth, has moulded the
earth to his necessity without violating it. . . .
   Yet Spring returns, and on the terrace lips, and in the stony
nooks between terraces, up rise the aconites, the crocuses, the
narcissus and the asphodel, the inextinguishable wild tulips. There
they are, forever hanging on the precarious brink of an existence,
but forever triumphant, never quite losing their footing. . . .
   The *tramontana* ceases, comes a day of wild February sunshine.
The clenched little nuggets of the aconite puff out, they become
light bubbles, like small balloons, on a green base. The sun blazes on,
with February splendour. And by noon, all under the olives are
wide-open little suns, the aconites spreading all their rays; and
there is an exquisitely sweet scent, honey-sweet, not narcissus-
frosty; and there is a February humming of the little brown bees. . . .

But in the morning it is quite different. Then the sun shines strong on the horizontal green cloud-puffs of the pines. . . . You cannot believe that the flowers are really still. They are open with such delight, and their pistil-thrust is so red-orange, and they are so many, all reaching out wide and marvellous, that it suggests a perfect ecstasy of radiant thronging movement, lit-up violet and orange, and surging in some invisible rhythm of concerted delightful movement.[1]

Lawrence was a puritan by conditioning, born in 1885 into a class-ridden industrial society. He inherited none of his coalminer father's uninhibited masculinity and had been nurtured by the consuming love of a mother who was on the side of the mind rather than of the body. His driving need was to emancipate himself from this inheritance and conditioning. 'You can have life two ways,' he wrote in the essay 'Democracy'. 'Either everything is created from the mind, downwards; or else everything proceeds from the creative quick outwards into exfoliating and blossom.' In Italy he found a land and people to whom he responded from 'the creative quick', and to me his writings about Italy are more alive and moving than his work as a would-be prophet, important though his achievement was to be as a leader among those who freed us of the hypocritical dross which had come to surround sex.

He came to Tuscany at a turning point in his life. In 1910 his second novel, *The Trespasser* had been rejected on the grounds of eroticism (William Heinemann had published his first, *The White Peacock*) and his mother had died horribly of cancer—a traumatic experience for him, from which he took long to recover. A year later he collapsed and almost died himself. The threat of tuberculosis had, however, the advantage of freeing him from teaching, and he decided to go abroad to Germany. In his native Nottingham he visited the celebrated etymologist Ernest Weekley, one of his former teachers, for advice, and the Professor's handsome, green-eyed German wife, the mother of three children and five years older than Lawrence, was struck by the 'long, thin figure, quick straight legs, light sure movements'. A month later they eloped to the Continent with the princely sum of £11 in their possession,

---

[1] *Selected Essays.*

as shocking to their contemporaries, and as brave, as Shelley and his little party had been before them.

Lawrence detested the militarism of Germany, where he finished the second draft of *Sons and Lovers*, and Frieda ached for her children, dreading the arrival of letters. Her husband wrote that unless she returned she would not see them again, and she says: 'I was beside myself with grief. But Lawrence held me, I could not leave him any more, he needed me more than they did . . . but I felt the separation physically as if something tore at my navel-string. And Lawrence could not bear it.' They can hardly be described as happy as they moved south towards Italy, so poor that they could scarcely afford enough to eat, but they were at the beginning of the relationship which would be central to both their lives. Lawrence's discovery of Italy coincided with discoveries about himself.

In the autumn of 1913 their wanderings brought them to a little cottage called Fiascherino, near Lerici. Frieda described it as having

> a large piece of land with olive trees and vegetables running down to the little bay where we bathed and kept a flat-bottomed boat, on which Lawrence went out to sea through the surf. I was on the shore watching like a hen who hatched a duckling and yelled in rage: 'If you can't be a real poet, you'll drown like one anyhow.'[1]

Lawrence loved messing about in boats, but like Shelley, he couldn't swim. And he somewhat resembled Shelley in another way as well: he expected women to rise above possessiveness when it suited him. He had been sending drafts of *Sons and Lovers* to Jessie Chambers, the close friend of his youth with whom he had almost fallen in love and who had wholly fallen in love with him, and he invited her to stay with them in Italy, saying 'Frieda and I discuss you endlessly'. With dignity she returned his letter, and their ten-year friendship, which had done a great deal for him, came to an end.

In October 1972, nearly sixty years after the Lawrences were there, a friend took me to Fiascherino—a tiny bay near Lerici,

---

[1] *Not I but the Wind*, by Frieda Lawrence, 1935.

the hillside now built-up with villas. The Lawrences' house, however, was still there, right on the beach—still the only one, unchanged except for the addition of a little wooden terrace on the top floor, and the remains of a concrete bunker from the Second World War. We went in at the back door down some charming stone steps, and a very young-looking, lovely, fair Italian girl came out, to be recognised by my companion as a friend. It was a simple colour-washed cottage with thick walls: on the ground floor there was now a child's playroom and up the staircase charmingly furnished interconnecting rooms with slightly vaulted ceilings, in the familiar Tuscan manner. One could easily imagine Lawrence there and see him cooking in the kitchen, endlessly fascinated by the view across the bay to Porto Venere. The lovely girl's grandmother, Signora Maria Azzarini, had known Lawrence; but had not approved of him, which was hardly surprising since he and Frieda were not married when they lived there.

Lawrence described it all vividly to Edward Garnett in 1913.

I am so happy with the place we have at last discovered. I must write smack off to tell you. It is perfect. There is a little tiny bay half shut in by rocks and smothered by olive woods that slope down swiftly . . . You run out of the gate into the sea, which washes among the rocks at the mouth of the bay. The garden is vines and fig trees and great woods on the hills all round.

And to Lady Cynthia Asquith:

But we've got an adorable place here, a beautiful palazzino in large grounds that descend in terraces to the sea—that's the Italian for it. I call it a little pink four-roomed cottage in a big vine garden, on the edge of a rocky bay. Frieda calls it a pink-washed sepulchre, because it is—or was—so dirty inside. Lord, what a time we've had, scrubbing it . . . so I tied my braces round my waist and went for it. Lord, to see the dark floor flushing crimson, the dawn of deep red bricks rise from out this night of filth, was enough to make one burst forth into hymns and psalms. . . .

And in the morning one wakes and sees the pines all dark and mixed up with perfect rose at dawn, and all day long the olives shimmer in the sun, and fishing boats and strange sails like Corsican

Lawrence and Frieda in Italy,
towards the end of his life.

Villa Mirenda, 'My heart went out to it.
I wanted that villa,' wrote Frieda Lawrence.

The Lawrences' house at Lerici: 'I call it a little pink
four-roomed cottage ... Frieda calls it a pink-washed sepulchre ....'

ships come out of nowhere on a pale blue sea, and then at evening all the sea is milky gold and scarlet with sundown. It is very pretty.[1]

It is still possible to see and feel this place exactly as Lawrence describes it. For instance, to W. E. Hopkin:

We have a great vine garden, all shut in, and lemons on the wall, and today, with a wind from the Apennines, the big heavy oranges swing gold in their dark green leaves. We've only one orange tree, but it's a beauty.

There is no road here that carts may pass—not even a mule road. Everything must go by rowing boat on the sea that is not carried on the heads of the peasants.

At this time of the year all the women are out in the olive woods—you have no idea how beautiful olives are, so grey, so delicately sad, reminding one constantly of the New Testament. I am always expecting, when I go to Tellaro for the letters, to meet Jesus gossiping with his disciples as he goes along above the sea, under the grey light trees. Now the hills are full of voices, the peasant women and children all day long and day after day, in the faint shadow of olives, picking up the fallen fruit off the ground, pannier after pannier full.[2]

The gate to the garden of that little paradise was closed when war threatened and the writer and his German wife had to return to England. At first, in July 1915, there was an attempted alliance between Bertrand Russell and Lawrence to plan the immediate reconstruction of the world on socialist lines. Lawrence visited Cambridge and stayed the night at Trinity College, but there was no *rapport* between the combination room and their guest. To Frieda's expectant queries he reported: 'In the evening they drank port, and they walked up and down the room and talked about the Balkan situation and things like that and they knew nothing about it'. But then, to be fair, Lawrence was always ill at ease in the world and moved by a spirit of contradiction, which is not to say that his wounds were self-inflicted. At the end of September 1915, his novel *The Rainbow* was suppressed as obscene. The war years brought nothing but disaster and

[1] *Collected Letters of D. H. Lawrence.*
[2] Ibid.

humiliation, and he and Frieda were hounded from Cornwall as if they were German spies.

Frieda had obtained her divorce from Ernest Weekley, and they were married at a London register office on July 13, 1914. They had continual and bitter quarrels during these dark years and afterwards, but Frieda stayed with him and their love survived. She herself explains his attraction:

> I certainly found him more delicately and sensitively aware of me than I ever imagined anybody would be. To be so enveloped in tenderness was a miracle in itself to me.[1]

Later, in 1926, Maria Huxley, wife of Aldous, tried to explain Frieda and Lawrence's relationship to Frieda's daughter, Barbara Weekley Barr, in words that while percipient are fetchingly businesslike:

> A great passion. Frieda is silly. She is like a child, but Lawrence likes her because she is like a child.[2]

When the war ended Lawrence was soon back in Tuscany. In 1919, after calling at Lerici, he arrived at Florence, and he was so enchanted—it was his first visit—that he took Frieda for a drive in the moonlit city immediately she arrived at 4 a.m. In *Aaron's Rod* he reveals the spell of Florence as it was after the First World War—a Florence that we shall never see as Lawrence saw it, now that it has been damaged by another war and changed by tourism, beautiful though it remains.

> There ran the Arno: not such a flood after all, but a green stream with shoals of pebbles in its course. Across, and in the delicate shadow of the early sun, stood the opposite Lungarno, the old flat houses, pink or white, or grey stone, with their green shutters, some closed, some opened. It had a flowery effect of the skyline, irregular against the morning light. To the right the delicate Trinita bridge, to the left the old bridge with its little shops over the river. Beyond, towards the sun, glimpses of green, sky-bloomed

[1] *Not I but the Wind*, by Frieda Lawrence, 1935.
[2] *D. H. Lawrence*, by Edward Nehls.

country: Tuscany. There was a noise and clatter of traffic; boys pushing hand-barrows over the cobble-stones, slow bullocks, stepping side by side, and shouldering one another affectionately, drawing a load of country produce, then horses in great brilliant scarlet cloths, like vivid palls, slowly pulling the long narrow carts of the district and men hu-huing!—and people calling: all the sharp clattering morning noise of Florence.

He continues:

Finding the Piazza della Signoria packed with men: but all, all men. And all farmers, land-owners and land-workers. The curious fine-nosed Tuscan farmers with their half-sardonic, amber-coloured eyes. Their curious individuality, their clothes worn so easy and reckless, their hats with the personal twist. Their curious full oval cheeks, their tendency to be too fat, to have a belly and heavy limbs. Their close-sitting dark hair. And above all their sharp, almost acrid, mocking expression, the silent curl of the nose, the eternal challenge, the rock-bottom unbelief, and the subtle fearlessness. . . .

In the afternoon, in the last of the lovely autumn sunshine. Below the square was already cold in shadow, the pink and white and green Baptistery rose lantern-shaped as from some sea-shore, cool, cold and wan, now the sun was gone. . . .

Sunlight, lovely full sunlight lingered warm and still on the balcony. It caught the façade of the cathedral sideways, like the tip of a flower, and sideways lit up the stem of Giotto's tower, like a lily stem, or a long, lovely pale pink and white and green pistil of the lily of the cathedral. Florence—the flowery town . . . the red lilies. The Fiorentini the flower-souled. Flowers with good roots in the mud and muck, as should be: and fearless blossoms in air, like the cathedral and the tower and the David.

Frieda tells how they found their house, the Villa Mirenda:

Friends told us of a villa to let in the country about Florence. So we took a car and went out by the Porta Federica through dreary suburban parts till we came to the end of the tramline. It was April, the young beans were green and the wheat and peas up and we drove into the old Tuscan landscape, that perfect harmony of what nature did and man made. It is quite unspoiled there still. Beyond Scandicci we passed two cypresses and went to the left on a small, little used road. On the top of one of those Tuscan hills stood a villa. My heart went out to it. I wanted that villa. It was rather large, but so perfectly placed with a panorama of the Valdarno in front, Florence to the left and the umbrella pinewood behind . . . Such a sweetness and perfection of successive flowering Florence meant to us. We walked in the afternoons, almost awed, through so much unknown unobtrusive loveliness . . . the white oxen so carefully ploughing, between the cypresses, the flowers in the wheat, the beans and peas and clover! At twilight we would come home, light our stove in the big sitting-room, the stove that had been there for centuries, used as it had been to keep the silkworms warm in winter . . . now it warmed us. We had no pictures on the walls but Maria Huxley had left some canvases behind and I said 'Let's have some pictures'. He enjoyed painting . . . with what intensity he went for it.[1]

By October 1926 they had settled down there, and Lawrence now wrote *Lady Chatterley's Lover*. Frieda continues:

After breakfast—we had it at seven or so—he would take his book and pen and a cushion, followed by John the dog, and go into the woods behind the Mirenda and come back to lunch with what he had written. I read it day by day and wondered how chapters were built up and how it all came to him. I wondered at his courage and daring to face and write these hidden things that people dare not write or say.

For two years 'Lady Chatterley' lay in an old chest that Lawrence had painted a greeny yellow with roses on it . . . Lawrence asked me 'Shall I publish it, or will it only bring me abuse and hatred again?' I said: 'You have written it, you believe in it, all right, then publish it'. So one day we talked it all over with Orioli [its Florence publisher] we went to a little old-fashioned printer with a little old printing shop where they had only enough type to do half the book—and 'Lady Chatterley' was printed. When it was done stacks and stacks of 'Lady C.,' or 'Our Lady' as we called it— were sitting on the floor of Orioli's shop. There seemed such a terrific lot of them that I said in terror: 'We shall never sell all these'.[2]

So, amidst hesitations and exhilarations, a modern classic was

[1] *Not I but the Wind*, by Frieda Lawrence, 1935.
[2] Ibid.

born, and there in Tuscany, said Frieda, the different culture of another race gave impetus to Lawrence's work.

At this time Osbert and Edith Sitwell paid a call. Says Osbert:

I only met Lawrence once, when he and his wife were living in Tuscany. I was staying near by and they asked my sister and myself to have tea with them so we drove through the blossoming countryside—for it was high May—to his farmhouse. This square, blue-painted house stood among gentle hills . . . Lawrence opened the door to us, and it was the first time I had ever realised what a fragile and goatish little saint he was: a Pan and a Messiah; for in his flattish face, with its hollow, wan cheeks, and rather red beard, was to be discerned a curious but happy mingling of satyr and ascetic; qualities too which must really have belonged to him, since they are continually to be found in his work. It was, certainly, a remarkable appearance. Unlike the faces of most geniuses, it was the face of a genius.

He was extremely courteous, I remember, and prepared the tea himself, doing all the work; which grieved one, for he looked so ill. The rooms were charming, simple Italian-farmhouse rooms, with none of that broken *gold* junk one so frequently encounters in the homes of the English in Italy; a great relief. On the other hand, they were hung with large canvases by Lawrence; pictures that he had just at that period begun to paint. These, though many wise people have since praised them, I thought then and still think crudely hideous and without any merit save that he painted them and in so doing may have rid himself of various complexes which might otherwise have become yet more firmly rooted in his books; useful, then, but not beautiful.

Two hours, two extremely delightful hours, we spent with them, and then he saw us off at the door, standing with the evening sun pouring down on that extraordinary face; but Lawrence, I am sure, must always have been glad to be alone once more. I left Italy a day or two later, and never saw him again, so that scarcely knowing him, I am left to fit those two hours and their impressions on to that solitary, delicate and ever interesting figure. . . . Some of his books bore me profoundly; others seem of an inspired nature that no one can deny. Exasperating is too mild a word to describe some of his repetitive passages. His use of language can be nauseating: viz. his fondness for the word 'winsome' and 'dainty'; nevertheless, he is a prophet and a poet. And yet even I think it is less in his novels that he is a great writer than in his miscellaneous books, his 'Studies in Classic American Literature', for example, in that wonderful, unpleasant, and even unintelligent preface to 'M.M.A. Memoirs of the Foreign Legion', in certain of his poems, and above all in his short stories.[1]

Frieda the earth mother, for her part, found something disturbing—perhaps it was their impeccable manners—about the visitors:

> On Sunday afternoon Osbert and Edith Sitwell came. They moved us strangely. They seemed so oversensitive, as if something had hurt them too much, as if they had to keep up a brave front to the world, to pretend they didn't care and yet they only cared too much. When they left we went for a long walk, disturbed by them.

Edith Sitwell, very prickly about it later on, felt that Lawrence was too obsessed by his own poor beginnings to realise that although she and Osbert came from the landed gentry their childhood was 'hell'. Afterwards she was convinced he had used their home, Renishaw Hall, near Sheffield, as the setting of *Lady Chatterley's Lover*, even though he had never visited it. With her gift for witty denigration she whipped Lawrence as the head of the Jaeger school of literature, 'hot, soft and wooly', to which the firm of Jaeger engagingly objected. Whatever it was she believed about Lawrence, her antagonism went deep, for in an interview on her seventy-fifth birthday she said she had hated only two people in her life, and one of them was D. H. Lawrence.

On a perfect Tuscan afternoon in mid-October 1972 I found the Villa Mirenda standing high, looking out over Scandicci, which is now a modern built-up suburb of Florence. It was once the property of an Army officer, Raul Mirenda, and is still owned by the same family. The suddenness with which one starts to climb into fold upon fold of the olive and vine-covered hills is amazing considering how near one is to Florence.

No wonder the Lawrences were excited to find the house: it is a dignified villa (not perfectly kept-up) divided now as then

---

[1] *Penny Foolish*, by Osbert Sitwell.

into two parts. Approaching from the back, one passes farmhouse buildings and goes through a formal garden of paths edged with bay, and opposite the back entrance is an enchanting domed structure covering the well, which is still working. The entrance from this side of the house is up steps shaded by a metal scalloped canopy in need of repair. Inside, the rooms retain their original brick-tiled floors, highly polished; there are high ceilings and pleasant rooms, not over-large. The rather sad remains of a terrace can be seen. Raul Mirenda, the then landlord, recorded that the Lawrences 'showed themselves particularly appreciative of the very beautiful view which one enjoyed from a broad terrace to the east of the villa'; he was unable to rent it to the Lawrences with the upper floor of the house as it formed part of his own apartment, but he urged them to feel free to use it whenever they wished. Raul Mirenda wrote:

In April 1926 . . . I became acquainted with David Herbert Lawrence, who was then staying in Florence at the Pensione Lucchesi on the Lungarno. Lawrence was thinking of renting an apartment or a villa on the hills which crown Florence, possibly to the south of the Arno, to reside there with his wife, Frieda von Richthofen . . . I offered him the suite on the second floor of the villa, furnished. It comprised an apartment of six rooms, with service. Three rooms, facing south, looked over a small park, three facing north-north-west, over a grass-covered court. From each side one enjoys a splendid view. . . .

The writer's day began quite early: in the morning it was his custom to go on foot to Scandicci, with a little basket to fetch the provisions necessary for his table. . . . Of profound human feeling and generous spirit, he lavished every form of assistance on the families of the peasants. . . . He used to help the wives of peasants when they had given birth to a child, providing a ration of milk for the mother for a period of two months.

The child of a certain peasant, Dino Bandelli, had been afflicted from birth with a double inguinal hernia. Lawrence made it possible for the child to enter hospital at Florence, and bore the entire expense of the operation, which was completely successful. Deep indeed was the gratitude felt by the parents of the child towards their benefactor.[1]

[1] Quoted from *D. H. Lawrence*, volume III, by Edmund Nehls, 1959.

The English puppet-master, Walter Wilkinson, who lived near by, gives yet another description of the house, a poetically romantic one:

If I remember, his letters from there were headed Scandicci, but his villa was far removed from that long sordid village on the plain. You took the tramvia from Florence right through Scandicci to the terminus at Ponte Vignone where the lovely hill country begins . . . You climbed the gently mounting road winding, without hedge or fence, between the orchards of olives and trailing vines and the beautiful cabbages and grains grown under the trees. Where the peasants, like works of art, laboured in the glittering shadow of the fragile olives—men in blue aprons and black hats, women in faded washed-out colours, and the holy, white oxen, hitched to the rose-coloured carts, meditated gently on the ways of peace and the art of slow movement. Rough grass and blue chicory flowers line the road and as you mounted you began to get that wide flat view over the plain of the Arno, away to Monte Morello, to Prato and Pistoia, and the glorious peaks of the Apennines. After a mile or so you mounted an abrupt and sharp hairpin bend (where I remember seeing Aldous Huxley once get stuck in a little car) and you then came out to one of those picturesque groups of Tuscan country buildings—a large cream-coloured villa, some peasant houses and a small church all stuck together, clustered over the hilltop under a jumble of crusty roofs. The handsome antique villa was the Mirenda at the top of which the Lawrences lived. It was not the sordid Scandicci at all. It was one of those large summer villas, rising with its peasant house and church out of a misty grey sea of olive trees. . . .

You entered the Mirenda, which means, more or less, a picnic, between high and splendid gate-pillars into a formal Italian garden, all very neglected Boccaccio, and approached a handsome panelled door . . . You pushed open the door, crossed a hall hung with very dull and badly painted Italian family portraits, and after two flights of stone steps you came into the Lawrence flat at the top of the building.

Both Lorenzo and Frieda would be busy about some simple chore—they always seemed to be busy and either or both as spontaneously as children would begin to talk about anything that happened to be in their minds. . . .

The second time I visited Lawrence was immediately after one of his fateful haemorrhages. I walked off the stairs into a bedroom absolutely bare but for a simple white camp bed, and found

Lawrence in his pyjamas stuffing something into a black leather bag
. . . 'My doctor's bag' he said with a grin . . . and led me through
the bare white kitchen with a pot or two, and Frieda at a charcoal
fire, through a bare white salotta furnished only with a piano, into
another white bedroom with another little white camp bed, a
small hanging bookshelf standing on the floor, a couple of straw
chairs and some of his own paintings, frameless canvasses hanging
on the white walls. There were no carpets, no curtains, no orna-
ments, no bottles, no ashtrays. It was all very clean and bare, like a
monastic cell, ascetic and aesthetic. It fulfilled his idea of living
completely. 'What I like is to get an empty room or two and live
in them for a bit—like this—until you're tired of them and then
move on.' And that is how he lived, skittering about the world,
travelling light, camping for a short time in some immense Landscape with no dragging social attachments, no conventional
routine.[1]

Much of this style of life can be attributed to the state of
Lawrence's health, to the eternal optimism of the ill who need
to hide from reality and transfer their concentration to the
weather or the surroundings. For Frieda it must have been very
hard: she who was never to have a permanent home with Lawrence
was sad when they packed up their belongings and left Scandicci
in June 1928.

There are always conflicting accounts of Lawrence's activities,
and some witnesses give an uninviting picture of the Villa
Mirenda. To Lawrence's publisher in Florence, for example, the
bookseller Giuseppe (Pino) Orioli, it was 'a distant and dilapidated
place among the hills with no water supply and only one small
fireplace'.[2] Orioli was the friend of both Lawrence and Norman
Douglas, and a bitter quarrel developed in Florence between the
author of *Sons and Lovers* and the author of *South Wind*. It
originated in remarks made by Lawrence about Maurice Magnus
in the long preface to the little book called *Memoirs of the Foreign
Legion*, by 'M. M.'[3] published in London by Martin Secker in
1924 and mentioned by Osbert Sitwell earlier in this section.

---

[1] Quoted from *D. H. Lawrence*, volume III, by Edward Nehls, 1959.
[2] *Adventures of a Bookseller*, by G. Orioli, 1938.
[3] Magnus at different times was manager for Isadora Duncan, a member of the
French Foreign Legion, and a journalist. He committed suicide in Malta on
November 4, 1920, having travelled there in the same ship as the Lawrences.

Norman Douglas, whose homosexuality made it convenient for him to live out of England, was epicurean in his tastes, and it was inevitable that at some time or other he would quarrel with Lawrence the puritan. Harold Acton thinks that Douglas 'belonged to the eighteenth century. . . . He had those qualities of order, lucidity, balance and precision for which the eighteenth century was distinguishable; he also had on occasion, its bawdy and downright bluntness.'[1] Many people admired Douglas, and over the years he has attracted the attention of some of the most vigorous and even quarrelsome (*pace* Mr Acton) memoirists of our time. Perhaps for that reason the Norman Douglas cult now wears rather a faded air. All it is necessary to say is that he was the antithesis of Lawrence, and his writing is an acquired taste which some can continue to resist.

It was in the spring of 1927 that Lawrence, still at the Villa Mirenda, visited the ancient Etruscan sites. He told his mother-in-law in a letter that he had been to Cerveteri, Tarquinia and Vulci, Grosseto and Volterra and that the 'Etruscan tombs are very interesting and so nice and lovable. They were a living, fresh, jolly people, lived their own lives without wanting to dominate the lives of others . . . I want to write some sketches of these Etruscan places.'

Etruscan Places, though written when he was very frail, at the same time as the second version of *Lady Chatterley* and *The Man Who Died*, was not published until after his death. To me the book *is* Lawrence—it is he as well as the Etruscans who come alive. The book did much to increase a general interest in the Etruscans.

Richard Aldington, in this year of 1927, found Lawrence 'particularly charming . . . he lived quietly in a genial climate near the Florence he loved'. Aldington thought that perhaps he was taking the warnings of the doctors seriously, and added: 'of all human beings I have known he was by far the most continuously and vividly alive and receptive'.[2]

With another writer, Aldous Huxley, Lawrence had developed a friendship which was the comfort of his last years. Huxley recognised Lawrence as a being of a superior kind, and he found

---

[1] *More Memoirs of an Aesthete*, by Harold Acton, 1970.
[2] *Portrait of a Genius but . . .*, by Richard Aldington, 1950.

that 'to be with Lawrence was a kind of adventure, a voyage of discovery into newness and otherness. For, being himself of a different order, he inhabited a different universe from that of common men—a brighter, intenser world of which, while he spoke he would make you free.'[1]

In July of 1927 Huxley wrote to his father from Forte dei Marmi:

> The heat is considerable; but we all flourish so far . . . We went to Florence the other day to see our poor friend D. H. Lawrence, the novelist, who was down with a nasty attack of haemorrhage from the lungs—long-standing tuberculosis, which has suddenly taken a turn for the worse. This is decidedly not a temperature to be ill in, and the poor wretch is not strong enough from fresh bleedings to move away from Florence into the cool of the mountains. He was with us at Forte, some three or four weeks ago, and I am afraid that bathing did him no good. The first attack came on shortly after he had left us. He is a very extraordinary man, for whom I have a great admiration and liking—but difficult to get on with, passionate, queer, violent. However, age is improving him and now his illness has cured him of his violences and left him touchingly gentle. I hope profoundly he'll get over this business.

Huxley's letters also give us a glimpse of the relationship between Lawrence and Frieda. After her death in 1956 he wrote of the miraculous way in which she raised Lawrence almost from death when he was ill.

> Thanks to Frieda, Lawrence remained alive for at least five years after he ought, by all the rules of medicine, to have been in the grave . . . Frieda and Lawrence had, undoubtedly, a profound and passionate love-life. But this did not prevent Frieda from having, every now and then, affairs . . . Lawrence for his part, was aware of these erotic excursions, got angry about them sometimes, but never made the least effort to break away from her; for he realised his own organic dependence upon her. He felt towards her as a man might feel towards his own liver; the liver may give trouble from time to time, but it remains one of the vital organs, absolutely necessary to survival.[2]

[1] Quoted from *D. H. Lawrence*, by Edward Nehls, 1959.
[2] *Letters of Aldous Huxley*, edited by G. Smith, 1969.

During their stay at Scandicci a friendship had developed between Frieda and Captain Angelo Ravagli, to whom she turned after Lawrence's death. Her love for Lawrence and her lifelong loyalty to his memory were not impaired by her infidelities. Lawrence, she knew, depended on her entirely, and in the same way she came to depend on Ravagli, who left his wife and family to live with her in New Mexico and built a chapel for Lawrence's ashes.

The invalid went to Switzerland, but he returned to the Villa Mirenda and on March 15, 1928, he wrote to the literary agent Curtis Brown:

> My novel Lady Chatterley's Lover, or John Thomas and Lady Jane, is at the printer's in Florence; such a nice little printing shop all working away by hand—cosy and bit by bit, real Florentine manner—and the printer doesn't know a word of English—nobody on the place knows a word—where ignorance is bliss! Where the serpent is invisible! They will print on a nice hand-made Italian paper—should be an attractive book. I do hope I'll sell my 1,000 copies—or most of 'em—or I'll be broke. I want to post them direct to purchasers . . . I shan't send the book unless the people send the two quid, else I'm left.

By June 28 he was writing to Pino Orioli:

> Lady Chatterley this morning, to our great excitement, and everybody thinks she looks beautiful outwardly. [It is] a handsome and dignified volume—a fine shape and proportion, and I like the terra cotta very much, and I think my phoenix is just the right bird for the cover. Now let us hope she will find her way safely and quickly to all her destinations.

But by July 31 he was in a deflated and despairing mood as is evident from this letter to his sister Ada:

> I suppose all the ordered copies of Lady Jane (Lady Chatterley's Lover) are in England: so the booksellers have hastily written to say we must take back their copies at once, they couldn't handle the Lady, and I must cancel their orders, and will we remove the offence at once. That is in all 114 copies we have to fetch back. Of course, these children of God haven't paid.—Then there are rumours that

police are going to raid the shops: I suppose people hope they will. At the same time the first batch has arrived safely at its various destinations in America.

I believe I have lost most of my friends in the escapade, but that is a small loss, alas! I never had any.

The row continued, his worries mounted. Despite his obvious need for rest he moved from Florence to France, and his persecution by the Establishment continued when thirteen out of twenty-five of his paintings exhibited at the Warren Gallery in London were seized by the police.

While Frieda was in London for the exhibition, Lawrence, who had struggled to Majorca, left there for Forte dei Marmi to be near the Huxleys. Thence he went to Orioli's flat in Florence, where he heard of the action against his pictures. Orioli was alarmed at his weak condition: he lay with head and arms hanging limply over the side of the bed, looking, as Orioli afterwards declared, 'like an old picture of the descent from the Cross'. The return of Frieda rallied him, and she took him to Germany first and then—both he and she realised he was a dying man—to Bandol, near Toulon. In January friends from England asked Dr Andrew Morland, a young physician who was becoming known for his treatment of tuberculosis, to examine him. On the doctor's advice he was moved up the mountains to Vence where he died on March 2, 1930, aged forty-four.

> Tuscan cypresses
> What is it?
> Folded-in like a dark thought
> For which the language is lost,
> Tuscan cypresses,
> Is there a great secret?
> Are our words no good?

> The undeliverable secret,
> Dead with a dead race and a dead speech, and yet
> Darkly monumental in you,
> Etruscan cypresses.

And how I admire your fidelity,
Dark cypresses.

Is it the secret of the long-nosed Etruscans?
The long-nosed, sensitive-footed, subtly-smiling Etruscans
Who made so little noise outside the cypress groves?[1]

[1] Verses from 'Tuscan Cypresses', by D. H. Lawrence.

CHAPTER XIII

The Sitwells

*The towers of Northern Italy in general, and of Tuscany
in particular, possess a beauty of their own, different
from that of towers in the south. They are taller, simpler
in line, but larger at the top, bursting into open platforms
under pointed arches, as the stalk of a flower bursts into
blossom. Indeed they have some resemblance in shape to
the Florentine lily . . . My Italian home, Montegufoni,
stands at the very centre of this country of towers, and
from time to time I climb up the steep stairs of my own
tower there, in the morning or at night, to allow the feeling of the country round to permeate my consciousness. . . .*

Osbert Sitwell: *The Four Continents*

ONE of the most eccentric Englishmen to live in Tuscany must
surely have been Sir George Sitwell, an English landowner who
represented Scarborough twice in Parliament. His frenzied activities included researches in genealogy and heraldry and the history
of the two-pronged fork! He was expert in the laying out of
formal gardens, about which he wrote a book called *The Making
of Gardens*, published in 1909 and republished in 1949, by when
the biography of his son Osbert had made him one of literature's
great comic characters. One of his lordly remarks is famous:
'I must ask anyone entering the house never to contradict me or
differ from me in any way, as it interferes with the functioning
of the gastric juices and prevents my sleeping at night'. To his
three brilliant children, Edith, Osbert and Sacheverell, he was at
once a depressant and an exhilarant: they were the victims of his
eccentricities and petty spites, but somehow he transcends his
weaknesses and emerges in Osbert's pages as a version of a
cracked Renaissance man—great taste, great artistic achievement,

175

great failures in his personal and business life, a clever, cruel, maddening fantasist.

Says Osbert:[1] 'It was ... during my first term at the crammer's that my father bought the castle, or rather half of it—in which in later years he was to live, thereby substituting for farce, with moments of tragedy, the purest Commedia dell'Arte. He apparently found it by accident in 1906 while motoring from Florence to Siena, when the driver took the wrong turning and the motor then broke down beneath the walls of an immense old castle ... On the terrace above the cellar doors were open, and the peasants could be seen treading the grapes, for it was the season of the vintage.' Nearly seventy years later, when I first saw the castle of Montegufoni, it was also the season of the vintage, but although two white bullocks drew the cartload of grapes, the peasants no longer trod them—they were pressed in a machine.

The Florentine family of Acciaiuoli had settled at Montegufoni in the eleventh century and had gone forth to conquer Malta, Corinth and finally Athens, on the Acropolis of which they built a castle out of antique ruins. They were, in all probability, the Dukes of Athens in whose territory Shakespeare set the scene for *A Midsummer Night's Dream*. In 1750 the British Minister at Florence agreed with Horace Walpole:

> You are certainly right about the bad taste of the Florentine villas. That of Acciajoli is a proof of it. One would think that their chief pride was to shew that they could prop up a house by vast walls and Intrenchments more expensive than the habitation itself.

But by the time Sir George and his beautiful but equally fantastic wife left England to settle permanently at Montegufoni, to the relief of their three children who desperately needed to live their own lives and develop their talents without interference, there had been, as Osbert[2] relates, 'perpetual discoveries and openings up, and renovating and repainting' in 'this vast labyrinth of a building ... which was being carried back, pinned down to a past that—like the present—only existed in my father's mind'.

---

[1] *Great Morning*, volume III of *Left Hand, Right Hand*, 1946-50.
[2] *Laughter in the Next Room*, volume IV of *Left Hand, Right Hand*, 1946-50.

Alice Keppel, drawn by Ellis Roberts.

Montegufoni: a castle magnificent enough to
house Sir George Sitwell's magnificent dreams.

Henry Moore at Carrara, with the Cava di Michelangelo in the distance.

The three hundred peasant families who had been in possession of the castle had been removed with their possessions, and a new era, one of magnificence mingled with decay, opened for Montegufoni, with the Sitwells' mother, Lady Ida, sleeping 'in an ancient gilded iron bed, painted with fantastic landscapes, gardens and villas, while the sky was full of swarms of cupids'.

During this period, both my mother and father were to find a comparative contentment, even happiness, they had never yet known, for my mother liked the climate and the life in Florence, and my father enjoyed the absence of life in the house . . . My mother . . . would ask twenty people to luncheon and forget to tell either my father or the butler or the chef, indeed it would pass from her mind altogether. Suddenly just as my father was having a quiet early luncheon, the guests would arrive, tired and hungry after their long mountain run—that was the sort of incident which could occur regularly.[1]

Sir George, however, became more and more eccentric, to the point where, as Osbert tells us, 'if he did not like what was going on round him, he just refused to perceive it, and then it could no longer exist'; and he failed to perceive that his wife, living in a world of her own creation, with no sense of the value of money, was in the hands of a criminal moneylender. Sir George refused to be blackmailed into paying her debts, and a series of lawsuits ensued—this was in England—which brought great suffering on the family.

Osbert grew to love Florence as well as Montegufoni. He came to feel that Florence stood apart from the medieval cities of Europe:

In the palaces and churches there is an unexpected tilt to every roof, an unexpected angle to every wall, especially to be noticed in the earlier buildings—the edifices of striped and chequered marble are in their surroundings as exotic as would be giraffe or okapi. The universality of the Renaissance itself never succeeded in banishing this alien element that had accompanied the inheritance of Etruscan blood; for who knows, even today, the ancestry of that mysterious race, or whence came the originals of those enigmatic

---

[1] Ibid.

effigies that can still be seen reclining upon their funerary urns in rock-sepulchre and museum?—figures with slanting eyebrows and brooding incalculable smiles: characteristics to be repeated . . . many hundreds of years later, in the Florentine pictures, and to be observed to this day, exemplified in the eager, rustic faces of the Tuscan peasants . . .[1]

He was enchanted by the gardens which in autumn seemed like an English garden in June:

> With *Ranunculus asiaticus*. . . . Father Agostino del Riccio in a manuscript in the Florentine library, dated 1592, lists the flower as then usual in the spring gardens of the city. The author, who names the Acciaiuoli as among the families particularly devoted to fine gardening and rare plants, is an authority on the *Ranunculus*.
>
> Then too on the first terrace, against the walls of the building in the high narrow flower beds, stone-bordered—the dark, blue-grey stone of Volterra is used here for all cornering of rubble, brick and stucco—the clustered light azure heads of the plumbago rioted with an exuberance unknown to its delicate sisters in English hot-houses.[2]

His description of the plumbago fits so well our own youthful two-year-old plant, already exploring the roof of the house; and on the walls of the Acciaiuoli castle, when I visited it in mid-October, theirs was still flowering vigorously. Inside the castle strange things were to be found: 'The finest collection of Saints' relics in Tuscany in the chapel beneath the cardinal's garden; and from the deep cellars which had been medieval dungeons, where the light filtered weakly through a grating and from an open door on to the vats which stood, two to each room, came music—played by La Societa Filarmonica di Montegufoni'. Here the peasants from the castle and the district practised with fierce concentration in the 'gracefully vaulted, rather low room, with its walls stained by age, draped with cobwebs' for the feast of the patron saint of the castle.

By the time that Fascism brought war to Italy in 1940 Sir George's castle had been furnished and the frescoes restored. The

---

[1] *Great Morning*, volume III of *Left Hand, Right Hand*.
[2] Ibid.

room which interested me most contained a series of heads of the illustrious (or notorious) Acciaiuoli family, painted high on the walls all round the room, now baroque in style. Among them was Donato Acciaiuoli, a cultured member of the Calimala Guild of manufacturers of woollen cloth, who was elected *Gonfalier* of Florence at the wish of Cosimo di Medici, who had become dictator of Florence.

We come back to the English in Tuscany, and the Sitwells, when Osbert reports the exodus of the British on the outbreak of the last war:

> The trains to the frontier were crowded with English invalids, retired governesses, and old people living on small pensions, who had spent whole decades in Italy and were now obliged to abandon the homes they loved, and the people they liked . . . Few English remained . . . few even in Florence, for centuries their chosen city. But my father stayed on, in his Castle . . . He never listened to the radio and I was told that when in the morning he heard the news that Italy had declared war on England, he climbed the Tower of the Castle—with some difficulty for he was over eighty and had been ill for a long time—and remained up there for an hour or more.[1]

Three years later Sir George died in Switzerland to which he had been persuaded to move.

During the war the treasures of the two great Florentine art galleries, the Uffizi and the Pitti, as well as those of many churches and museums throughout Tuscany, were stored at Montegufoni by the Italian Government. The *contadino* in charge was Guido Masti, whose daugher showed me round the house with some pride, thirty years later, and whose family has been in charge of the castle for over a century. Among the first paintings to arrive were four of the greatest of all art treasures: Uccello's Battle of San Romano, the Virgin Enthroned and Prophets of Cimabue, and the Madonna of Giotto, together with Botticelli's Primavera. Seventeen lira a day was the salary of the custodian, and the value then of the paintings was 320 million dollars. When the Allied

---

[1] *Laughter in the Next Room.*

armies invaded the mainland of Italy and the war approached Siena and Florence, Professor Fasoli, who had been appointed curator, walked through the army lines to Montegufoni, it is said, finding there in the cellars hundreds of terrified and homeless people, to whom the historic fortress seemed to offer protection as it had so often done before. The paintings were on the ground floor, and when the Germans took over the castle they threw out the refugees and threatened to burn the pictures. Happily they were deterred by the Professor and Guido Masti, who persuaded them that the pictures belonged not to one nation but to the whole world.

Subsequently New Zealand, English and Indian troops took over the castle, and Eric Linklater has described in his book, *The Art of Adventure*, how he and his party flung open the doors to find an Aladdin's cave. Only one picture was damaged badly, a circular Ghirlandaio from the Uffizi, which the Germans had used as a table, placing it upwards on an ordinary table top; it was stained with wine and food, and deep knife-scratches made it difficult to restore.

When Sir Osbert Sitwell died in May 1969, at the age of seventy-six, he was living at Montegufoni—which, incidentally, had been bought in his name in 1906. There he wrote the five volumes of his majestic autobiography, *Left Hand, Right Hand*. The artist John Piper, who had been with Linklater in the British Army in Italy, went to stay with Osbert, and worked on the pictures which illustrate the book. Osbert's ironic portrait of his father is marvellously sustained but the supreme irony is that there was more of the father in the son than the son suspected. Sir George had to be the grandee, and both Osbert and his sister Edith were addicted to having their own 'court', counting everyone who opposed them as mere heathen. No matter; with their brother Sacheverell, they were brilliant in several artistic spheres, and the 'poor young people' deplored by their society acquaintances went on to become accepted as outstanding artists by less frivolous judges.

Harold Acton, who owns the famous Villa La Pietra at San Domenica in Fiesole (not far from Walter Savage Landor's home) was a friend of Osbert Sitwell's, and like him had a difficult father; as he reveals in *More Memoirs of an Aesthete*, that indis-

pensable work for all who want more than guide-book information about Tuscany. Mr Acton was delighted to find on his
return to La Pietra after the war that Osbert was already installed
at Montegufoni. Of Edith, who often visited her brother, Mr
Acton writes in the same book:

> Fundamentally shy, she was more on the defensive with strangers
> in private than in her public recitals, when, superbly self-confident,
> she became the perfect medium of her poems. To my mind she
> was the purest English poet since Yeats . . . So majestic a figure was
> bound to attract publicity and some of the hostility that goes with
> it. No lecturer at the British Institute in Florence has drawn a
> larger public.[1]

Osbert, who had perfect manners, entertained his friends
generously, lively conversation and good wine flowing simultaneously: Harold Acton regarded Montegufoni's red and white
chianti as the purest in Tuscany—'the musty aroma from the vats
in his cellars greeted one like a bibulous crony. After the austeri-
ties of post-war Britain, English guests felt they had entered the
land of Cockaigne.'
Osbert became a sufferer from Parkinson's disease, and when
in 1965 he decided to live permanently in Italy he made over his
interest in his English estate Renishaw to his nephew, Reresby
Sitwell, who also succeeded to Montegufoni on Osbert's death
four years later. Mr Sitwell is a partner in a London wine business,
and he sells the chianti here, retaining its distinctive and beautiful
label which shows an old engraving of Montegufoni and says
that the wine has been produced by 'Barone Osbert Sitwell'.
Unhappily Montegufoni is a vastly expensive property to keep
up, and Reresby Sitwell was unable to continue his attempts to
do so. In the spring of 1973 he disposed of it to an Italian indus-
trialist, and his friends are saddened now that the Sitwells are no
longer an ornament to Tuscany.

---

[1] *More Memoirs of an Aesthete*, by Harold Acton, 1970.

CHAPTER XIV

Henry Moore

IN the summer of 1972 there appeared at the fortress Belvedere, overlooking Florence, a breath-taking exhibition of the sculpture of Henry Moore, the greatest English sculptor of our times and one of the foremost in the world. For a modern artist Florence, with its unrivalled accumulation of works of genius, provides a formidable challenge. In a letter to the mayor of the city Moore explained:

> I want to tell you how happy it makes me to have been invited to hold this exhibition of my work in your great city.
> I have loved Florence since my first visit in 1925, as a young student spending a five-months' travelling scholarship to Italy. It was the most impressionable stage of my development. Out of the full five months I stayed three months in Florence. At first it was the early Florentines I studied most, especially Giotto, because of his evident sculptural qualities. Later Masaccio became an obsession, and each day I paid an early morning visit to the Carmine Chapel before going anywhere else . . . Towards the end of my three months it was Michelangelo who engaged me most, and he has remained an ideal ever since. . . .
> No better site for showing sculpture in the open-air, in relationship to architecture and to a town, could be found anywhere in the world than the Forte di Belvedere with its impressive environs and its wonderful panoramic views of the city. . . .
> For the last seven years my family and I have made our home in Tuscany for two months every summer, where I work on my marble sculptures,—and when I need refreshing in spirit, in little over an hour from our house I can be in Florence surrounded by the great paintings and sculptures I love. . . .[1]

What strikes one most about Henry Moore, who was seventy-

[1] *Catalogo della Mostra, Firenze, Forte di Belvedere,* 1972.

four at the time of this exhibition, is his Englishness. He is a Yorkshireman who has retained an immense and undeviating ability for hard work and a northern directness and courage to look the world in the face and continue on his own purposeful way. Part of his charm lies in his sense of fun and part in the fact that he has never acquired the synthetic polish of many of his southern compatriots, or their accents of speech; nor has he succumbed to the flattery which always goes to the successful. There is a clear rock-hard purpose in his work which springs from his native region and upbringing, as well as an assurance arising from the background of a happy childhood. His youthfulness and his undiminished enthusiasm for his materials and for the sources of his inspiration, accompanied by an unsophisticated joy of life, are irresistibly infectious. Yet he is totally self-contained and this, one feels, is his strength. At the formal opening of his exhibition in Florence by Princess Margaret, when long speeches were made by the mayor of Florence and the director of the British Council, which was sponsoring the exhibition, everyone longed for one word from the most important person there—the sculptor himself—but Henry did not break his habit of not making public speeches, although he writes most articulately.

From his home at Forte dei Marmi, at the foot of the Apuan Alps, Henry takes us up the mountains, on a sunny summer day, to the marble quarries which he himself uses. They are capped with a whiteness of chippings which, from the sea-front, looks like snow. He conducts us up the narrow roads, with their ever-increasing gradients and sharp bends, in a car driven by a member of the staff of Henraux, one of the last of the marble-owning companies to remain in private hands. (The original Henraux was a lieutenant in Napoleon's army, Henry explains.) With the delight of a guide who enjoys the trip more every time he makes it, he explains that we are lucky because there is no cloud high up to obscure the best marbles. On the way he points out the quarries Michelangelo used. At last we stand, awed, on a platform with a sheer vertical wall of marble in front of us and a cloudless blue sky above that. He explains how the marble is cut by wires and tells us what they are doing, those figures above us who look so tiny. These are experts who pit their skills and experience against the dangers of the massive rock, which was pushed volcanically to the surface of the earth millions of years ago. The best marble, it seems, is always at the top, where the greatest geological pressures were built up.

Henry is excited and fascinated by the variations in colour and explains that last year he came up to look for a piece of white marble with some, but not too much, marking. A block was finally chosen, and after the difficulties of cutting and transporting it down the mountain, where it was cleaned up, it was discovered that there was a bad vent in it and he had to abandon it. This happened to Michelangelo, too, in his day: the absence of a leg on the Christ in the Pieta in the Duomo, Santa Maria dei Fiori, in Florence, was due to the deficiency of the marble, though in so brilliantly executed a work one is not conscious of it. To Moore the marble itself is a challenge, especially in its natural state, and an inspiration.

Such is the danger here, where the marble is cut, that there are always men on duty, whether in the heat of the day at siesta time or during the night. Before gunpowder was invented wooden water-soaked wedges driven into natural fissures broke loose the pieces; and today, when one might imagine dynamite would be used, they still use gunpowder so as not to shatter the marble.

Usually modern motorised trucks transport the marble to the yards at Pietrasanta below for the finishing processes, but in 1844, when Dickens visited Carrara, the scene was different:

Some of these caves were opened by the ancient Romans, and remain as they left them to this hour. Many others are being worked at this moment . . . marble enough for more ages than have passed since the place was resorted to, lies hidden everywhere; patiently awaiting its time of discovery.

As you toil and clamber up one of these steep gorges (having left your pony soddening his girths in water, a mile or two lower down) you hear, every now and then, echoing among the hills, in a low tone, more silent than the previous silence, a melancholy warning bugle—a signal to the miners to withdraw. Then there is a thundering and echoing from hill to hill, and perhaps a splashing up of great fragments of rock into the air; and on you toil until some other bugle sounds, in a new direction, and you stop directly, lest you should come within range of the new explosion.

There were numbers of men, working high up in these hills—
on the sides—clearing away, and sending down the broken masses
of stone and earth, to make way for the blocks of marble that had
been discovered . . . Imagine the clumsy carts of five hundred years
ago, being used to this hour, and drawn as they used to be, five
hundred years ago, by oxen, whose ancestors were worn to death
five hundred years ago, as their unhappy descendants are now, in
twelve months, by the suffering and agony of this cruel work!
Two pair, four pair, ten pair, twenty pair, to one block, according
to its size; down it must come, this way. In their struggling from
stone to stone, with their enormous loads behind them, they die
frequently upon the spot; and not they alone, for their passionate
drivers, sometimes tumbling down in their energy, are crushed to
death beneath the wheels.

It strikes me that Dickens was rather wallowing in the pain of
the oxen goaded on by their driver, as if reporting for the
RSPCA in inflammatory terms, but later he relaxes a little:

Carrara, shut in by great hills . . . Few tourists stay there; and the
people are nearly all connected in one way or other with the working of the marble. There are also villages among the caves where
the workmen live . . . a beautiful little Theatre, newly built; and
it is an interesting custom there to form the chorus of labourers in
the marble quarries, who are self-taught and sing by ear. I heard
them in a comic opera and in an act of *Norma*, and they acquitted
themselves very well; unlike the common people of Italy generally
who (with some exceptions among the Neapolitans) sing vilely
out of tune, and have very disagreeable singing voices.

So wrote our great but insular novelist in *Pictures from Italy*;[1]
but then, as we all do, he succumbed to the beauty of the view:

From the summit of a lofty hill beyond Carrara, the first view of
the fertile plain in which the town of Pisa lies—with Leghorn a
purple spot in the flat distance—is enchanting. Nor is it only distance
that lends enchantment to the view; for the fruitful country and
rich woods of olive-trees through which the road subsequently
passes, render it delightful.

[1] A new edition, edited by Edward Paroissen, has just been published by
André Deutsch.

Half a century after Dickens's visit to the marble mountains, Henry Moore was born in 1898 at Castleford in Yorkshire, where at the proper time he won a scholarship to the grammar school. During the First World War he served in the Army in France, was gassed at Cambrai and sent back to England. He entered the Leeds School of Art and then, after two years, went to the Royal College of Art at Kensington, where he spent three or four days a week for four years drawing from life, trying to understand the human figure.

It was to be a long hard road before recognition came. 'Afterwards I had seven years teaching life-drawing and modelling at the Royal College and another seven years at Chelsea Art School . . . Altogether I had twenty years of continually concentrated observation and attempt at understanding the human figure. I've always had a liking for squareness . . . This may be the reason why I appreciate Mexican and particularly Aztec sculpture.'[1] About 1928 he experimented with cement in case he should need to connect a piece of sculpture to the newly introduced reinforced concrete for architecture.

> The first method of using concrete I tried was building it up on an armature and then rubbing it down after it had set. This I had to do very quickly because the cement and the gritty aggregate mixed with it set so hard that all my tools used to wear out. Secondly I tried casting it in concrete.[2]

At a dinner-party for Henry's seventy-fourth birthday in July 1972, in the hills near Forte dei Marmi, he was amused by our account of how we attempted unsuccessfully to apply some cement to the approach to our garage at our farmhouse in the neighbourhood, where the existing steep incline was a trial to our little Fiat. Henry explained in detail just what we should have done and offered—and characteristically—meant it—to help!

Undoubtedly much of his inner confidence and serenity can be traced to his happy marriage. In 1929 he married Irina Radetsky, and this union provided and continues to provide all the stable companionship which a struggling or a successful artist needs. Irina is essentially a private person with an inner calm and

[1] *Henry Moore*, by John Hedgcoe/Henry Moore, 1968.
[2] Ibid.

she and Henry have managed to defend their privacy without ever being discourteous.

Henry explains that his oft-repeated mother and child theme had been a universal one from earliest times, but I think the Tuscan Primitives and especially Giovanni Pisano, who, as Henry said, 'used the body to express his deep philosophical understanding of human nature, human tragedy', and whose work he loves, had a great influence on him. Contrary to his usual custom of not being deflected from his own work he took time off in 1967 to encourage the production of a book on Pisano by Michael Ayrton, for which he wrote an instructive introduction.

By 1931 Henry Moore 'had a real desire to make a three-dimensional form by thinking of it also from within, and not only as a solid object like a tree-trunk'[1]. For fifty years he collected flintstones, pebbles, shells and driftwood, all of which influenced his ideas; 'but far more important to me has been the human figure and its inner skeleton structure. You can feel that a bone has had some sort of use in its life; it has experienced tensions, has supported weights and has actually performed an organic function, which a pebble has not done at all.'[2]

In 1928 he had his first one-man exhibition, at the Warren Gallery, where in the following year they courageously exhibited the paintings of D. H. Lawrence. Moore was a little more fortunate than Lawrence. It was bad enough to have *The Morning Post* saying that 'the cult of ugliness triumphs at the hands of Henry Moore', but at least his exhibition wasn't raided by the police, with the approval of *The Daily Telegraph*.

Of all the notable people alive then, Lawrence was the man whom Moore, who also came from a mining family, would most have liked to meet. He told me that he felt he would have understood Lawrence, since their backgrounds were so similar; he thinks that Lawrence's tuberculosis gave him a sense of urgency and added a sort of excitement and tension to his work. It was ludicrous, Moore thought, that the police should have been allowed to remove some of Lawrence's paintings. He himself

[1] Ibid.
[2] Ibid.

187

had seen the exhibition, and it was innocuous even by the standards of the time.

Sir William Rothenstein, director of the Royal College of Art, stood firm against attempts to have Moore dismissed from his teaching post. At this time Henry remembers Epstein's support and his buying of Henry's work. Epstein, Moore recalls, had taken the whole of the Philistine attitude to sculpture on his shoulders from 1910 to 1940.

In the autumn of 1940, when the nightly raids of German bombers shook London, Henry began his drawings of the patient population sheltering in the Underground railway, where they gathered to talk, eat and sleep throughout the rest of the war. His studio in London was bombed and he discovered a house in Hertfordshire called Hoglands, in which he still lives. Appointed an official war artist, he would spend nights in the Underground, returning home to finish the near-completed drawings. For the War Artists' Committee he produced some ten works and they chose four or five—the remainder were his own.

> I sketched with pen and ink, wax crayons and watercolour, using the wax-resistant technique which I had discovered by accident before the war. I had been doing a drawing for my three-year-old niece using two or three wax crayons. Wishing to add some more colour, I found a box of watercolour paints and was delighted to see the watercolour run off the parts of the drawing that had a surface of wax. It was like magic, and I found it very useful when doing my sketchbooks.[1]

These drawings, which were exhibited inside the Forte Belvedere itself, are with their economy of line and sculptural quality the silent witnesses of the disciplined way in which the ordinary people of London faced their ordeal. The exhibition, which drew over 300,000 visitors, must have opened the eyes of many of Moore's admirers to this other side of his involvement with sculpture.

Henry says that he has always been more interested in the female form than the male, but one could not tell this from the 'King and Queen', which normally dominates the Scottish

---

[1] *Henry Moore*, by John Hedgcoe/Henry Moore, 1968.

lowlands landscape belonging to John Keswick, the owner. There are both purity and strength in this sculpture which fill me with joy and reassurance, and in imitation of it the two of us jokingly sit up very straight as we gaze from the stone seat in our Tuscan garden, enclosed as we are by the mountain ranges sloping towards the sea. We even call the huge dip before us the 'Moore Hole'!

When Henry is working in Tuscany he lives at his one-storey house in the pinewoods at Forte dei Marmi, and he never misses his daily swim. He works on a big figure in the open at the Henraux property at Querceta from ten till one each day. 'I like chopping and cutting things rather than building up. I like the resistance of hard material . . . While I still believe in keeping a stone-quality, I am not as afraid of hurting the stone or damaging it as I used to be. Hence there is more freedom in my compositional ideas . . . White marble is a more pure and elegant material. In carving a sculpture it is very important to match the right material with the particular subject in mind. In using white marble I give the forms a precision and refinement and a surface finish that I wouldn't try to obtain with a rough-textured stone such as travertine.'[1] He also prepares lithographs in his studio at Forte for printing in Florence.

In 1946, after seventeen years of marriage, the Moores had their only child, Mary, who grew up very close to her parents. She teases Henry, who says, 'She doesn't let me put on false dignities and I am glad'.

A more unaffected, unassuming 'great man' than Henry Moore would be difficult to find. When I teased him about the single word MOORE having been attached to every signpost leading to his great Florence exhibition, he said his greatest success had been recognition by his local newspaper shop: formerly they could never guarantee him a copy of The Times daily, now they were honoured to do so.

---

[1] Ibid.

CHAPTER XV

The Floods of 1966

THE reality of Anglo-Tuscan friendship was never more clearly demonstrated than in 1966, when Florence was so catastrophically flooded.

Florence was asleep on the night of November 4 when the Arno began to rise. There had been no warning: since the last disastrous flooding of the city had taken place as long ago as 1557 the Florentines were perhaps too complacent about the necessity of an early warning system. But the view was widely held afterwards that if a warning *had* been given that night, there would have been many deaths arising from the ensuing panic to leave the city.

The powerful rise in the level of the river in the city itself began at about 3 a.m., and as it spread over the banks and pavements it flooded cellars and burst oil tanks for central heating which, in large buildings, were of considerable size; it choked the antiquated sewer pipes beneath the city so that the stench became unbearable, and became worse as butchers' and fruit shops and all kinds of perishable provisions were engulfed; it smothered everything in a mass of thick mud which the inhabitants termed the *fango*.

The moving mass, gaining momentum as it invaded the streets and squares of the city, flooded the cellars and ground floors, threatened the foundations and structures of the less solidly built houses, and put the greatest art treasures in the world in peril. The very able mayor of the city, Piero Bargellini, became marooned in his office in the Palazzo Vecchio. In the Uffizi Palace personal possessions of the curator of the gallery were completely destroyed on the ground-floor while she was leading a desperate attempt to remove works of art to the higher floors— with only two hours grace before the flood rose so high as to prevent further work. Both the wings of the Uffizi, used by the staff for restoring, were damaged and a third of the archives, all the prints, and ten per cent of the photographic negatives were lost.

At 9.10 a.m. the telephones of the Uffizi went dead and they found themselves without electricity, without water and without radio bulletins. Everywhere the rescue of people was given priority, but even so four of the prisoners in the Murate gaol were swept away as they were being moved out.

The outside world seemed, to the inhabitants of the city, to be completely unaware of their plight; but at least, by the fifth day, the rest of Italy and the world began to realise the magnitude of the disaster and the individual efforts to clear the oily filth with fragile and inadequate tools, which were going on in every shop, workshop and home, began to be supplemented by the arrival of suitable machinery.

The British colony, true to tradition, were at their best in this great emergency. The British Consul, Mr Pirie-Gordon, delivered two-gallon containers of fresh water to those who were cut off. A team soon formed round him and organised a nursing service; an Italian-speaking senior medical officer arrived from London to assist, and started to give vaccination against typhoid.

Amongst other help of the same kind Britain's Art and Archives Rescue Fund raised £40,000, contributed without publicity through private letters of appeal, and a further £155,000 for restoration of works of art. The British and American consulates co-ordinated their efforts, using the British Consulate as their first headquarters. The Anglican church in Florence, whose vicar, George Church, was a former Royal Air Force padre, set up an emergency canteen and served the hungry and homeless. Mineral water was everywhere direly needed: for shaving, washing and for cleaning sculptures. A twenty-three-year-old student of the Courtauld Institute in London, hearing of the disaster on the radio, collected his farmer brother-in-law and the farm Landrover and set off for Florence towing a pump. This was first used to pump out the basement of the Uffizi and then ground its way through the mud to the Baptistery, where they loaded Donatello's priceless sculpture in wood of Mary Magdalene on to the truck and transported it to the Uffizi for restoration. This same student, Patrick Mathieson, worked voluntarily until

Christmas, cleaning bronzes in the National Museum, the Bargello. This was only one of the many immediate and spontaneous responses to the need for outside help in the stricken city.

John Pope-Hennessy, then Director-Designate of the Victoria and Albert Museum, went officially for the British Relief Fund to study the possibilities of restoration. He made a swift tour of the objects removed to safety in order to report personally to the Art and Archives Rescue Fund, and he assured the Italians that all aid was unconditional—a gesture of friendship. With business-like forethought he insisted that an Italian accompany him to catalogue the content of the crates as they were unpacked. Each object sent to the Uffizi restoration rooms had to be carefully labelled on arrival.

Six years after these heartrending scenes of desolation in Florence, marks on the walls showing the level to which the mud rose are a constant reminder of what was achieved. In Santa Croce the water rose to the tombs of Michelangelo, Macchiavelli and Galileo, and in the adjoining museum Cimabue's great crucifix painting on the wall was ruined. In the Cathedral square the beautiful bronze doors of the Baptistery, the Doors of Paradise, suffered, particularly the five panels of Ghiberti. The doors were forced off their hinges and battered against a fence surrounding the building. Yet they survived.

When President Saragat visited the scene of disaster ten days after it happened, the Florentines shouted, 'Give us pasta—not words'. Ten thousand of them were out of work and almost as many rendered homeless by the flood.

Yet with the almost miraculous patience and hard work of the Florentines and their friends, in a matter of months the city had resumed an almost normal life; and in the summer of 1973 a fascinating exhibition in the Fortezza da Basso showed in detail how the restoration of the art treasures had been carried out. Soon the delicate guilding of Donatello's Magdalene, never even suspected before, was seen for the first time, and she was put back in her place in the Baptistery in the heart of the city whose palaces and buildings had been lovingly and carefully cleaned of the filthy oily mixture which had stained them. Florence had been saved for future generations.

Proudly displayed in the Restoration Exhibition was a superbly executed wood carving which England's greatest artist in this craft, Grinling Gibbons, had made for Charles II and which he sent, in 1682, to the Grand Duke of Tuscany, Cosimo III, as a symbol of friendship.

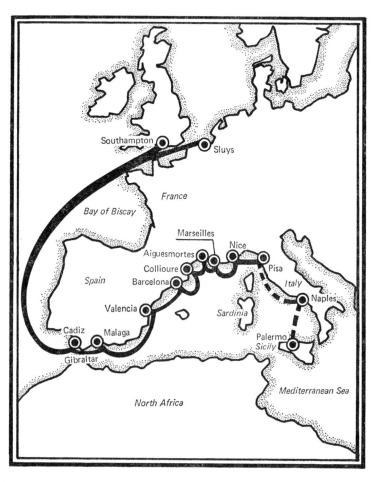

THE ROUTES OF THE FLORENTINE GALLEYS
AS ESTABLISHED IN 1447

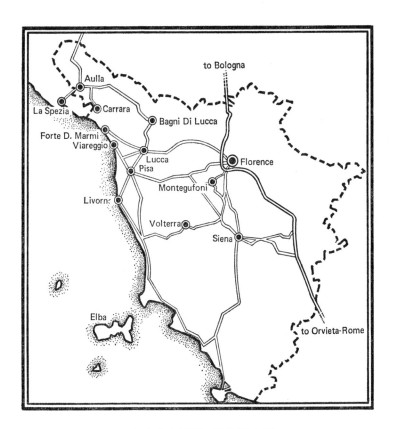

TUSCANY TODAY

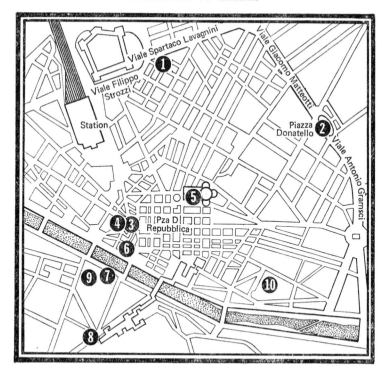

FLORENCE (*Centre*)

1. Villino Trollope, on the northern corner of Piazza Independenza.
2. The English Cemetery, Piazza Donatello.
3. Palazzo Dudley, Via della Vigna Nuova and Via della Spada.
4. Church of San Pancrazio, Via della Spada.
5. The Duomo.
6. British Consulate, Lungarno Corsini, 2.
7. British Institute, Lungarno Guicciardini 9.
8. Casa Guidi, Piazza San Felice, 8.
9. Casa Manetti, Via Santo Spirito, 23.
10. Santa Croce.

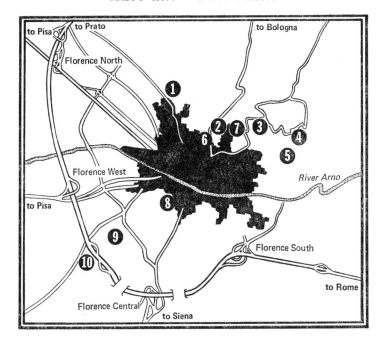

THE FLORENTINE COUNTRYSIDE

1. Villa Rinieri, near Castello and 100 yards south of Petraia.
2. Villa la Pietra, Via dei Bruni, off Via Bolognese.
3. Villa Landor, previously Villa Gherardesca, now La Torraccia. Via delle Fontanelle, San Domenico.
4. Vincigliata. Castle rebuilt by Temple-Leader.
5. I Tatti, above San Martino a Mensola.
6. Villa Fabricotti, off Via Vittorio Emanuele, 11.
7. Villa Palmieri, Via Boccaccio, south-west of San Domenico.
8. Villa Ombrellino, Bellosguardo.
9. Villa Farinola, Alto Scandicci.
10. Villa Mirenda, S. Paolo a Mosciano, Vignale.

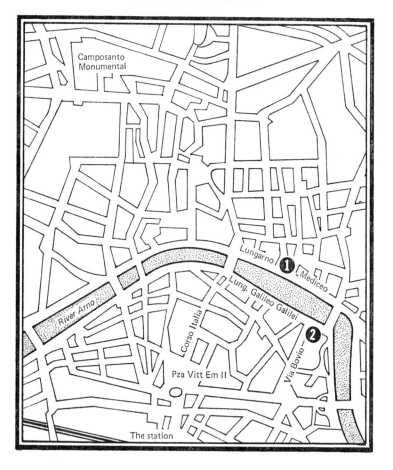

PISA

1. Palazzo Lanfranchi (*Byron*)
2. Tre Palazzi (*Shelley*)

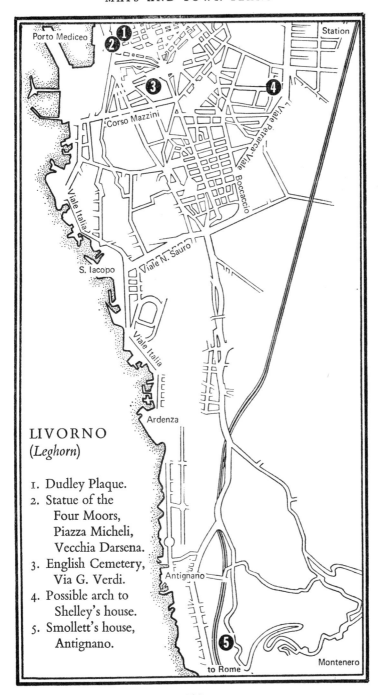

LIVORNO
(*Leghorn*)

1. Dudley Plaque.
2. Statue of the
   Four Moors,
   Piazza Micheli,
   Vecchia Darsena.
3. English Cemetery,
   Via G. Verdi.
4. Possible arch to
   Shelley's house.
5. Smollett's house,
   Antignano.

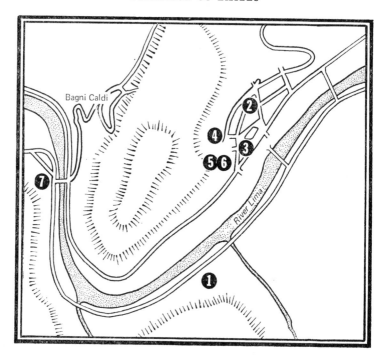

BAGNI di LUCCA

1. English Cemetery.
2. Grand-Ducal Villa.
3. English Church
4. Bagni.
5. Palazzo Buonvisi.
6. Casa Bertini.
7. Ouida's house with plaque.

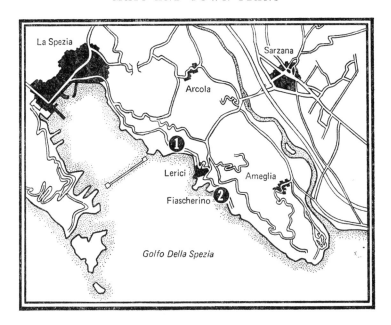

BAY OF LA SPEZIA

1. Shelley's house.
2. D. H. Lawrence's house, Fiascherino.

A List of Books

GUIDES AND MAPS

1. *Collins Companion Guides* to:
Tuscany	Archibald Lyall	1973
Florence	Eve Borsook	1966
Umbria	Maurice Rowdon	1968

2. *Blue Guide to Northern Italy* by Russell Muirhead (Benn)

3. The Dent Series on Medieval Towns, started in the late nineteenth century, is still today incomparable. They can be found in second-hand bookshops and have just been reprinted by Kraus-Thomson. The relevant titles are:

Assisi	Lina Duff Gordon	1901
Florence	Edmund Gardner	1900
Lucca	Janet Ross and Nelly Erichsen	1912
Perugia	Margaret Symonds and Lina Duff Gordon	1900
Pisa	Janet Ross and Nelly Erichsen	1909
Siena	Edmund Gardner	1903

4. The series by Edward Hutton in this century, now printed by Hollis and Carter, is also excellent. They include:

Florence (revised)	1966
Siena and Southern Tuscany	1910

   Other, but out of print, titles by Hutton, are worth the search:

Cities of Umbria	1905
Country Walks about Florence	1908
The Valley of the Arno	1927
A Wayfarer in Unknown Tuscany	1909
Florence and Northern Tuscany	1907

5. The Italian Touring Club publishes several series of maps. Tuscany is available in three maps (numbers 11, 13 and 15) on the scale of 1 : 200,000.

There are special maps at 1 : 50,000, published by the Litografia Artistica Cartografica.

The Instituto Geografico Militaire publishes detailed maps of Tuscany at 1 : 25,000. There is an excellent map of Florence and Environs.

BOOKS ON TUSCANY AND THE ENGLISH

The following is a list of books I have read in the course of preparation for this book and which now form my Anglo-Tuscan Library. I have hardly mentioned the immense number of books on art and architecture written by British scholars and authors.

ACTON Harold	*Memoirs of an Aesthete*	1948
	More Memoirs of an Aesthete	1970
ALDINGTON Richard	*D. H. Lawrence. Portrait of a*	
	Genius but. . . .	1950
	Pinorman	1954
ALKETT John G.	*Milton and the Idea of Matrimony*	1970
ANDERSON M. S.	*Europe in the Eighteenth Century*	1961
AYRTON Michael	*Giovanni Pisano*	1969
BARETTI Giuseppe	*Account of the Manners and*	
	Customs of Italy	1769
BARSALI Isa Belli	*Guida di Lucca*	1970
	La Villa a Lucca dal XV al	
	XIX Secolo	1964
BARTLETT Vernon	*Tuscan Retreat*	1964
	Tuscan Harvest	1970
BATTISCOMBE Georgina	*Queen Alexandra*	1969
BEARDWOOD A.	*Alien Merchants in England*	1931
BEERBOHM Max	*More (essays)*	1899
BERENSON Bernard	*The Passionate Sightseer*	1960
BERRY Mary	*Journals*	1784
BIGLAND Eileen	*Ouida: the Passionate Victorian*	1950
BLANCH Lesley	*The Wilder Shores of Love*	1954
BLESSINGTON The		
Countess of	*The Idler in Italy (3 vols.)*	1839
BLUNDEN Edmund	*Shelley*	1946
BLUNT Wilfred Scawen	*My Diaries 1888-1914*	1919

BOSWELL James	*Boswell on the Grand Tour:* Italy, Corsica and France, edited by Frank Brady and Frederick Pottle	1935
	Life of Samuel Johnson	1791
BOULAY F. R. H. Du	*An Age of Ambition*	1970
BRAND C. P.	*Italy and the English Romantics*	1957
British Institute of Florence	*Inghilterra e Toscana nel Ottocento*	
	Congress at Bagni di Lucca	1968
BROWNING Robert	*Letters*, edited by Ewan Kintner	1969
BROWNING Elizabeth Barrett	*Letters* (2 vols.), edited by F. C. Kenyon	1897
BURLAMACCHI Maurizio	*Le Antiche Case del Bagno Alla Villa*	1969
BURROWS Louie	*Lawrence in Love: Letters from D. H. Lawrence to Louie Burrows*	1968
BUXTON John	*Byron and Shelley*	1968
BYRON	*Letters of George Gordon, 6th Lord Byron*, edited by R. G. Howarth	1933
CAMERON Mary Lovett	*Old Etruria and Modern Tuscany*	1909
CAMPBELL Harriet Charlotte Beaujolais	*A Journey to Florence in 1817*	1951
CARMICHAEL Montgomery	*In Tuscany*	1901
	Francia's Masterpiece	1909
CHAMBERS R. W.	*Sir Thomas More*	1935
CHERUBINI B.	*I Bagni di Lucca*	1972
CHURCH Richard	*Mary Shelley*	1928
CLARK Kenneth	*Ruskin Today*	1964
COWLES Virginia	*Edward VII and his Circle*	1956
CRAWLEY C. W. ed.	'War and Peace in Age of Upheaval', *New Cambridge Modern History*	1965
CRINO Anna Maria	*Fatti e Fiure dei Seicento, Anglo Tossano*	1957
CROMPTON Margaret	*Shelley's Dream Women*	1967
CRUICKSHANK J. W. and A. M.	*Smaller Tuscan Towns*	1912
CUNARD Nancy	*Grand Man*	1954
DEISS Joseph Jay	*Captain of Fortune*	1966
DENTLER Clara Louise	*Famous Foreigners in Florence 1400–1900*	1960

DENNIS George	*Cities and Cemeteries of Etruria*	1907
DICKENS Charles	*Pictures from France and Italy*	1846
DORAN Dr J.	*Mann and Manners at the Court of*	
	Florence, vols. 1 and 2	1876
DOUGLAS Norman	*Looking Back*	1914
	South Wind	1924
DOWDEN Edward	*Life of Shelley*	1886
DUFF David	*Queen Victoria Travels*	1970
EINSTEIN Lewis	*The Italian Renaissance in England*	1902
ELWIN Malcolm	*Walter Savage Landor*	1941
EVELYN John	*Diary*, edited by William Bray	
	(4 vols.)	1889
FIELD Kate	'Landor's Last Years in Italy',	
	Atlantic Monthly, April, May,	
	June	1868
FIELDING Daphne	*Emerald and Nancy*	1968
FORSTER John	*The Life of Charles Dickens*	1872
	The Life of Walter S. Landor	1869
FROISSART Jean	*Chronicles*	1525
FRENCH Yvonne	*Ouida*	1938
FULLER Jean Overton	*Shelley*	1968
GAGE John	*Life in Italy at the Time of the*	
	Medici	1968
GAMBA Pietro	*Byron's Last Journey to Greece*	1825
GRAHAME Georgina	*In a Tuscan Garden*	1902
	Under Petraia	1908
GRYLLS R. Glynn	*Mary Shelley*	1938
HALE J. R.	*England and the Italian*	
	Renaissance	1954
HARE Augustus	*Cities of Northern Italy*, vol. 1	1876
	Cities of Central Italy, vol. 1	1876
HAYTER A.	*Mrs Browning*	1962
HEINE Heinrich	*Italian Travel Sketches*, trans.	
	E. Sharp	1927
HELE Desmond King-	*Shelley, His Thought and Work*	1960
HISCOCK W. G.	*John Evelyn and his Family Circle*	1955
HOGG Thomas Jefferson	*Life of Shelley*	1858
	Letters to Jane Williams,	
	edited by Norman Sylvia	1934
HOLT Edgar	*The Risorgimento*	1970
HOLLAND Lord	*Memoirs*	1850
HOWELLS W. D.	*Tuscan Cities*	1884

HUNT Leigh	*Autobiography*, edited by	
	J. E. Morpurgo	1949
HUXLEY Aldous	*Along the Road*	1925
	Letters, edited by G. Smith	1969
	Letters of D. H. Lawrence	1932
INGRAM John H.	*Elizabeth B. Browning*	1892
JOHNSTON Edgar	*Charles Dickens: his Tragedy*	
	and Triumph, vol. 2	1952
KETTON-CREMER R. W.	*Horace Walpole*	1940
KNAPP Lewis Mansfield	*Tobias Smollett*	1949
KNIGHT G. Wilson	*Lord Byron: Christian Virtues*	1952
KNIGHT E. Cornelia	*Autobiography*	1861
LANDOR W. S.	*High and Low Life in Italy*, vol. XI	
	Imaginary Conversations	1824
	The Shorter Poems, edited by	
	J. B. Sidgwick	1941
	Letters, edited by S. Wheeler	1899
LAWRENCE D. H.	The following titles relate to	
	Tuscany and to Italy:	
Novels	*Aaron's Rod*	1922
	The First Lady Chatterley	1972
	John Thomas and Lady Jane	1972
	Lady Chatterley's Lover	1928
	Sons and Lovers	1913
General	*Etruscan Places*	1932
	Twilight in Italy	1916
	Flowery Tuscany (in collected	
	essays)	1926
	Sea and Sardinia	1923
Poems	*Selected Poems*	1928
Letters	*Edited by Aldous Huxley*	1932
LAWRENCE Frieda	*Memoirs and Correspondence,*	
	edited by E. W. Tedlock	1964
	Not I But the Wind	1935
LEADER Temple	*Rough and Rambling Notes*	1899
	Life of Sir Robert Dudley	1895
LEE Elizabeth	*Ouida*	1914
LEE Arthur Gould	*The Son of Leicester*	1964
LEES Dorothy Neville	*Tuscan Feasts and Tuscan Friends*	1907
LESLIE Anita	*Edwardians in Love*	1972
LINDSAY Jack	*J. M. W. Turner*	1966
LUCAS E. V.	*A Wanderer in Florence*	1912

LUCAS Joseph	*Our Villa in Italy*	1913
LUCAS Robert	*Frieda Lawrence*	1973
MALCOLM Alexander	*Letters of an Invalid from Italy*	1897
MALENS Edward	*Samuel Palmer's Honeymoon*	1968
MALLETT Michael E.	*The Florentine Galleys in the Fifteenth Century*	1967
MALONEY Brian	*Florence and England*	1964
MARCHAND Leslie A.	*Byron's Poetry*	1966
	Byron—A Biography	1957
MAUROIS André	*Byron*	1936
MEAD W. E.	*The Grand Tour in the Eighteenth Century*	1917
McKISACK May	*The Fourteenth Century* 'Oxford History'	1959
MILLER Betty	*Robert Browning*	1952
MOORE Harry T. and WARREN Roberts	*D. H. Lawrence and his World*	1966
MOORE Henry	*Catalogue of Exhibition, Belvedere, Florence*	1972
	Photographs by John Hedgcoe, text by Henry Moore	1968
MORE Sir Thomas	*Selected Letters*, edited by Elizabeth Francis Rogers	1961
NEHLS Edward	*A Composite Biography of D. H. Lawrence* (3 vols.)	1958
NEWBY Eric	*Love and War in the Apennines*	1971
NICHOLSON Harold	*Byron, The Last Journey*	1924
OMAN Carola	*Nelson*	1947
ORIGO Iris	*The Merchant of Prato*	1957
	A Measure of Love	1957
	The Last Attachment	1949
ORIOLI G.	*Adventures of a Bookseller*	1938
OUIDA	*Under Two Flags*	1867
	Idalia	1867
	Friendship	1878
	Pascarel	1873
	Moths	1880
	Views and Opinions	1895
PATMORE Derek	*Italian Pageant*	1949
PIOMBANTI Guida	*Storica ed Artistic di Livorno*	1903
PLUMB J. H.	*Men and Places*	1963
PONSONBY Henry	*A. A. Ponsonby*	

POPE-HENNESSY James	*Queen Mary*	1959
	Anthony Trollope	1971
POPE-HENNESSY Una	*Charles Dickens*	1945
POWICKE Sir Maurice	*Oxford History of the Thirteenth*	
	Century	1953
PRIESTLEY J. B.	*The Prince of Pleasure*	1969
QUENNELL Peter	*Byron in Italy*	1941
	Byron, a Self Portrait (2 vols.)	1935
ROGERS Samuel	*The Italian Journal of Samuel Rogers,*	
	edited by J. R. Hale	1956
	Italy, illustrated by J. M. W.	
	Turner	1830
ROSS Janet	*Italian Sketches*	1887
	Three Generations	1911
	Florentine Palaces	1900
	Old Florence and Modern Tuscany	1904
RUSKIN John	*Mornings in Florence*	1908
RUSSELL John	*Henry Moore*	1968
SADLEIR Michael	*Blessington d'Orsay*	1933
SARDI Cesare	*Vita Lucchese nel Settecento*	1968
SELLS Lytton	*The Paradise of Travellers*	1964
SHELLEY Percy Bysshe	*Letters*, edited by Roger Ingpen	1913
SITWELL Edith	*Selected Letters*, edited by John	
	Lehmann and Derek Palmer	1970
	Autobiography: Taken Care Of	1965
SITWELL Osbert Sir	*Tales My Father Taught Me*	1962
	Autobiography (5 vols.)	
	Left Hand Right Hand	1946-50
	Four Continents	1955
	Penny Foolish	1935
	Winters of Content	1951
SMITH Robert M.	*The Shelley Legend*	1945
SMITH Warren Hunting	*Horace Walpole*	1967
SMOLLETT Tobias	*Letters*, edited by Edward S. Noyes	1969
	Travels Through France and Italy	1766
Novels	*Humphrey Clinker*	1770
	Adventures of Peregrine Pickle	1751
	Roderick Random	1748
STEVENSON R. Scott	*Famous Illnesses in History*	1962
STIRLING Monica	*Ouida The Fine and The Wicked*	1957
STISTED H. Mrs	*Letters from the Byeways of Italy*	1830
SULLY James	*Italian Travel Sketches*	1912

SYMONDS John Addington	*Sketches and Studies in France and Italy*	1886
TAYLOR Katharine Kressman	*Florence: Ordeal by Water*	1967
THOMAS Vaughan	*Italian Biography of Sir Robert Dudley*	
	written	1649
	published	1861
THOMPSON James Westfall	*Economic and Social History of the Middle Ages*	1928
TREASE Geoffrey	*The Condottieri*	1970
TRELAWNY E. J.	*Records of Shelley, Byron and the Author*	1878
TREVES Guiliana Artom	*The Golden Ring of the Anglo-Florentines*	1956
TROLLOPE Anthony	*Autobiography*	1883
TROLLOPE Francis (Fanny)	*Visit to Italy* (2 vols.)	1842
TROLLOPE Thomas Adolphus	*What I Remember* (3 vols.)	1887
	Decade of Italian Women (2 vols.)	1859
	The History of the Commonwealth of Florence	1865
TROLLOPE Francis Eleanor	*Homes and Haunts of Italian Poets*	1881
WALPOLE Horace	*Letters*, edited by Mrs Paget Toynbee	1903
WATERFIELD Lina (Lina Duff Gordon)	*Home Life in Italy*	1908
	Castle in Italy	1961
WELLARD James	*The Search for the Etruscans*	1973
WHELPTON Eric	*Florence and Tuscany*	1965
WHIPPLE Evangeline E.	*A Famous Corner of Tuscany*	1920
WHITING Lillian	*The Florence of Landor*	1905
WILLIAMS Egerton	*Hill Towns of Italy*	1903
WOOD Jessie Chambers	*A Personal Record*	1935
WOOLF Virginia	*Flush*	1933
VIGO Pietro	*Nelson a Livorno*	1903
VILLARI Pasquale	*History of Florence*	1905

INDEX

Index

Ablett, Joseph, 107
Acton, Harold, 155, 170, 180-1
Acton, Sir John Francis Edward, 57
Adam, James, 63
Adam, Robert, 63
Addison, Joseph, 50, 62
Ainsley, Samuel, 149
Albizzi, Luca di Maso degli, 23-5
Aldington, Richard, 170
Alexandra, Queen, 155
Alice, Grand Duchess of Hesse, 153
Alice of Battenberg, Princess, 155
Ancona, 66
Anne of Denmark, Queen Consort, 39
Arnold, Matthew, 149
Arrighi, Professor Gino, 34, 35
Asquith, Lady Cynthia, 160
Austin, Alfred, 149
Ayrton, Michael, 187
Azzarini, Signora Maria, 160

Baciocchi, Elise, 68
Bagnacavallo, 29, 87
Bagni di Lucca, Shelley on, 68; thermal springs of 68, 69; Protestant church at, 69; British Institute of Florence at, 69; social life at, 144; the Brownings at, 140; Landor at, 111; Ouida at, 133, 136; the Shelleys at, 67-8, 70; Fanny Trollope in, 144
Bargellini, Piero, 190
Baretti, Giuseppe, 63-64
Barrett, Elizabeth, *see* Browning, Elizabeth Barrett
Baths of San Giuliano, 74
Battenberg, Prince Henry of, 150, 151
Battista da Pisa, 14
Beatrice, Princess (Princess Henry of Battenberg), 150, 151

Beerbohm, Sir Max, 121
Bellosguardo, Ouida at, 132; the Brownings at, 140
Bentham, Jeremy, 95
Berry, Mary, 64
Bertini, Domenico, 68
Bicchierai, Alessandro, 64
Blagden, Isa, 140, 141, 148
Blanch, Lesley, 123
Blessington, Charles, 2nd Viscount Mountjoy and 1st Earl of, 94, 106
Blessington, Marguerite, Countess of, on Byron's bad taste, 88; Byron and, 94-5; and Landor, 106, 107, 112; and D'Orsay, 107; has a house-warming party, 112; death of, 113
Blunt, Wilfred Scawen, 121, 125, 134-5
Boissy, Marquis de, 96
Bonaparte, Joseph, 100
Bonaparte, Napoleon, 99, 100, 127
Bonvisi, Antonio, 33-4
Borgia, Lucrezia, 103
Bradley, James, 50
Brown, Charles Armitage, 102-3, 111
Browning, Elizabeth Barrett, 15; in Siena, 115; death of, 117, 141; her grave, 119, 141; her appearance, 139; her ideas, 139; on Casa Guidi, 142-3; and Pen Browning, 140; and Robert Browning, 138; and Cavour's death, 140-1; and Theodosia Garrow, 145; and Landor, 116; on Mazzini, 140; and the Trollopes, 146
Browning Institute, 142
Browning, Penini, 140, 142
Browning, Robert, 15; his character, 139; leaves Florence, 143; and Elizabeth Browning, 117, 138, 141; and Pen Browning, 140; and Lan-

dor, 113, 115-16; and the Trollopes, 146; and Tom Trollope, 147-8

Burton, Isabel, Lady, 121, 123

Burton, Sir Richard, 121, 123, 132

Bute, John Stuart, 3rd Earl of, 53, 54

Byron, Allegra, her death, 29, 78, 79; gossip about her paternity, 67; in Venice, 70; Byron's views on her upbringing, 83, 86; in Bagnacavallo convent, 87

Byron, Anne Isabella, Lady, 84

Byron, George Gordon, 6th Baron Byron, 124; at Lucca, 35; his work, 86; traits of character, 88; challenges Masi to a duel, 89; death of, 95-6; Turner's illustrations for, 148; and Allegra, 70, 83, 86; and Claire Clairmont, 67, 70, 78, 86; and Teresa Guiccioli, 75-6, 78, 84-6, 87, 95; Guerazzi on, 77-8; and Hunt, 90, 91-2; and the Hunts, 77; and Landor, 103; Ouida on, 121; and Mary Shelley, 94; and Shelley, 66, 70, 76, 77, 78, 81, 86-7, 90; Trelawny on, 89

Caesena, 'massacre' of, 29

Camaiore, 136

Campbell-Bannerman, Sir Henry, 136

Carlyle, Dr Alexander, 52-3

Carlyle, Thomas, 140

Carmichael, Montgomery, 71-2, 134, 136

Caroline, Queen, 75

Carrara, marble quarries of, 14, 184; Dickens on, 184-5

Casini, Prof. Dott. Bruno, 77

Catherine of Siena, Saint, 28-9

Cavendish, Margaret (Mrs Robert Dudley), 38

Cavendish, Captain Thomas, 38

Cavour, Count Camillo Benso di, 140

Chaloner, Sir Thomas, 37, 44

Chambers, Jessie, 159

Charles, Archduke of Austria, 40

Charles II, King of Great Britain, 193

Chiostri, Dr Ferdinando, 41

Christina, Grand Duchess of Tuscany, 40, 42, 43

Church, George, 191

Church, the; Smollett on pageantry of, 57-8

Cimabue, Giovanni, 192

Clairmont, Clare; and Byron, 67, 70, 83, 86; and Shelley, 70, 73, 75; and the Shelleys, 71, 72

Clarence, Lionel, Duke of, 28

Cockerell, Sir Sydney, 134, 135

Coleridge, Samuel Taylor, 90

Corelli, Marie, 136

Corsini family, 41, 42

Cortignola, 29

Cosimo I, Grand Duke of Tuscany, 55

Cosimo II, Grand Duke of Tuscany, family connections, 40; and Dudley, 41, 47; death of, 42; and Galileo, 46, 49

Cosimo III, Grand Duke of Tuscany, 193

Cowper, George Nassau, 3rd Earl, 64

Crispi, Francesco, 152, 153

Cumberland, William Augustus, Duke of ('Butcher' Cumberland), 53

Dance, Nathaniel, 53

D'Annunzio, Gabriele, 134

Dante Alighieri, 56; and moneylenders, 17; exiled, 21; Byron and, 77, 86; Taafe's translation of, 78

Davy, Sir Humphrey, 149

Dennis, George, 149

Dickens, Charles, on marble-quarrying at Carrara, 184-5; and Hunt, 90; and Landor, 112-14; and Smollett, 61; and Tom Trollope, 145

Donatello, 191, 192

D'Orsay, Alfred Guillaume Gabriel, Count, 94, 106

Douglas, Norman, 169-70

Drake, Sir Francis, 38

Dudley, Anna, 42

Dudley, Cosimo, 42

Dudley, Lady (Alice), 38, 39

Dudley, Maddalena, 42

Dudley, Sir Robert, Earl of Warwick and Duke of Northumberland, and port of Livorno, 35, 36; *Arcano del Mare*, 36, 43, 46, 47; family background, 37; marriages, 38; interest in maritime affairs, 38, 45-7; and Elizabeth I, 38, 39; appearance, 39, 46; tries to establish his rights, 39, 43-4; and Elizabeth Southwell, 39-40, 41, 43; in Florence, 40, 41-3; his death, 43; his interest in medicine, 46

Eden, Sir Ashley, 131, 132
Edward I, King of England, 17, 18, 19
Edward III, King of England, 26, 28
Edward VII, King of Great Britain, 133, 155
Eliot, George (*prop.* Mary Ann Evans), 133, 146
Elizabeth I, Queen of England, 35, 37, 38, 39
Epstein, Jacob, 188
Erichsen, Nelly, 129
Essex, Robert Devereux, 2nd Earl of, 38, 39
Este, 70
Etruscology, 149, 170
Evelyn, John, 36, 51, 55

Faraday, Michael, 149
Fasoli, Professor, 180
Ferdinand I, Grand Duke of Tuscany, Dudley and, 35, 40, 43, 45; statue of, 36; and Livorno, 51; and aqueduct at Pisa, 55
Ferdinand II, Grand Duke of Tuscany, 40, 46, 47
Ferdinand IV, King of Naples, 66
Fiascherino, Lawrence's cottage at, 159-61
Field, Kate, 100
Fielding, Henry, 50
Fiesole, Landor's home in, 107-9, 113-14, 115; Dickens in, 113-14
Florence, mediaeval, 19, 20, 21, 23; wool trade, 22; Florentine galleys, 23, 24; strict supervision of mercenaries, 30; under Grand Duke Ferdinand I, 40; British Institute of, 69-70; University of Europe in, 70; entertainments and excursions in, 127; English cemetery in, 147; Turner's paintings of, 148; *Scoppia del Carro*, 152; Moore's sculpture exhibition at Forte Belvedere, 182; the 1966 floods, 190-3
Buildings and gardens (*see also* Houses): Boboli Gardens, 73; Cascine, 73; the Duomo, 27, 32, 120, 147, 184; Pitti Palace, 73, 152, 179; San Giovanni, 32; San Pancrazio Church, 41, 43; Uffizi Gallery, 50, 179, 190-1
Quotations on Florence from: Landor, 118; Lawrence, 162-3; Ouida, 120; Osbert Sitwell, 177-8; Smollett, 56, 57
Residents and visitors: Addison, 50; the Brownings, 116-17, 138-40, 143; Claire Clairmont, 75; Lord Cowper, 64; Dante, 21; Dickens, 145; Dudley, 40, 41-3; Hare, 102; Hawkwood, 28, 30-1; Hazlitt, 105; Hunt, 103; Alice Keppel, 154-6; Kirkup, 102; Landor, 98, 101-2, 115, 116, 119; the Lawrences, 162, 167; Sir Horace Mann, 62; Mario, 130; Nelson and party, 66; Florence Nightingale, 149; Ouida, 124, 132; the Shelleys, 72, 73; the Trollopes, 144, 145-7; Queen Victoria, 64, 150-4; Horace Walpole, 62, 63; other distinguished visitors, 148-9, 154
Florentines, Landor critical of, 104, 109, 118
Ford, Sir Clare, 151
Forster, John, 112, 113, 114, 115, 116
Forte dei Marmi, 82; Moore's home at, 183, 186, 189
Fox, Charles James, 99
Frederick II, Holy Roman Emperor, 44
Frere, John Hookham, 100
Frescobaldi, Amerigo, 18
Froissart, Jean, 27

Galilei, Galileo, 46, 49, 50, 109, 192
Gamba, Count Pietro, and the Carbonari, 86; and Byron, 89, 95; moves

to Livorno, 90; and the servants' quarrel, 91, 92; on death of Byron, 95-6

Gamba, Count Ruggero, 86, 90

Gamba, Count Vincenzo, 96

Garibaldi, Giuseppe, 140; Landor and, 116, 117; Ouida and, 127; Peard on, 146; the Trollopes and, 146; and Queen Victoria, 146

Garnett, Edward, 160

Garrick, David, 53

Garrow, Joseph, 145, 146

Genoa, boat building at, 79; Byron and others at, 94; Hunt at, 79, 94; Landor's effects sent to, 114; Mary Shelley at, 94

George II, King of Great Britain, 62

George IV, King of Great Britain, 75, 90

George V, King of Great Britain, 155

Gibbons, Grinling, 193

Gisborne, John and Maria, 74

Goad, Harold, 70

Godwin, Mary Wollstonecraft (Mrs Shelley), on Villa Valsovona, 71; on 'The Witch of Atlas', 74; miscarries, 79; in later life, 82; and Byron, 94; and Claire Clairmont, 75; on la Guiccioli, 76; and Shelley, 67, 70, 72, 73, 76, 79

Godwin, William, 67, 74, 94

Gordon, Peter, 52

Grahame, Georgina, 153

Grand Tour, the, 16, 62, 63-4, 78, 83

Greek Committee, 95

Greenlees, Ian, 70, 136

Gregory XI, Pope, 29

Grifoni, Elizabeth, 63

Grosfils, Mme, 134

Guerazzi, Francesco Domenico, on Byron, 77-8

Guiccioli, Count, 84, 86

Guiccioli, Teresa, Countess, opinions about, 76; and death of Shelley, 80; after Byron's death, 96-7; *Vie de Byron en Italie*, 97; and Byron, 75-6, 78, 84-6, 87, 88, 95; Byron on, 83-4, 85 and Lady Blessington, 94, 95, 96; Hunt on, 91, 92-3; and Shelley, 76-7, 87

Hakluyt, Richard, 38

Halley, Edmund, 50

Hamilton, Emma, Lady, 66

Hamilton, Sir William, 66

Hardy, Thomas, 149

Hare, Augustus John Cuthbert, 128, 137

Hare, Francis, 102, 105

Hawkins, Sir John, 38

Hawkwood, Lady Donnina, 29, 31

Hawkwood, Sir John, knighted, 26; and his mercenaries, 26-7, 28, 29, 30; his appearance, 27-9; payments and grants to, 28, 30-1; and St Catherine of Siena, 28-9; at Bagnacavallo, 29; his marriage, 29-30; his funeral, 31-2

Hazlitt, William, 90, 105

Henry VI, King of England, 25

Henry VIII, King of England, 33, 35

Henry, Prince, of Great Britain, 41, 44

Hillard, George, 137

Hilliard, Nicholas, 39

Hobhouse, John Cam, 83, 95

Hogg, Thomas Jefferson, 66-7, 105

Holland, Henry Richard Fox, 3rd Baron, 64

Hopkin, W. E., 161

Houses: Acciaiuoli castle, 176-7; 178-9; Casa Guidi, 116, 138, 141, 142-3; Il Giardino, 59-60, 79, 108; Palazzo Dudley, 41; Palazzo Lanfranchi, 76, 77, 79, 88, 89, 92, 93, 108, 127; Palazzo Medici, 101, 104; Tre Palazzi di Chiesa, 76; Villa Castagnolo, 127, 129; Villa Castiglione, 104; Villa della Corona, 132; Villa Dupuy, 78; Villa Fabricotti, 151; Villa Farinola, 125-7, 128, 130, 131; Villa Gherardesca, 107, 108-9, 113-14, 115; Villa Guinigi, 20; Villa I Rinieri, 41-2, 43; Villa La Pietra, 180; Villa Massoni, 133, 134; Villa Mirenda, 163-4, 165, 166-7, 168-9, 170; Villa Ombrellino, 155, 156; Villa Palmieri, 64, 108, 150-1, 152, 153; Villino Trollope, 146, 147; Villa Valsovona, 71-2

Hume, David, 56

Humphrey, Duke of Gloucester, 25

Hunt, John, 90

Hunt, James Henry Leigh, on Villa Dupuy, Livorno, 78; arrives at Genoa, 79; his copy of Keats's poems, 80; his friends, 90; the journey to Italy, 90; on Pisa, 93-4; and Armitage Brown, 103; and Byron, 77, 91-2; on Kirkup, 102; and London, 103; and Shelley, 77, 81; on Trelawny, 91

Hunter, Dr William, 60

Hutton, Edward, 69

Huxley, Aldous, 168, 170-1, 173

Huxley, Maria, 162, 164, 173

Irving, Sir Henry, 123

James I, King of Great Britain, 39, 43, 44, 45

Jenkins, Elizabeth, 121

Johnson, Dr Samuel, 35, 49, 62

Jones, Nancy, 99

Keats, John, 75, 80, 90, 102-3

Kenilworth Castle, 37, 38, 44

Keppel, Alice, 154-6

Keswick, John, 189

Kinnaird, Douglas, 95

Kirkup, Seymour, 102, 108

Knight, Ellis Cornelia, 66

Knollys, Sir Francis, 37

Knollys, Lettice, Countess of Essex, 37, 39

Lamb, Charles, 66, 90

Lambton, Henry, 51

Landor, Charles, 119

Landor, Henry, 111, 115, 116

Landor, Julia (Landor's daughter), 113, 115, 116

Landor, Julia (née Thuillier), 101, 110, 111, 112, 114

Landor, Walter (Landor's son), 113, 115, 119

Landor, Walter Savage, 181; appearance and personality, 98; early life, 99-101; his work, 104; on Florentines and Tuscans, 104; his impetuosity, 104, 107, 108; his interest in pictures, 104-5; and his children,

105, 111, 112, 113, 114; his marriage, 110-12; in London, 112; his devotion to his dog, 113; returns to Italy, 114; in old age, 114-19; on Florence, 118; death of, 119; his grave, 141; and Armitage Brown, 103, 111; and Lady Blessington, 106, 107, 112; and the Brownings, 115-17, 141; and Byron, 103; and Dickens, 112-13, 114; on Count D'Orsay, 107; and Hare, 102; and Hogg, 105-6; and Hunt, 103; and Kirkup, 102; on Napoleon, 99, 100; and Shelley, 98-9; and Southey, 100, 104; and Story, 115; Treves on, 118-19

Lawrence, David Herbert, on Tuscany, 157-8; his way of thought, 158; at Fiascherino, 159-61; his work suppressed as obscene, 161; on Florence, 162-3; at Villa Mirenda, 164; and Lady Chatterley's Lover, 164, 170, 172, 173; his generosity, 167; his interest in Etruscology, 170; ill, 171, 173; his pictures exhibited, 173, 187; persecuted, 172-3; his death, 173; 'Tuscan Cypresses', 173-4; Aldington on, 170; and Douglas, 169, 170; and Frieda, 158-9, 162; and Aldous Huxley, 170-1; Mirenda on, 167; and Edith Sitwell, 166; and Osbert Sitwell, 165-6; Walter Wilkinson on, 168-9

Lawrence, Frieda (née von Richtofen), and her children, 159; and Villa Mirenda, 163-4; on Lady Chatterley's Lover, 164; in London, 173; and Aldous Huxley, 171; and Lawrence, 158-9, 161-2, 167, 169, 173; on Edith and Osbert Sitwell, 166; Walter Wilkinson on 168

Leader, John Temple, 41, 47-8

Leicester, Douglas Dudley, Countess of, 37, 39

Leicester, Robert Dudley, Earl of, 37

Leicester, Robert Sidney, Earl of, 44

Leigh, Augusta, 84, 96

Leopold, Prince, Duke of Albany, 127

Lerici, Claire Clairmont at, 78;

Shelley and Williams at, 79; Casa Magni, 79, 81; *Ariel* does not return to, 80; *Coppa Byron*, 82; Lawrence's cottage near, 159-61
Lewes, George Henry, 146
Linklater, Eric, 180
Linton, Mrs Lynne, 116
Livorno, mediaeval, 22, 23; the port, 35, 42, 45, 47, 65; *I Quatro Mori*, 35-6; English cemetery at, 50-1, 141; British 'factory' at, 51; English merchants at, 63, 65; French occupy, 65; bombed, 72; Byron and la Guiccioli at, 78-9; Claire Clairmont leaves, 75; Dudley at, 40, 46; Hunt at, 90; Luca di Maso at, 25; Nelson at, 65; Shelley at, 66, 71-72, 74, 79; Smollett's house on Monte Nero, 59-60, 79, 108
London, Italian merchants in, 19; Luca di Maso in, 25; Crosby Hall, 33, 34; Landor in, 112, 113; Ouida in, 121-3; Garibaldi in, 146; Warren Gallery, 173, 187
Lotti, Ambassador, 43, 44
Lucca, 14-15; mediaeval, 17, 19, 20, 21; San Frediano's basilica, 34, 35; on the Grand Tour, 64; Bonvisis of, 33, 34; grants citizenship to Hawkwood, 28; Milton at, 50; Napoleon occupies, 66; Old Pretender at, 34-5; Ouida at, 133
Lucini, Jacopo, 47
Lynham, Edward, 47
Lytton, Robert Edward Bulwer, Ist Earl of (*pseud.* Owen Meredith), 121, 131-3, 146

Magnus, Maurice, 169
Malcolm, Alexander, 59-60
Mallett, Michael E., 24
Mann, Sir Horace, 62-3, 65, 176
Maria Carolina, Queen of Naples, 66
Maria Maddalena, Archduchess of Tuscany, 40, 42, 43, 44
Marie Louise, Empress of France, 68
Mario, Giuseppe, 124, 125, 130
Mario, Jessie White, 146
Mary Adelaide, Princess, 154
Masti, Guido, 179, 180

Mathieson, Patrick, 191
May of Teck, Princess, 154
Mazzarosa, Ouida at, 136
Mazzini, Giuseppe, 140
Medici, Caterina de, 40
Medici, Cosimo de, 179
Medici family, 40, 147
Medici, Giuliano de, 147
Medicina, 29
Medwin, Thomas, 75, 76, 88
Memorials, Bagni di Lucca: to Ouida, 136; Ferento: to George Dennis, 149; Florence: to Elizabeth Browning, 141, 146; to Dudley, 41, 42, 48; to Theodosia Trollope, 146; Lerici: to Shelley, 81; Livorno: to Dudley, 37, 48; to Ferdinand I (*I Quatro Mori*), 35-6; to Smollett, 51; Lucca: to Bonvisis, 34; to Byron, 35; Viareggio: to Shelley, 15, 81
Meredith, Owen, *see* Lytton, Earl of
Michelangelo, 183, 184, 192
Mignaty, George, 142
Milan, 28, 29, 30
Milnes, Richard Monckton, 105
Milton, John, 49-50
Mirenda, Paul, 166, 167
Montegufoni, 176-81
Montgomery, Bernard Law, Viscount, 28
Moore, Henry, in Tuscany, 14; his letter to the mayor of Florence, 182; his personality and charm, 183, 189; visits the marble quarries, 183-4; early history, 186; experiments with concrete, 186; his happy marriage, 186-7; his work, 187; and Lawrence, 187-8; Epstein and, 188; official war artist, 188; 'King and Queen', 188-9; on his sculpture, 189; and his daughter, 189
Moore, Sir John, 100
Moore, Mary, 189
Moore, Tom, 90
More, Sir Thomas, 33, 35
Murat, Joachim, 100
Murray, John, 83, 85, 96

Naples, 70
Napoleon I, *see* Bonaparte, Napoleon

Napoleon III, Emperor of France, 139
Nelson, Horatio, Viscount Nelson, 65, 66
Nevill, Lady Dorothy, 132
Newton, Sir Isaac, 50
New York Browning Society, 142
Norfini, Giuseppe, 136

Oman, Carola, 65
Orford, Lady, 124, 125
Origo, Iris, 97
Orioli, Giuseppe, 164, 169, 173
Oswald, James, 53
Ouida (*prop.* Louisa Ramé), on Florence, 120; her clothes, 121, 125, 128, 129, 131; early life, 121; her passion for dogs, 121, 123, 131, 134, 136; in London, 121-3; in Florence, 124, 132; at Villa Farinola, 125-6, 127; and Marchese della Stufa, 127, 128, 130; and Janet Ross, 129-30; a visit to England, 131-2; financial difficulties, 132, 134, 135; and death of her mother, 133; her advanced opinions, 133; her case against the Grosfils family, 134, 136; illness, poverty and death, 136

Pacchiani, Francesco, 75
Padua, 49
Paget, Lady, 131-2, 136
Papacy, wool trade and, 18; Hawkwood and, 28, 29; and Protestant church at Bagni di Lucca, 69; and the Guiccioli's separation, 86
Parkin, Robert, 72
Patmore, Derek, 156
Pazzi Plot of 1478, 147
Peacock, Thomas Love, 68, 94
Peard, Col. John, 146
Peter Leopold, Grand Duke of Tuscany, 64
Philip III, King of Spain, 40
Piacenza, 20
Pietrasanta, 14, 184
Piombina, Prince of, 42
Piper, John, 180
Pirie-Gordon, Mr, 191
Pisa, 63; mediaeval trade routes to,

15, 18; walls of, 20; port for Florence, 22, 23; draining of marshes, 36, 45; the Brownings in, 138; Byron in, 88-92; Byron and la Guiccioli in, 76, 77, 88, 90-4; Dudley in, 40, 46; Galileo and, 46, 49; Hawkwood and, 28; Hunt in, 77, 79; Hunt's description of, 93-4; Landor on, 98, 101; Shelley in, 73, 79; the Shelleys in, 74, 75, 76; and death of Shelley, 80; Smollett on, 55; Smollett in, 59
Pisano, Giovanni, 186
Pius IX, Pope, 117
Plague, 19, 20, 42
Polo, Marco, 21
Ponsonby, Sir Henry, 150
Pope-Hennessy, John, 192
Porto Pisano, 22-3
Porto Venere, 82
Puccio, Jacopo, 68

Querceta, 189
Quercia, Jacopo della, 35

Radetsky, Irina (Mrs Henry Moore) 186-7
Ramé, Louis, 121, 122
Ravagli, Captain Angelo, 172
Ravenna, 77, 78, 84-6, 87
Rhodes, Dennis, 149
Riccio, Fr. Agostino del, 178
Richard II, King of England, 27, 32
Risorgimento, 17, 139
Roberto, Count of Geneva, 29
Rogers, Samuel, 137, 148
Rome, Lady Blessington in, 106; Keats's death in, 75; Landor in, 106; Ouida in, 130; the Shelleys in, 71; Trelawny's daughter in, 80; the Tom Trollopes in, 148
Ross, Henry, 129
Ross, Janet, 69, 128, 129-30
Rothenstein, Sir William, 188
Ruskin, John, 137, 148
Russell, Bertrand (3rd Earl Russell), 161

Sackville-West, Vita, 156
Salisbury, Robert Cecil, 3rd Marquis of, 131-2

Salvetti, Amerigo, 44
Saragat, President Giuseppe, 192
Scandicci, 168; Lawrence at, 167; the Lawrences at, 172; Ouida at, 125-32
Science, Dudley's interest in, 46; 17th and 18th century developments in, 49, 50; 'fashionable topic of conversation', 64; Lord Cowper's laboratory, 64; scientists in Florence, 149
Scott, Sir Walter, 149
Shelley, Clara, 67, 70
Shelley, Harriet, see Westbrook, Harriet
Shelley, Mary, see Godwin, Mary Wollstonecraft
Shelley, Percy Bysshe, 51, 144; his friends' opinions of, 66-7; his marriages, 67; in Bagni di Lucca, 67-8, 70; death of his children, 70, 71; in Livorno, 71; in Florence, 72; attitude to women, 72-3; relationships with women, 75, 79; death of, 80-1; his rejection of England, 83; his generosity of spirit, 87; absorbed in Gebir, 105-6; and Browning, 143; and Byron, 70, 76, 77, 78, 86-7, 88, 89, 94; and Claire Clairmont, 70, 75; and la Guiccioli, 76-7, 87; and Hunt, 77, 90; Landor on, 99; Lawrence compared with, 159; and Mary Shelley, 79
Shelley, Percy Florence, 72, 82
Shelley, Sir Thomas, 82, 94
Shelley, William, 67, 70
Siena, 64, 115
Sitwell, Edith, 165, 166, 175, 180, 181
Sitwell, Sir George, 175, 176, 177, 179
Sitwell, Ida, Lady, 176, 177
Sitwell, Osbert, 169; on castle of Montegufoni, 176; on Florence, 177; on exodus of British from Tuscany, 179; as host, 181; on Alice Keppel, 155-6; on Lawrence, 165-6; on Sir George Sitwell, 175, 176, 177, 180
Sitwell, Reresby, 181
Sitwell, Sacheverell, 175, 180
Smollett, Tobias George, in Florence, 20; his death, 50; his monument, 51,

his history, 51-2, his work, 52-4; his illnesses, 54, 60-1; on Genoese thrift, 54; on travel in Italy, 54; on Florentines, 56-7; on Florence, 56, 57; on Church pageantry, 57-8; and cicisbei, 58, 85; on Italian women, 59; his house near Livorno, 59-60, 79, 108; Dr Gentili on, 61; his death, 61; Sir Horace Mann and, 63
Soper, William, 24
Southampton, 19-20, 24
Southey, Robert; and Byron, 103; and Hunt, 90; and Landor, 100, 104, 111; on Landor and his bride, 101; on Shelley, 66
Southwell, Elizabeth (Robert Dudley's wife), 39-40, 41, 42-3
Stacey, Sophia, 72, 73
Steele, Sir Richard, 50
Stisted, Mrs Henry, 69
Story, William Wetmore, 115, 131, 140-1
Stuart, Charles Edward, 'the Young Pretender', 63
Stuart, James Edward, 'the Old Pretender', 34-5
Stufa, Marchese Lottaringa della, 127-8
Swifte, Jane ('Ianthe'), 100, 110, 113, 117
Swinburne, Algernon Charles, 119, 149

Taafe, John, 78, 89
Talleyrand-Périgord, Charles de, Prince of Benevento, 127
Tchaiatcheff, Emilie de, 124-5
Tennyson, Alfred Tennyson, 1st Baron, 149
Thackeray, William Makepeace, 149
Tracey, Andrew, 44
Trefusis, Violet, 156
Trelawny, Edward, his appearance, 78; and Byron, 79, 88-9; Hunt on, 91; and Mary Shelley, 82; and Shelley, 79, 80-1, 88-9
Trieste, 66, 132
Trollope, Anthony, 144, 147

Trollope, Beatrice (Bice), 146, 147, 148
Trollope, Frances (Fanny), 144, 145, 147, 148
Trollope, Frances Eleanor (*née* Ternan), 144, 147, 148
Trollope, Theodosia (*née* Garrow), 144, 145-6, 147
Trollope, Thomas Adolphus, 69; in Florence, 144, 145; and Theodosia, 145, 147; on Garibaldi, 146; his works, 146; and death of his mother and wife, 147; his second marriage, 147-8; his death, 148
Turner, Joseph Mallord William, 137, 148

Uccello, Paolo, 27
Umberto I, King of Italy, 127, 131, 151, 152, 153
Urban VIII, Pope, 45

Venice, 70, 76, 84
Verelst, William, 53
Viareggio, 15, 80, 81, 134, 136
Victoria, Queen, 127; in Tuscany, 150-4; and Garibaldi, 146; Ouida and the death of, 133

Villani, Giovanni, 22, 26
Villari, Professor Pasquale, 146
Visconti, Bernabo, 29, 30
Visconti, Galeazzo, 28
Visconti, Gian Galeazzo, 30
Visconti, Violante, 28
Vivian, Charles, 80
Viviani, Emilia, 73, 75

Walpole, Horace, 62, 63, 176
Walpole, Sir Robert, 62
Warwick, Robert Rich, Earl of, 44
Waterfield, Lina, 69, 128-9
Weekley, Ernest, 158, 159
Westbrook, Harriet, 67, 73, 75
Wilkes, John, 53
Wilkinson, Walter, 168-9
Williams, Edward, 73, 76, 79
Williams, Jane, 73, 76, 79, 80
Wood, Anthony à, 45
Wood, Captain Benjamin, 38
Wordsworth, William, 103, 149
Wortley, Charles Stuart, 148
Wyndham, Sir Charles, 123

Zita, Santa, 35